Assessing Teacher Effectiveness

Developing a differentiated model

Jim Campbell, Leonidas Kyriakides, Daniel Muijs and Wendy Robinson

RoutledgeFalmer
Taylor & Francis Group

LONDON AND NEW YORK

First published 2004
by RoutledgeFalmer
11 New Fetter Lane, London EC4P 4EE

Simultaneously published in the USA and Canada
by RoutledgeFalmer
29 West 35th Street, New York, NY 10001

RoutledgeFalmer is an imprint of the Taylor & Francis Group

© 2004 Jim Campbell, Leonidas Kyriakides, Daniel Muijs and
Wendy Robinson

Typeset in Sabon by BC Typesetting Ltd, Bristol
Printed and bound in Great Britain by
TJ International Ltd, Padstow, Cornwall

British Library Cataloguing in Publication Data
A catalogue record for this book is available from the British Library

Library of Congress Cataloging in Publication Data
A catalog record for this book has been requested

ISBN 0–415–30478–4 (hbk)
ISBN 0–415–30479–2 (pbk)

Contents

PART IV
**Differentiated teacher effectiveness research:
the model in practice**

Preface

In writing this book we have tried to achieve two broad aims.

We are attempting to explore a theory of teacher effectiveness that is differentiated, rather than generic, along five dimensions: range of work activity; curriculum subject; pupil background; pupil personal characteristics; and organisational context of teaching. In this sense we are working within the established teacher effectiveness research paradigm, but with a strong revisionist ambition. We accept that the dichotomy between the generic and the differentiated is somewhat contrived, but we think that research investigating and testing a more differentiated model is needed to counterbalance, or to add dimensions to, the more conventional generic model.

We are also attempting to connect teacher effectiveness theory with more broadly based educational theorising, including studies of teachers' work, historical perspectives, the analysis of educational values, teacher evaluation and appraisal, and policy studies. Educational effectiveness has developed, almost as a field in its own right, within a very strong paradigm, but one that has become separated from – and not sufficiently influenced by – other kinds of educational research, analysis and theorising. To take three consequences only, effectiveness research has not drawn as much as it could on qualitative methods, has been somewhat ahistorical, and has tended to ignore value assumptions. We think that connecting broader educational theorising with educational effectiveness research could strengthen both.

These are ambitious aims, on which we hope we have made a start, but it is only a start. We see the book as containing something closer to a set of tentative hypotheses than a fully established theoretical model. We hope that it will encourage more research and theorising in the direction of differentiated teacher effectiveness and further empirical testing of the model we have explored here.

Acknowledgements

We are grateful to colleagues at the Universities of Warwick and Cyprus for discussing aspects of this book in draft.

We are grateful to the University of Warwick for study leave granted to two of us (Campbell and Robinson) to work on ideas in this book.

We are grateful to the Ministry of Education in Nicosia, Cyprus for permission to conduct the study that forms Part IV of this book, and to the teachers and pupils who participated in it.

Part I

The background to teacher effectiveness research

1 Differentiated teacher effectiveness: framing the concept

The purposes of this chapter are to illustrate the influential ideas in teacher effectiveness, to argue the case for a differentiated model of teacher effectiveness, and to justify the structure of the book. We draw the ideas from key research studies, but there is no attempt to provide a comprehensive review of the literature, because the field has been systematically reviewed by others (see for example Creemers 1994, 1996, Mortimore 1998, Reynolds *et al.* 1994, Scheerens 2000, Scheerens and Bosker 1997, Teddlie and Reynolds 2000). The research studies we particularly draw upon are: Coleman *et al.* 1966, Jencks *et al.* 1972, Bernstein 1971, Brookover *et al.* 1979, Brophy and Good 1986, Rutter *et al.* 1979, Mortimore *et al.* 1988, Wittrock 1986, Creemers 1994, Mortimore 1998, Teddlie and Stringfield 1993, Reynolds *et al.* 1994, Teddlie and Reynolds 2000, Scheerens 2000, Wright *et al.* 1997.

The three terms, school effectiveness, teacher effectiveness and educational effectiveness, are used inconsistently in the literature, but are interrelated. We are taking school effectiveness to mean the impact that school-wide factors, such as leadership, school climate, and school policies, have on students' cognitive and affective performance. Teacher effectiveness is the impact that classroom factors, such as teaching methods, teacher expectations, classroom organisation, and use of classroom resources, have on students' performance. Educational effectiveness can refer to either of the above, but we are using it to mean the interactions between the school, classroom and individual student levels and their contributions to students' performance. (Educational effectiveness can refer also to the functioning of the system as a whole, but we are not treating this aspect substantively.)

There is an issue of definition. The *Shorter Oxford English Dictionary* (*SOED*) defines effectiveness as 'the quality of being effective' which is not terribly helpful, especially as effective is defined as 'concerned with, or having the function of, effecting'. The use of the term as an idea in research is much closer to the *SOED*'s definition of efficacy, defined as 'the capacity to produce effects; power to effect the object intended'. Thus we propose a definition of teacher effectiveness as follows: *the power to realise socially valued objectives agreed for teachers' work, especially, but not exclusively, the work concerned with enabling students to learn.*

Four matters flow from this definition. The contexts and conditions in which students are enabled to learn can differ; students differ; the extent to which objectives for learning are achieved can differ; and the values underlying learning and effectiveness can differ. For these reasons we are working towards a concept of effectiveness which is differentiated.

By this we mean a concept of teacher effectiveness that moves beyond the generic to incorporate the idea that teachers can be effective with some students more than others, with some subjects more than others, in some contexts more than others, with some aspects of their professional work more than others. The task of research is to build concepts and methodologies that recognise this differentiation. We argue that a next stage for research development is a model of *differentiated teacher effectiveness*. We use 'differentiated' rather than 'differential', since the latter is used in the literature to mean different extent of achievement of effectiveness on the same dimension, whereas we mean effectiveness across different dimensions of teaching.

The background to educational effectiveness research

The conventional starting points for research into school effectiveness are the studies in the United States of America by Coleman *et al.* (1966), and Jencks *et al.* (1972), whose general findings were echoed in the early work of the English sociologist, Bernstein (1971). These studies were essentially sociological in perspective, attempting to un-ravel the uncertain relationships between society (defined in concepts of the economy, linguistic and cultural capital, the moral order, or social class relations) and the performance of its schools. One funda-mental question they addressed was about the extent to which schools might 'compensate for society', to use Bernstein's phrase.

The general position portrayed in these studies was that, compared to social influences such as the family, media, poverty, or peer group culture, schools were relatively ineffective. Analysing the UK evidence, Musgrove (1971) considered that schools were 'impotent' to achieve the range of goals set for them. In the USA, Coleman and his colleagues

(1966: 21) concluded, 'when socio-economic factors are statistically controlled, it appears that differences between schools account for only a small fraction of the differences in pupil achievement'. According to Katz (1975: 142), 'it is clear that the powers of schooling have been vastly overrated. Despite substantial financing and a captive audience, the schools have not been able to attain the goals set for them, with remarkably little change, for the last century and a quarter.'

In the UK, the focus was on social class. For example, with a national sample studied longitudinally, Douglas (1964) had shown that class-related differences in attainment at age eight had increased by age eleven. Moreover, at age eleven there were significant differences in attainment between manual and non-manual workers' children whose attainment had been identical at age eight. In the United States, socio-economic status (SES) was increasingly, though problematically, conflated with race. The harshest judgement came from Katz, who argued that for poor, especially black or brown, children, education continued to control rather than to educate. Educational improvement was an illusion.

An influential meta-analysis using economic modelling (Carnoy 1976) covered studies of Puerto Ricans and Mexican/Americans as well as Afro-Americans. Carnoy (1976: 215) showed that it was possible to alter the school input allocation, including quality of teaching, but that equalising the input would not equalise the academic performance, as judged by exam scores, of 'ethnic and racial minorities'. This judgement anticipated later work in the UK in which it was shown that improving the effectiveness of schools generally would not lead to reductions in social class differences in attainment and might even increase group differences (see Mortimore 1998).

Despite the significance attached to these studies, they embodied five problematic assumptions, the investigation of which helped to set the school effectiveness research agenda.

First, the fact that there was relatively little contribution at the level of the school to variance in pupil attainment was not the same as saying that there was none, so that the school-level contribution needed to be investigated rather than written off.

Second, the use of measures of student cognitive gain as a proxy for effectiveness ignored other possible measures, for example the extent to which schools were effective in transmitting social, cultural and moral values. As Jencks (1972: 185) put it, 'the best index [of a school's effectiveness] may not be reading scores but the number of rocks thrown through its windows in an average month'.

Third, the conclusion that schooling in general did not appear to reduce social class differences in achievement was interpreted as meaning that the school had no effect. However, it could be argued that without the intervention of schooling the differences in attainment between groups would have been even greater.

The fourth point is, in retrospect, obvious. The unit of analysis was the school, rather than the classroom: effectiveness would be demonstrated in a whole-school mode. Later work (Creemers 1996, Scheerens and Bosker 1997) showed that the greatest contribution to attainment from in-school factors was the classroom.

Fifth, the studies generated an attitude of resigned scepticism (a 'climate of despair' as Brookover *et al.* (1979) put it) about the potential for educational reform based on the school; only wholesale social and economic reform would improve the educational life chances of the disadvantaged. According to Jencks (1972: 185), changing the performance of schools would be at best a marginal activity.

Although revisionism through school effectiveness research has altered the social determinism in these studies, their strength was to remind us that there were limits to improved effectiveness, a point sometimes ignored in the contemporary zeal for increasing effectiveness.

The search for evidence of educational effectiveness

Not all educational researchers shared the pessimism, or social determinism, of the social theorists. Significance was attached by some to curriculum and teaching. In the UK, Bernstein's work included a language intervention programme designed to improve working-class children's access to the extended codes considered prerequisite for educational success (see Gahagan and Gahagan 1970). In the USA, Katz (1975) advocated that schools should offer a renewed emphasis on basic literacy skills and abandon goals associated with moral socialisation, in order to empower poor children.

Moreover, there was conceptual confusion in the American studies between education reform and educational effectiveness; the argument was that educational reform was difficult to achieve. But effectiveness might be demonstrated outside reform programmes. Secondly, the focus on overcoming social disadvantage diverted attention from an important but neglected question about the extent to which all schools, including those catering for socially advantaged intakes, were effective.

In the USA, Brookover and his colleagues (1979) investigated the impact of three school-based variables: *input* (student composition and teacher characteristics), *school structure* (parental involvement, differentiation in student programme, classroom organisation, time allocation, staff satisfaction) and *school climate* (norms, expectations and beliefs within the school) on the achievement, academic self-concept, and self-reliance of the students. They reported that, in combination, the three school variables explained most of the variance between schools in measures of achievement, self-concept and self-reliance. They found the data on the association between school climate and student achievement particularly impressive in three sub-samples of school (high SES white, low SES white, and majority black schools (Brookover *et al.* 1979: 141–142).

Most importantly for the direction of later research and policy, they identified schools with similar student social or racial composition, but with very different climate variables, associated with different 'sense of futility' among students. The relevant variables reflected value-orientations: teachers' belief in their students' ability to learn, high expectations, and discriminating reinforcement of learning behaviour.

There are five methodological and conceptual issues in the Brookover *et al.* study. The test result data were pre-existing, state-wide, data collected for other reasons, and did not necessarily reflect curriculum coverage. Secondly, the data on climate and structure were, with the exception of four case studies, *perceptions* of climate and structure held by students, teachers and principals, which raises issues of validity. Third, the significant association between climate and attainment may be in part explained by the inclusion of teacher expectations in the climate variables. Fourth, the test data were attainment data, not progress data. Fifth, the school effect looked strong when the three school variables were used in combination, but treated separately the largest contribution came from the input variable in the sample as a whole, though climate made the largest contribution in the majority black schools.

In the UK, the seminal studies were by Rutter *et al.* (1979) and Mortimore *et al.* (1988), examining the school effect in secondary and junior schools respectively. In the Rutter *et al.* study, twelve secondary schools were studied, using four clusters of measures: intake, process, outcomes and ecology. The outcome measures were attendance rates, behaviour in school, examination success, employment, and delinquency. As with Brookover, Rutter found the combined effect of school process measures to be greater than any one measure and proposed that a distinctive school 'ethos' (again a value-orientation) might be necessary to explain the combination. The Mortimore *et al.* study involved 50 junior (i.e. 7–11 year olds) schools in London. Although the main concentration was upon school-wide factors, such as leadership, participation, and consistency, influencing pupil attainment, the study reported findings referring to teaching effectiveness. These included the unexceptional idea that lessons should be structured and intellectually challenging, work-centred, have high levels of communication, and a limited subject focus.

Important methodological implications for later studies were the fact that data were collected longitudinally on the same students as they progressed through school, so that causal explanations for progress could be essayed, and that classroom observation was involved so that direct evidence about teaching methods was available. Moreover, data on outcomes was not restricted to test scores, but included practical tasks, speaking and writing activities, self-concept measures, and measures of attendance and behaviour.

Models of teacher effectiveness

In America, a different perspective was being developed, which had a much lower dependence on school context for explaining teacher effectiveness. A series of key studies, culminating in the publication of the *Handbook of Research in Teaching* for the American Educational Research Association (Wittrock 1986), attempted to identify the characteristics of effective teacher behaviour in the classroom. The underlying model, referred to as the process-product model, led to a range of other models of teacher effectiveness (see Chapter 4).

The findings of this set of studies were influential for two reasons. They were able to identify the classroom behaviour of teachers most likely to lead to good student attainment, and thus to propose a set of context-free principles of teacher effectiveness. Also, some researchers had created intervention programmes based on the research. They thus linked analysis of classroom practice with its improvement.

Important though these studies were, there remained three principal problems: the model of teaching effectiveness was generic, lacking any sense that teachers could be effective with some students, in some contexts, in some subjects, but not in others; there was little explicit evocation of values underlying effectiveness; and the studies neglected the influence of school contexts on teachers' classroom performance.

The American studies may have been re-inventing wheels, since they reflected a much earlier tradition. Robinson (2004) shows that similar models of effective teaching were being developed in England in the early decades of the last century, as educationists attempted to move teaching on to a more scientific basis, in tune with the emergent scientific rationalism of the time. These are discussed fully in Chapter 3, but a distinctive characteristic was 'power to teach', that is, the ability of the teacher to adjust general pedagogical principles in the light of her judgement about the needs of individuals or of particular contexts.

Methodologies for identifying differentiated effectiveness

From 1990 onwards the field has been dominated by technical developments in measuring effectiveness. These have been brought about by the invention of two techniques, namely Multi-level Modelling (MLM) (see Goldstein 1995) and Structural Equation Modelling (SEM) (see Raykov and Marcoulides 2000). Multi-level modelling has enabled researchers to tease out the interacting variables at the social, school, classroom and individual student levels. This has been particularly important for identifying the contribution to variance made by the classroom level, including the effect of teaching. Important developments occurred in the Netherlands (Creemers 1994, 1996) with the generation of a comprehensive model of educational effectiveness. This was able to predict that classroom variables would have the greatest effect of any school-based factors. It is early to evaluate these developments (but see Thrupp 1999, 2001a, 2001b, Slee *et al.* 1998, Lauder *et al.* 1998 for some critiques) because the modelling has tended to outstrip empirical testing. However, when Creemers' model was tested empirically (e.g. by Kyriakides *et al.* 2000), the prediction that the classroom effect was the largest turned out to be supported.

Partly as a result of these technical developments, researchers in the UK and the USA (e.g. Borich 1996, Harris 2001, Watkins and Mortimore 1999, Hopkins and Reynolds 2001, Muijs and Reynolds 2000, Teddlie and Stringfield 1993) have been able to identify the issue of differentiated effectiveness. This has included different subjects (Askew *et al.* 1997, Medwell *et al.* 1999), different organisational structures (Harris 2001, Sammons *et al.* 1997) and different socio-economic contexts (Teddlie and Stringfield 1993, Borich 1996). Educational effectiveness research was beginning to incorporate what Hopkins and Reynolds (2001) call 'context specificity'.

Towards a model of differentiated teacher effectiveness: five possible dimensions of difference

It follows from the foregoing outline that there may be five potential dimensions of differentiation in teacher effectiveness.

The *range of role activities* expected of teachers in modernising education systems is extremely broad. These include social, pastoral, welfare dimensions and leadership of other adults, and other work outside classrooms, in addition to the formal instructional dimension.

Second, there is the issue of differentiated effectiveness across *different subjects* in the curriculum, or across different components (algebra as against number in mathematics).

Third, teachers may be differentially effective in promoting the cognitive progress of different groups of students according to *background variables*. The principal ones are ability, age (or developmental stage), sex, socio-economic status and ethnicity.

Fourth, teachers may be differentially effective in promoting the learning of students according to the students' *personal characteristics*, such as their personality, cognitive learning style, and extent of motivation and self-esteem.

Fifth, teachers may be differentially effective in response to the different *cultural and organisational contexts* in which they work, such as the school culture, department structure and school size.

The nature and structure of the book

The book is organised in four parts.

Part I presents an overview of theory and research, examining the nature of teaching as work, historical antecedents and empirical research findings. After this introductory chapter, Chapter 2 examines the different roles that teachers occupy and proposes that these should be included in a differentiated model. Chapter 3 traces the historical antecedents of ideas on teacher effectiveness illustrating resonance with current models. Chapter 4 evaluates the main approaches to teacher effectiveness research.

Part II proposes a tentative technical model of differentiated teacher effectiveness, in terms of concepts and methodologies. Chapter 5 develops a critique of this research leading to suggestions for a differentiated model. In Chapter 6 the five dimensions of differentiation are elaborated as a theoretical model. Chapter 7 examines the relatively small amount of existing research on differentiated teacher effectiveness, to support the argument that the model has some potential for realisation. Chapter 8 develops the theoretical model further in terms of concepts and methodologies.

Part III explores the implications for values and educational policy of a differentiated model. Chapter 9 exemplifies the value assumptions underlying teacher effectiveness while Chapter 10 examines the implications for teacher appraisal, in so far as these can be discerned. Chapter 11 explores the implications of a differentiated teacher effectiveness model for educational policy. In these three chapters we are deliberately and, we would argue, appropriately, illustrative rather than comprehensive in our approach.

In Part IV, in Chapter 12, we illustrate the application of the model in a specific research project conducted to test some aspects of the model as a research design.

By using the singular noun 'model' we do not mean a single inflexible and overarching model. We mean something much more tentative and exploratory, since the current state of concept and research development in differentiated teacher effectiveness is emergent rather than established. Another reason for tentativeness is that we do not mean statistical modelling exclusively, since we believe that qualitative elements in research in this field have a significant part to play in understanding the meanings that teachers attach to teaching effectiveness, and the appropriate forms of combination of quantitative and qualitative paradigms are also at an exploratory stage. What we are proposing is more like a set of research-based hypotheses and methodologies that need substantial testing and refining. However, the term 'model' is widely used in the literature and for that reason we have adopted it, though *models* might be thought more suitable.

2   The range of teachers' work

The purpose of this chapter is to analyse the findings of research investigating the nature of teachers' work, its range and activities, and to examine the implications of such research for the development of a model of differentiated teacher effectiveness. We have largely excluded studies of pedagogy, i.e. studies concerned with the effectiveness of different approaches to classroom behaviour. This may at first sight seem perverse, but there are two reasons for it: our primary intention here is to examine the range of activities that make up teachers' work; and studies of pedagogy occupy most of the rest of this book.

Investigations into the work of teachers: a typology

Studies of the work of teachers can be constructed as falling into five broad categories, though there is some overlap.

First there are theoretical, mostly neo-Marxist, analyses investigating the concept of work intensification. The most influential have been from Apple (1986) in the United States, from Connell (1985) in Australia and Ozga and Lawn (1981, 1989) in England. Their theoretical positions can be traced to an American sociologist, Larson (1980), who argued that non-manual professional workers – 'educated labour' – experienced, under late twentieth-century capitalism, increased pressure for efficiency and productivity in the delivery of their services. This had led to reduced collegiality in work relations, less time for relaxation in official breaks and pressure to cut corners leading to deterioration in the quality of service provided. Apple argued that intensification represented one of the most tangible ways in which the work privileges of educational workers were eroded. These ranged from the apparently trivial – not being allowed a coffee break – to a total absence of time to keep up with one's field and a chronic sense of work overload. In England, Ozga and Lawn interpreted the thesis as reflecting the de-professionalising and de-skilling of teachers. Attempts to test the thesis empirically (see Campbell and Neill 1994a, Chapter 10, for a review) suggested that it was highly problematic and that the evidence did not support the thesis in many aspects. Campbell and Neill also argue that the particular association of work intensification with late capitalism was unconvincing, since similar indicators of intensification occurred in both capitalist and socialist societies.

Second, there are studies of teaching as a profession, and the nature of teacher professionalism (e.g. Lortie 1969, Etzioni 1969, Hoyle 1974, 1995, Hoyle and John 1995, Little and McLaughlin 1993, Helsby 1999). These tend to be analytical studies, concerned with the nature of a profession and the extent to which school teachers typically experience the same degrees of autonomy and control over their work as other professions. Those in the UK predate the formation of the first formal professional body for teachers, the General Teaching Council, in 2001, and therefore are in some respects anachronistic. Some of these studies analyse the feminisation of the profession (e.g. Evetts 1990, Sharpe 1984), while others examine different professional roles (e.g. Whitaker 1983, Nias 1989, Webb and Vulliamy 1996).

Third, there are studies examining the affective and personal aspects of teaching, i.e. sources of morale, motivation, stress and burn-out. These are both analytical and normative in nature, seeking ways of improving the first two and reducing the last two characteristics (Dunham 1984, Kyriacou 1980, Varlaam *et al.* 1992, Travers and Cooper 1993, Vandenberghe and Huberman 1999). These tend to portray teaching as relatively high in stress as an occupation, partly due to the frequency or intensity of the classroom interactions that teachers have with pupils, and partly due to the high degree of teachers' ego identification with their work. The more recent of these studies, such as those in Vandenberghe and Huberman (1999), conclude that 'performativity' (Ball 1999) has exacerbated stress, reduced morale, and led to high levels of burn-out.

Fourth, there are studies of the functions of teaching for society. These are often supra-national studies, drawing on sociology and policy analyses, in which the changing role of education, and therefore teachers, is examined. They are meta-analyses, drawing on official data rather than generating new primary evidence. The main function of these studies is to trace macro-changes in the relationship between education systems and the work of teachers, and to identify issues associated with conditions and pay (see International Labour Office 1981, 1991, OECD 1990, Louis and Smith 1990, Reyes 1990).

Finally, there are empirical surveys of the use of teachers' time on work. These are atheoretical, descriptive modelling, or mapping, exercises concerning themselves with the hours spent on work, and comparing them with previous studies or with studies of teaching in other countries, or of other professional workers. They also report on the balance of time spent on different aspects of work, such as planning, marking, teaching, professional development, communicating with parents, working on committees, so as to provide a profile of the teacher's workload. There has been a strong tradition of such studies in the United Kingdom. Duthie (1970) and Johnstone (1993) examined the position in Scotland, while Hilsum and Cane (1971) and Hilsum and Strong (1978) looked at English teachers. The interest probably arises because the working conditions of teachers in the UK have not had an upper limit on working hours, in contrast to other systems (see for example Campbell and Neill 1994a, 1994b, Hilsum and Cane 1971, Hilsum and Strong 1978, Galton and MacBeath 2002, Office of Manpower Economics 2000, PriceWaterhouseCoopers 2001).

Profiles of teaching as work

The studies have in common an interest in teaching under systemic change, whether change of the school curriculum, of school management or of the system as a whole. For this reason we draw upon some evidence and analysis from all of the categories of study, but the predominant focus is upon the last one. Studies in this category have typically produced profiles showing the overall working time of teachers, the main categories of work activity involved, and the proportions of time spent on them. From these profiles it is possible to identify which activities might be used for research relating to differentiated effectiveness and to analyse the profiles in relation to teacher effectiveness generally.

There is no perfect agreement about how to categorise different aspects of teachers' work, and different studies have used different methodologies and instruments, so that measurement errors could be high because of activity overlap. (The majority of studies use diary logs, self-reports, and/or questionnaires, though the studies for the Office of Manpower Economics (2000) were able to triangulate these with follow-up interviews. Two studies (Phillips 1997, Galton and MacBeath 2002) used direct observation to triangulate diaries. Despite these differences in methodology and instruments, there is impressive agreement about the extent of working time overall in the studies conducted in England since 1990. The principal studies (Campbell and

Neill 1994a, 1994b, Office of Manpower Economics 2000, Price-WaterhouseCoopers 2001, Galton and MacBeath 2002) tend to agree that English teachers work on average somewhere between 50 and 55 hours per week in term time. The range is largely accounted for by phase or role responsibility, with head teachers and other senior staff working longer hours than junior staff and secondary teachers working longer hours than primary teachers, partly because of the latter's shorter teaching week. Scottish teachers work fewer hours than those in England and Wales, according to a survey for the Scottish Council for Research in Education (Johnstone 1993). Galton and MacBeath (2002) point out that the figure for English teachers is considerably more than managers in other professions, who typically work a 45 hour week, though teachers have compensatory longer vacation time. Overall working time has increased since Hilsum and Cane (1971) reported as typical a 45 hour working week in term time.

There are three general implications for measuring teacher effectiveness. First, teachers instruct pupils in classrooms for about 18 hours a week, approximately one third of their total working time. If instruction-related activity, such as planning and marking, is taken into account the proportion rises to about two thirds, still leaving a third of teachers' work not directly related to classroom teaching. This suggests that activities beyond the classroom might be taken account of in appraisal and research. To take a specific example, teachers spend time with parents in consultation about pupils' work. It is widely believed that this activity contributes to improvement in pupil learning, especially in schools in areas of high levels of economic and social disadvantage. To ignore this activity in conceptualising effectiveness simply because it does not normally occur in classrooms seems to us perverse. Secondly, all the studies show that the overall working time has increased even though the time spent instructing pupils has remained broadly constant. The increase in working time is accounted for by extra-classroom activities associated with 'modernisation' of teaching, and to ignore it in a model of effectiveness would be anachronistic. Third, counting hours is a banal activity if undertaken for itself; it has point only if it can be used to contribute to understanding teacher effectiveness. To illustrate the point, it can be shown that teachers spend some substantial time in the school day on low level routines such as photocopying or putting up displays or registering pupils, which in principle could be undertaken by adults other than teachers, thereby freeing the latter to concentrate on more directly instructional activities.

There is a further, more specific, point concerning the differences in profiles that emerge from different phases of school teaching. Primary teachers work in flatter structures, with relatively little hierarchical differentiation between class teachers, differences in profile being largely between head teachers and deputies on the one hand and other staff on the other. Most primary teachers spend most of the school day teaching, with little time allowed in the school day for administration, preparation or marking. In secondary schools, the hierarchical structures are more differentiated with increasingly reduced time in the school day spent on teaching and increased time on administration and leadership activities as teachers move up the hierarchy (see Campbell and Neill 1994a, 1994b). These organisational and contextual differences might be incorporated in a differentiated model of teacher effectiveness.

Categories of work activity

There is also considerable agreement among the studies on the broad-brush categories of teachers' work. These are: teaching; planning, preparation, marking and giving feedback; pastoral and welfare activities; communications with parents and other stakeholders; professional development and training; leadership and management, including meetings with colleagues; and other activities. However, there is much less secure agreement about how to measure these activities and, once measured, how to allocate particular activities to any given category. For example, the apparently least problematic category is teaching, but during the time that they are teaching teachers frequently give feedback to pupils, set tests and sometimes mark pupils' work.

Teaching

Teaching pupils in classrooms is the work activity to which most importance is attached in current models of teacher effectiveness. This is understandable given the recent evidence that pupil learning, in the sense of the value-added learning generated by the school, is largely associated with classroom-level factors (e.g. Creemers 1994, Scheerens and Bosker 1997, Kyriakides *et al.* 2000). However, there are some complexities about teaching of which existing models do not take adequate account. They call for a more differentiated model. The principal complexities are to do with the pupils in the class and the nature of the subject. Teaching effectiveness is responsive, to an as yet unknown degree, to the age of the pupils, the ability of the pupils, the composition of the class, the subject being taught, and the extent to which the teacher has appropriate subject knowledge. These complexities are not likely to be discrete in their effect but may often interact and combine in the classroom setting. For example, being effective with a class of 25 five year olds, who have not yet been socialised into turn-taking, and who include four or five pupils whose behaviour is disruptive, is likely to take a different form from effectiveness with a class of ten eighteen year olds following a high-salience examination course in a specialist subject, which they have opted to study on the basis of their previous high attainment in earlier examinations, and who have demonstrated capability for independent learning. Similarly the nature of the subject being taught is likely to affect teaching. An Art class in a studio, with most of the time being spent by pupils on the production of a piece of pottery, might call for different teaching from that required to teach communicative skills in a modern foreign language class. In the former class we might expect a large amount of 'individual monitoring' (Galton *et al.* 1980), as the teacher goes round the class helping individuals as they produce the pottery. In the latter we might expect large amounts of 'class enquiry' (Galton *et al.* 1980) as the teacher interacts with the whole class developing communicative competence through talk in the target language.

Also, a significant amount of teaching is carried out by teachers who have relatively low levels of subject knowledge, and we ought to attempt to understand what effectiveness means for teachers put into that position, and whether there are subjects in which effectiveness is less hampered by lack of subject expertise than others. Teaching subjects requiring high levels of skill, such as music and foreign languages, or knowledge of safety issues, such as physical education and laboratory-based science teaching, might be more dependent on strong subject knowledge than others calling upon more generally available knowledge, such as History, Social Studies, Citizenship and English Literature. However, we simply do not know. Thus any model aiming to incorporate differential effectiveness will need to be able to show how these factors relating to pupils and subjects have been allowed for.

Furthermore, the existing research has been helpful in distinguishing between teaching that is effective and that which is not. There has been no sustained attempt to distinguish between different quality or levels of effectiveness among those identified as effective. The exception is the Hay McBer model of teacher effectiveness (DfEE 2000) in which teacher performance is placed on one of three levels. However, the connection between these levels and pupils' cognitive gain is unclear and the methodology by which the model overall was created and tested empirically has been difficult to verify (BERA 2001). A model that is able to distinguish the outstanding teachers from the merely competent in a transparent, reliable and valid way is now needed.

Planning, marking and feedback

It can be shown that, under conditions of curriculum reform, teachers spend almost as much time planning as they do teaching (Campbell and Neill 1994a, 1994b, Office of Manpower Economics 2000, Galton and MacBeath 2002). In current models the effectiveness of planning is conflated with teaching: teaching effectiveness acts as a proxy for effectiveness in planning. There is sense in this; in research and appraisal, there is a pressing need to avoid time-consuming bureaucracy that contributes little extra to our understanding. Moreover, in appraisal it would be a problem in practice, if not logically, if a teacher were to be judged effective at planning but ineffective at teaching or vice versa. However, in principle, it is possible to envisage teaching that could be improved by more effective planning, and planning made more effective by the evaluation of teaching. Perhaps a particular focus might be the effectiveness of marking, much of which occurs outside the classroom but which, through formative feedback, may differentially contribute to pupil learning, depending upon its quality. We would argue therefore that a differentiated model should, as far as is technically feasible and efficient in use of time, incorporate the role of planning, preparation and marking.

Pastoral and welfare activities

There is increasing European interest in the role of teachers in pastoral activity, and the interest worldwide has grown very significantly. This is especially true in societies undergoing radical cultural shifts in values or economic modernisation, and intergenerational differences in social attitudes to authority, such as China and the Pacific Rim countries or Eastern Europe or Africa. Nearly all teachers engage in pastoral and welfare activities, designed to respond to the emotional and social needs of pupils. Such activities normally have as their objectives the development of the affective aspects of pupils, such as moral values, self-esteem, and behaviour considered to be desirable by the school. For some senior staff in the UK, pastoral duties occupy a major part of their working week, while in the USA counselling can be a full-time responsibility. Broadly speaking, secondary school teachers engage in pastoral and welfare activities outside teaching time as well as in the classroom. Thus there are House systems with pastoral time, counselling and careers advice, as well as activity which is more overtly disciplinary in purpose. In primary schools, pastoral work is frequently integrated into classroom learning activities, such as when young children are invited to tell their class about their news, or when children are comforted by the teacher after some mishap, or praised in front of their classmates for some action they have taken, but the emergence of programmes such as Circle Time (see Mosley 1996) is beginning to separate out pastoral time from academic time.

There are substantial difficulties, both conceptual and methodological, in incorporating pastoral activities into a model of teacher effectiveness. The first is a matter of definition. Pastoral work tends to be defined by what it is not, namely academic or cognitive learning, which in theory could allow any activity outside classroom cognitive tasks to be included, giving rise to the possibility that supervising pupils at break times, or in detentions, could be included. This would pose serious problems of measurement of quality. Even where it is constructively defined, it could be considered as encompassing the whole work of the school, since success in learning is thought to be associated with self-esteem and self-concept, and with values such as industriousness (see Chapter 7).

Second, there is little in the literature to help us tease out pastoral activity that contributes to pupil learning from that which has no effect. Brookover *et al.* (1979) in the USA associated positive self-esteem with particular school climate and attainment, but the direction of the effect is unclear. In England, Her Majesty's Inspectorate has consistently praised primary schools for their positive moral climate and for supporting pupils' emotional and social development, yet it has been hard to show how, if at all, these factors contribute to effective learning. It may be that positive climate and self-esteem arise from effective learning, or that both interact, rather than that the climate and raised esteem impact directly upon academic performance.

Third, it is not clear that pastoral activity should be judged on the basis of its contribution to learning. It is often argued (Mosley 1996) that it has to be justified in its own, affective terms, in the ways it contributes to behaviour and self-confidence, irrespective of whether it contributes to learning. On this basis we would need a model whose criteria were significantly broader than pupil cognitive gain, including effectiveness in developing values and self-esteem.

Finally the literature makes clear that much of the effectiveness in pastoral activity depends more upon the effectiveness and appropriateness of school-wide policies than does effectiveness in teaching. This means that a model would need to be able to identify the contribution that teachers make, either to the development of pastoral policy at the level of the school, or department within the school, or to the achievement of pastoral goals at the level of the class, or individual pupils.

These problems are daunting, but there is a research base, especially in respect of the development of pupil self-concept and self-esteem, sufficiently robust to enable the measurement of pupil growth in these areas to be undertaken convincingly. Equally, the development of multi-level modelling should enable the different contributions to school, department, class and pupil to be identified. Bearing in mind the argument above, we would want a model that recognised that effectiveness in this area might be judged in relation to gain in cognitive outcome, where this could be shown to have occurred, but a differentiated model could also incorporate criteria more directly related to affective aims, irrespective of impact on cognitive gain.

Working with parents and other stakeholders

Time spent working with parents and other stakeholders such as school governors and members of the school's community occupies a relatively small part of a teacher's working year. Moreover, it takes different forms in different systems. In most systems, and notably in the USA, parent–teacher associations support the school through social activities designed to raise funds, but it is unclear how this kind of activity contributes directly to effectiveness. In Australia, the 'new work order' according to the analysis by Grundy and Bonsor (2000) involves intensive reporting to parents (though less intensive involvement with other stakeholders). Across Europe, three different functions are discernible, according to Galton and Blyth's (1989) review for the Council of Europe. These are to participate in school decision-making, to support teaching, and to engage in child-oriented socialisation. In Italy, according to HMI (1994), parental involvement is highly formalised into school committees with a corporate focus which take strategic decisions about textbooks, and about the evaluation and development of curriculum in particular years of the school. In England, it is less formal and more individualised, since parents can set up meetings with teachers to discuss the progress of their own children at any time agreeable, as well as having highly formalised contexts such as governors' meetings and parents' evenings. In addition, many schools in areas of social and economic disadvantage run programmes for parents to train them in supporting their children's learning, for example in how they should help them with homework, or help them to develop literacy and numeracy.

Both Rutter *et al.* (1979) and Mortimore *et al.* (1988) found parental involvement and amounts of homework to be positively associated with school effectiveness. This gives us some empirical basis for arguing that a model of teacher effectiveness also should incorporate working with parents. However, it is clear from the research that some aspects, such as specific programmes to enable parents to support pupil learning, are more closely associated with pupil cognitive gain than others, such as involvement in formal meetings with parent bodies. The implication here is that we would need to be selective about which aspects were incorporated into the model. However, selectivity might need to vary by age of pupil, with child-oriented socialisation activity being seen as important for teachers of young children, and support for teaching and learning being more important for teachers of older pupils.

Professional development and training

Modernised professionalism requires continuing professional development in order that the teacher can keep up to date with academic and professional developments in their field. In some systems of appraisal, such as in universities in England, evidence of commitment to continuing professional development is taken as a proxy for aspects of effectiveness generally. Teachers generally spend increasing amounts of time on professional development, particularly as systemic reforms are being implemented. This is to ensure that teachers are informed and up-skilled in relation to the reform initiatives. On the face of it, such activity should feature in any model of effectiveness.

The major problem, however, is that it is difficult to demonstrate that time spent on professional development impacts directly on pupil learning, or, if it does, which elements of professional development activity make the significant contributions. In their sample of 189 primary head teachers, Campbell *et al.* (2002) argue that even where teachers were committed to evaluate the effect of professional development on pupils' behaviour and learning, and even though they believed that there had been an impact, they were unable to do so. The second problem is that it would be possible to measure proportions of time, or indicators of certification, spent on professional development but such measures on their own would not be very useful since length of time spent is not an indicator of worthwhileness. It is particularly unhelpful where teachers are required to participate in professional development contractually by the state or its agencies. It would be useful, though much more problematic from the point of view of reliability and validity, to incorporate a measure of the quality or usefulness of time spent on professional development, by self-report instruments. There are therefore good reasons for including professional development activity in a model of effectiveness, but we think that the methodological difficulties in this area are currently substantial.

Leadership and management

The research evidence, especially from Mortimore *et al.* (1988), is that effective schools are characterised by positive leadership especially in relation to academic matters such as requiring teachers to produce planning forecasts, establishing consistency and clear policies, and supporting professional development in a discriminating way. Positive leadership also contributed to school climate and to participatory decision-making. Clearly, on this model of school effectiveness, some teachers, mainly the senior staff, would need to have their leadership qualities incorporated into a model of teacher effectiveness. Leadership, however, is not conceptually, or in practice, the monopoly of senior staff, since under forms of distributed leadership, all staff exercise leadership in matters such as curriculum development, in quality of relationships with others in the school, and in matters such as holding and demonstrating high standards and expectations. We would argue therefore that leadership activity should be incorporated into a model of effectiveness, though the problems of what counts as leadership might vary strongly by the nature of the role responsibilities held by the individual. Measuring leadership is also problematic, and many of the characteristics in the Mortimore *et al.* study have an element of tautology about them.

Towards a model including a range of teacher role activities

From the above analyses, it is clear why previous models of teacher effectiveness have been generic and have generally limited ways of measuring effectiveness to pupil cognitive performance in mathematics and the national language. Economy of effort, the high salience of mathematics performance, the availability of tests with established levels of reliability and validity are all real advantages in educational research.

Yet there have been exceptions to this narrowness. Mortimore's (1998) review of his work showed that he had included a relatively wide range of measures extending beyond cognitive performance. As he argues in a chapter rebutting many of the alleged defects of school effectiveness research:

> we have collected and used a much broader range of outcomes than most critics acknowledge . . . in addition to reading and mathematics tests, practical mathematics tasks, speaking assessments and writing assessments, as well as measures of self-concept, attitude to school, attendance and behaviour.
>
> (Mortimore 1998: 321)

The main differences in a differentiated model will relate to pupils and subjects. Pupil characteristics, such as age, the composition of a class, the different kinds of pupil, such as those with SEN, those defined as very able, those from different social and cultural backgrounds, are all problematic for a generic model of effectiveness. Likewise with subjects, where differences in terms of appropriate pedagogy and levels of expertise need to be incorporated.

However, as we have argued earlier, the contribution of different aspects of the work of teachers to their effectiveness extends beyond the classroom. There is very little research which shows the contribution of these different aspects of teachers' work to their effectiveness, but three dimensions in particular should be encompassed in modelling teacher effectiveness: planning, marking and feedback; pastoral care; and working with parents. These should not be excluded from a model simply because they occur outside classrooms. Secondly, in some of these activities there ought not to be a requirement that effectiveness should be defined by reference to pupil cognitive gain. There are other outcomes – for example, improved parental confidence, improved pupil self-concept – that should be valued even where it cannot be shown that teachers' achievement feeds directly into pupil academic performance.

There are two dimensions, namely professional development and leadership, which are increasingly seen as significant in improving educational effectiveness but in which the research base is comparatively weak. In these, further research is called for in order to generate appropriate methods and instruments, but potentially these two dimensions also can be incorporated into a differentiated model.

3 Historical models of teacher effectiveness

The purpose of this chapter is to begin to redress some of the historical neglect of pedagogy and to probe the question as to whether there might exist any principles about effective teaching and learning which transcend time, context and place and which therefore might have something to say to today's teachers, researchers and policy-makers. Inspired by Simon's identification of the late nineteenth/early twentieth century period of pedagogical advance in Britain, the main focus of the chapter is on the development of a practical, experimental pedagogy among leading teacher trainers in the UK during the period 1900–1920 who were interested in finding a rational basis for teaching, moving it from intuitive craft to a science of pedagogy (Robinson 2004). Embryonic forms of pedagogic enquiry and research in this period sought an integration of knowledge about teaching and its practical application in an attempt to bridge the already firmly established theory/practice divide.

In his presidential address to the British Training College Association (TCA) in 1912, Professor J. A. Green of Sheffield University argued that it was time for teachers and teacher trainers to move away from the construction of teaching as technical craftsmanship towards a more critical engagement with the principles which underpinned effective teaching practice. Envisaging the potential of a partnership between trained practitioners in the classroom, staff in the new University Departments of Education and teacher trainers, Green and many of his colleagues looked forward to the development and refinement of educational theory by experienced practitioners and researchers. Educational theory was not something to be imposed upon the teaching profession by academic or scientific experts, but would be rooted in a 'more systematic study of pedagogics' which was classroom-based and concerned with the lived realities of teachers' work (Green 1913: 50).

Nearly 100 years on from Green's proposition, at a time when pedagogy has been rediscovered in educational debate and policy-making, a widely held view is that this promise of a 'more systematic study of pedagogics' was never fully sustained and certainly was not something to which practising teachers ever contributed in any serious way (Mortimore 1999). Simon's critique of the historical denigration of pedagogy, written in the early 1990s, argued that in Britain, 'The most striking aspect of current thinking and discussion about education is its eclectic character, reflecting deep confusion of thought, and of aims and purposes, relating to learning and teaching – to pedagogy' (Simon 1994). He claimed then that aside from a brief flourishing of professional interest in pedagogy in the late nineteenth and early twentieth centuries, Britain's education system had long suffered from a lack of an all-embracing, universalised, scientific theory of education relating to the practice of teaching.

As we now know, this situation has changed. Much of the current research into effective teaching, however, has failed to take account of the historical development of educational theory and teaching method. Interestingly, much earlier historians of pedagogy have also been subjected to the vagaries of fashion as interest in pedagogy has waxed and waned. In 1886, Gabriel Compayre in his history of the subject observed that, 'pedagogy, long-neglected . . . has regained its standing, nay more, it has become the fashion' (Compayre 1886: xii). This has some resonance with current developments. His justification for studying the history of pedagogy in his own time, however, raises some important questions for historians of education today. Compayre argued that: 'The history of pedagogy is a necessary introduction to pedagogy itself. It should be studied not for purposes of erudition or for mere curiosity, but with a practical purpose for the sake of finding in it the permanent truths which are the essentials of a definite theory of education' (Compayre 1886: xviii). The notion of permanent pedagogical truths might seem at best quirky and old-fashioned and at worst anachronistic to current research and policy on effective school teaching in the twenty-first century. Yet, just as Compayre sought to look back at the history of pedagogy for greater understanding, it is arguably as instructive now to examine pedagogy historically, not least because this might have some bearing upon current research and practice.

Historical context

If, as has already been suggested, pedagogy has recently emerged from a long exile from educational research and policy-making then it will be helpful to briefly situate this development within its historical framework. In order to understand this pedagogical legacy, it is necessary to turn to the historical development of educational theory (Robinson 2000). Simon has blamed a combination of social, political and ideological factors for the dearth of a truly scientific basis to the theory and practice of education. Yet, he also suggests that there was once a brief moment in our educational past when a rigorous and coherent system of pedagogy was being developed and refined by the teaching profession itself in the UK. This emergent pedagogical system which sought the systematic integration of theory and practice flourished as the mass system of elementary schooling expanded and became more sophisticated in terms of scope and purpose by the end of the nineteenth century. It was premised on a positive belief in the innate educability of all children and in the importance of effective teaching to realise their potential. This was supported by improved training both in the pupil–teacher centres and church and municipal training colleges, which provided professional and academic training for elementary teachers, and also by the gradual establishment of education as a subject of university study in the early university day training colleges, which sprang up during the 1890s. The interruption of war and the ensuing rise of psychology, psychometrics and intelligence testing in the inter-war period highlighted and categorised the limitations of human potential and destroyed those earlier pedagogical gains whose roots were found in the lowly-esteemed elementary school tradition. A *laissez-faire*, highly individualised, private pedagogy emerged after the Second World War as teachers tried to negotiate their way around a confusing and contested muddle of ideological rhetoric. The unhelpful dichotomisation of progressive versus traditional teaching methods and child-centred versus subject-centred frameworks, according to Simon, caused the real question of the integration of theoretical knowledge with the practice of education to be side-stepped.

Professional pedagogical debate at the turn of the twentieth century

Professional pedagogical debate at the turn of the twentieth century which led to the elaboration of principles of effective teaching has to be situated within a much wider movement across the UK, the rest of Europe and America which attempted to base the study of education on a much more rational, scientific basis. The chequered and often contested history of the establishment of education within academe and the ensuing implications for status, theory and practice have been variously charted by writers such as Aldrich, De Paepe, Lagemann, Labaree, Selleck, Simon and Wooldridge. In examining this development and the way in which the science of education went on to influence ideas about teaching in the early years of the twentieth century, however, it is important to distinguish between general ideas about a science of education and more specific ideas about the science of teaching. In England, in the early years of the twentieth century, there was particular concern to connect theories of education with its practice. For those educationists seeking, amid the flurry of scientific interest and activity in the various paradigms of child study, applied psychology and intelligence testing, a stronger connection between the science and practice of education, experimental pedagogy offered some sort of solution. In 1907 Adams urged the profession to seek to answer pedagogical questions by engaging in systematic observation and experiment conducted upon scientific principles (Adams 1907: i). Experimental pedagogy was just one branch of the movement to place educational theory on a more secure scientific basis (De Paepe 1987: 279). A committee under the presidency of Findlay and Green reported to the 1910 meeting of the British Association for the Advancement of Science in an attempt to promote the cause of experimental pedagogy. Experimental pedagogy, according to them, was different from child study or observation because it specifically sought answers to questions of educational method and was concerned with processes of teaching. The experimental pedagogy movement spread rapidly through Europe and America, with corresponding experimental or laboratory schools, such as Binet's laboratory school in France, the Fielden Demonstration schools in England and the Horace Mann, Speyer and Dewey schools in America, being set up to investigate the relation of theory and practice in teaching (Claparede 1911: 3). The movement was not, however, conceptually, theoretically or practically coherent and has to be understood in the context of the mêlée of activity associated with education at that time. One of the chief obstacles to the development of a theory of teaching which was fully integrated with its practice lay in the difficulty in finding an appropriate branch of established applied science with which to identify. Should the science of teaching be located in physiology, psychology, logic, ethics, philosophy, child study or some other branch of scientific enquiry, and furthermore how should it be constructed in relation to actual practice and the lived realities of serving teachers?

If the combination of scientific method and practical experience was lacking in the earlier attempts to set education on a scientific footing, by the early years of the twentieth century teacher educators in England were calling for a science of teaching which was rooted in, not separate from, the art or craft of teaching. Previously, the gulf between teachers who practised the art or craft of their business, and theorists who developed erudite but inaccessible and remote theories had appeared intractable and formed the heart of a professional tension between theory and practice in teaching. According to Findlay, the combination of scientific method and practical experience had historically been lacking. 'The sharp separation between theory and practice in the examination papers merely emphasises the wide gulf which has severed "the theory" of the lecture-room from "the practice" of the daily toil in the classroom. This gulf somehow must be bridged; so long as it exists it remains as a standing reproach both to those who practise and to those who theorise' (Findlay 1903: 23). For Findlay, any science of teaching had to be drawn from its practice:

> we are seeking all the time for links by which we may bind together the Theory of Education with the Practice of it. We see that in our science, as in every other principle, abstract principles can only be attained by the slow process of experience; books on Education, lectures on Education and Psychology have their value, but only so far as they touch the practical experience and observation of the student. Hence then the importance of assigning a due place to that portion of the student's work which is called Practical Training; for Practical Training is essentially Laboratory Training, the lecture room and the text book can do nothing apart from this constant experience in the schoolroom.
>
> (Findlay 1903: 23)

Most of the chapter focuses upon the contribution to this systematic study of pedagogics of three particular teacher trainers – Joseph Findlay, Thomas Raymont and James Welton. They were all experienced teachers of children and trainers of teachers and had specialised in method teaching to student teachers. Welton and Findlay were appointed as Professors of Education at Leeds and Manchester Universities respectively and Raymont was Professor of Education at the University College of South Wales and Monmouthshire at Cardiff. They all contributed to the *Journal of Experimental Pedagogy*, set up in 1911 by leading members of the Training College Association (TCA) to promote pedagogic research, and disseminated their ideas at various conferences and meetings of the Training College Association as well as through their publications and professional work.

In search of general principles

The critical professional issue for Findlay, Welton and Raymont, as it still is for educationists today, was the relationship between theory and practice. They argued that the science and art of teaching had for too long been falsely dichotomised. This had resulted in a confusion of disparate theories of education which consisted either of dubious scientific claims divorced from experience or practical hints and tips for teachers which were unrelated to existing understanding about teaching and learning. Findlay argued that 'Theory without practice is wind; Practice without theory is quackery' (Findlay 1902: 11). Raymont was worried about the piecemeal and haphazard application of psychology to education in the name of science. Psychology at this time was itself in a state of flux with the notion of Alexander Bain's faculty psychology which had offered a scientific approach to curriculum and pedagogy, which dominated late nineteenth-century educational theory and practice and sought to develop the intellect and character through a careful system of teaching through the training of the senses, memory and imagination, now redundant. The rigid polarisation of what Welton defined as 'knowing' and 'doing' in education was therefore identified as a real hindrance to the proper development of a theory of teaching and learning (Welton 1906: 9).

Rather than being set in antithesis to each other, it was suggested that theory and practice should be considered in terms of a symbiotic relationship. Raymont argued that 'Theory and practice are not opposed, but complementary, not different things, but different sides of the same thing, each meaningless without reference to the other' (Raymont 1904: 24). The two extremes between theory and practice were to be avoided: the mere theorist adept at spinning fine webs of doctrine who then collapses on contact with the hard facts of experience; and the mere empiricist, or rule-of-thumb practitioner, who seeks no rational basis for his practice.

Any theory of education which was not rooted in practice and which had not been tested in the mettle of the classroom could not be upheld. What was being sought was a 'sane' theory of education which harmonised the results of experience. This should command the respect and inform the practice of teachers and bear a direct relation to the lived realities of classroom life. Anticipating the ideas that these activities might be differentiated, Raymont argued, 'A good practical teacher must have a theory behind his practice, whether implicit or explicitly, and a sane theorist must have constant regard to existing circumstances' (Raymont 1904: 24). A crucial test for the validity of any theory was whether its proponent could teach. It is significant that these educationists had all served their time in the classroom and had distinguished themselves as practising teachers before moving into higher education. Findlay was particularly keen to demonstrate that his ideas about education were not proclaimed from the remove of the lecture room, but were drawn from and exemplified by his own practice and experience. He argued that 'theory is practice become conscious of itself, and practice is realised theory' (Findlay 1902: 17).

'Essence, rules, integrity'

In elucidating this 'sane theory' of education, Findlay, Raymont and Welton were seeking to identify core principles of teaching and learning. They were concerned with capturing and disseminating fundamental truths or rules of practice which could be embraced by teachers. These generic principles expressed and formulated from experience, practice and research were to form the bedrock of any proper theory of education (Findlay 1902: 11).

In the preface to Welton's book for students on the forms of criticism lessons, W. Scott Coward, Her Majesty's Inspector for Training Colleges, wrote: 'Mr Welton does not lose sight for a moment, however, of the necessity of principles; they are luminous everywhere throughout his book, and they form, as should ever be the case, the basis and groundwork upon which the whole of the practical superstructure stands' (Welton 1902: i). In writing this book, it was Welton's aim to produce a pro forma for criticising a lesson which would encourage students to record specific applications of general principles. Welton clearly believed that there existed principles which transcended time and context and which had been embodied in the practice of educators who, having reflected and meditated upon their work, found a rational basis for the successful application of certain modes of teaching.

Engaged as they were in the business of training teachers, Findlay, Raymont and Welton wanted the generic principles of teaching to be understood by young teachers. In the relative calm of a period of training away from the immediate responsibilities of a class, trainee teachers could be grounded in the principles and practice of their work. Training provided an opportune time for the problems of school life and work to be thought out in the light of the wisdom both of the past and of the present. The TCA endorsed this belief in the value of learning principles at the training stage so that students should emerge 'with a real grip of first principles and with a genuine desire to keep critically abreast of pedagogic inquiry and research' (Green 1913: 51). Raymont argued that good teaching was the function of many variables, of which the study of the principles and methods was only one. However, he regarded it as essential that young teachers should study and assimilate principles and methods to protect them from becoming blind imitators either of their own past selves or of other people and to improve upon bad practice. If young teachers began their professional careers armed with a firm grasp of the principles of practice and able to engage critically with a theory of teaching, then this, it was hoped, would go some way in raising the status of the teaching profession (Raymont 1904: 23). These principles of practice encompassed a range of key teaching skills, including effective lesson planning, differentiation, questioning, exposition and narration, classroom and behaviour management skills, subject knowledge and personal qualities.

However important the application of generic principles was to Findlay, Raymont and Welton, they were not advocating a mechanistic or imitative mode of practice and were highly suspicious of the notion of neat prescription or rigid formulae. This raised an interesting tension. They recognised that there was a potential conflict between a methodical approach to teaching and an individual teacher's professional judgement about their application in particular contexts. Teachers could not be viewed as mere machines, yet at the same time their teaching needed to be methodical. In seeking to systematise the daily practice of teachers there would be some risk of unthinking, mechanical application on the part of some practitioners. 'Teaching is emphatically skilled work. It may be done mechanically – but then the result is inferior' (Welton 1906: 18). The slavish imitation of unthinking method was the antithesis of the theory of education being sought.

Welton deplored unthinking prescription and verbal reproductions of textbook methods and rather promoted the need for teachers, both experienced and novice, to develop themselves as critical, reflective practitioners. Indeed, Welton would probably have regretted the initial practice of implementing the national literacy and numeracy strategies, with their prescriptive and rigid formulae, in English primary schools. He argued that the model for a work on teaching should not be like a cookery book, with its detailed recipes directing the reader how to produce by rule of thumb certain specific results. The unique individuality of teachers was to be celebrated and the idea was that thinking and informed professionals would apply principles of teaching according to their own understanding and in keeping with the particular circumstances of their work, which would vary according to the age and ability of the children, the location of the school – whether in an urban or rural environment – and the size of class. Effectiveness, in modern terminology, would have to be differentiated. The escape from mechanism in teaching, according to Welton, rested on teachers' willingness to engage in earnest reflection upon the purpose and nature of teaching. The outcome of such a process would be a theory of teaching which sprang out of actual school work, 'not an insubstantial vision spun out of the clouds of an untrammelled imagination' (Welton 1906: 18). It was teachers themselves, in partnership with other educational professionals and researchers, who were to be responsible for the development of a theory of education and who were to secure professional security through their own intellectual, practical and critical engagement with the principles.

Towards a practical pedagogy

It was in their discussion of the forms and process of teaching an individual lesson that Findlay, Raymont and Welton began to probe the nature of a set of fundamental propositions about teaching. While they each tackled the issue in a slightly different way, it is possible to identify common characteristics. They were all influenced by Herbartianism which replaced the earlier emphasis on Bain and modified faculty psychology. Herbart, a Prussian philosopher interested in psychology and education, had published his work on the science of education in the early years of the nineteenth century but his ideas did not become influential until they were taken up and modified for practical use by his followers at the University of Jena in the 1890s. Herbart tried to explain the process of human development through a model of a staged, systematic and sequenced approach to teaching and constructed a method derived from psychological analysis, with the starting point for teaching to be found in the pupil's own experience and knowledge. He placed considerable emphasis on the role and importance of the teacher in the process of education (Leinster-Mackay 2002). Raymont was interested in Herbart's tried and tested maxims but wanted to draw upon the wisdom of the past and integrate it with a more practice-based analysis (Raymont 1904: 21–22). They were all interested in the nature of children's learning and called for more research in this field. They all emphasised the need for interaction between the teacher and the child. Welton suggested that the three chief factors in education were the child to be taught, the subject matter and the teacher. A theory of teaching must bring these into effective union and the role of the teacher as mediator and guide was critical (Welton 1906: 19). Our examination of their work suggests five broad propositions for effective practice on the part of the teacher. These are: planning; teacher–pupil interaction; lesson structure; core teaching skills; and the power of the individual teacher to teach. These five propositions are interdependent and only really make sense when considered as a unit.

The first was based on the need for meticulous forward planning and preparation. Teachers were encouraged to think through the stages of a lesson and write these down in detail. The usefulness of a model or pro forma for lesson planning to student teachers in training was highlighted. In particular, teachers were urged to consider how the subject matter related to the class in terms of their previous knowledge, range of ability and interest. Findlay urged experienced teachers to write detailed lesson notes to provide the basis for a systematic evaluation of a lesson and a reworking of planning for further lessons. The keeping of a planning diary or notebook for each course study was advised.

The second concerned interaction between teacher and taught. This demanded an ability to be flexible and adaptable on the part of the teacher. Meaningful planning could only emerge from a thorough knowledge and understanding of the children and an ability to adapt to particular educational contexts. There was no place for old-fashioned, didactic 'chalk and talk' in this model of teaching. Teachers were required to determine the flow, pace and dynamic of a lesson and to respond appropriately to the needs of the class. According to Welton, 'it is the power of putting oneself in the mental place and attitude of the pupils, that marks off the true artist in teaching from the mere mechanical grinder of facts and formulae. To know where the pupils are and where they should try to be are the two first essentials of good teaching' (Welton 1906: 57).

The third involved the logical construction of a lesson. It referred to the shape and sequence of a lesson in which material was systematically organised into manageable and orderly sections. Each of these sections would be thoroughly revised before moving on with the lesson. Progression between stages was crucial. According to Findlay, 'the quality of teaching, in the sphere of method, is largely determined by the skill with which a teacher is able to analyse and group his subject matter into sections' (Findlay 1902: 268). This idea was drawn from the Herbartian theory of formal stages from which the five-step model of teaching a lesson was devised. The difficulty with this model was its assumption that the five steps themselves reflected what was going on in the minds of the pupils and that the pupils kept pace with the teacher. Findlay particularly urged teachers not to fall into the trap of constructing staged lessons without an adequate investigation of the needs of the class. Findlay argued that the main unit in education was not the school or the class but the single pupil and that teachers should be attuned to the needs of the individual child (Findlay 1902: 13). An introduction would prepare children for the lesson in which the teacher would offer explicit aims and objectives and show the purpose of the work. Drawing on children's existing knowledge and recapping on previous lessons, the teacher would focus and concentrate the children's minds and stimulate their interest. There would be opportunity for cross-curricular links at this stage. The next stage would consist of the presentation of new subject matter. There was particular emphasis on new information being presented in such a way that it connected with existing knowledge. Following the presentation of new knowledge, two further parts of the lesson would seek to systematise and apply this knowledge to the practical needs of daily life. Similar ideas would be compared, dissimilar ideas contrasted with problem-solving using new knowledge. Finally, a recapitulation would draw together the main threads of the lesson, rehearsing main teaching points and checking understanding. This model, which emphasises the importance of a proper plenary session, would not be unfamiliar to teachers working to the national literacy and numeracy strategies in English primary schools today.

The fourth proposition, without which none of the previous three could exist, highlighted certain core teaching skills. Broadly, these related to questioning, exposition or explanation, narration and illustration. Oral questioning was clearly a critical skill for a young teacher to develop but it was important to recognise that questioning should not be the dominant mode of instruction in a lesson. Different types of question were promoted including preliminary 'experimental' questions usually asked at the start of a lesson to probe children's knowledge, recapitulatory or résumé questions to test understanding and interrogatory questions for examination purposes. According to Raymont, good questions should incite a pupil to genuine activity of mind and should cause him to observe, remember and think. The emphasis should not be on a rapid fire and response style and questions should be framed so as not to encourage guesswork or simply 'yes or no' answers. Teachers should construct questions in relation to the ability of the children and should distribute them carefully across the class (Raymont 1904: 259). The atmosphere of a classroom should be friendly so as to encourage children to ask questions.

The skill of effective exposition was also highlighted as a necessary constituent of effective teaching. Raymont suggested that power to describe clearly, to narrate vividly and to tell a story well was just as important as skill in oral questioning. A fundamental part of the skill was the ability to narrate or tell a story well and to illustrate teaching points in a vivid and lively fashion so as to excite and maintain children's interest. Welton argued that 'the teacher should therefore, cultivate the power of effective and vivid narrative – terse, pointed and clear' (Welton 1906: 80). Like the structuring of a whole lesson, the points of a narrative should also be well structured and orderly with essential points being stressed as appropriate. Teachers should be mindful of their use of language and ensure its relation to children's comprehension. They should enter the spirit of the story and their voice and manner should be varied, with a balance between detail, repetition (particularly for younger children) and description. Supporting this view, Green and Birchenough argued that narration and the ability to tell stories was the oldest instrument of formal education: 'The power to tell a story might not unfittingly be regarded as an essential qualification of the teacher. If dealing with issues outside children's own experience, description which leads them to imagine and call up images is important and teachers need to make use of what children already do know' (Green and Birchenough 1911: 40).

The final proposition brought together all of the previous four ideas and focused on the personal characteristics of the teacher. The individual uniqueness of the teacher was the safeguard against slavish imitation and mechanistic teaching. If teachers did not have the power to stimulate and sustain the interest of their class through their use of language, expression, tact, sympathy, tone of voice and overall demeanour, then a well-planned, carefully sequenced lesson would be worthless. The onus was placed on the teacher to harness their professional knowledge and their understanding of individual children to ascertain their readiness for new information and experiences. This growing interest in the needs of individual children was in itself a relatively underdeveloped area and was reflected more widely in other aspects of the scientific study of education, including child study, child hygiene and child psychology. Rudimentary and developmental as this focus on the individual child was, it formed an essential part of the emergent model of teacher effectiveness then, just as it does today.

Personal power, often referred to as the moral dimension in teaching, is perhaps the most difficult aspect of teaching power to quantify. It is implicit in the other more technical, managerial or intellectual powers, none of which could properly function without some individual personal flair, instinct or intuition. It is perhaps in the quality of personal power that the intangible mystery and magic of teaching, alluded to in art or craft designations, can be found. In personal power can be found something of the natural, born or innate qualities of teaching – those qualities often referred to as gifts. Personal power in teaching might be understood as the mysterious 'x factor' without which the other essential skills and qualities were incomplete. In one very important respect it was very different from the four propositions in that it would be much more difficult to train or influence. Significantly, current policy on the necessary skills and competences required of trained teachers has recently re-emphasised the importance of personal qualities, previously neglected in the standards-driven National Curriculum for ITT in England, and one of the challenges in incorporating this dimension of teaching into a training scheme is measuring its presence or impact.

While Findlay, Raymont and Welton found it instructive to formulate these general propositions for teachers, they were not claiming to afford definite and detailed guidance. Rather, they wanted the careful application of general methods to particular teaching contexts and hoped that young teachers would appropriate the 'spirit' of a systematic approach to teaching without becoming enslaved to it. Welton summed up this belief when he wrote: 'teaching, then, is educative as far as it is stimulating. And in this the personality of the teacher counts for more than the method of teaching' (Welton 1918: 179). Power to teach was the nub of what these five propositions were trying to describe. It was a linguistic term frequently used by teacher trainers, inspectors and teachers when judging a teacher's person, capacity and effectiveness. The notion of power to teach somehow welded together art, craft and science elements and embraced the personal, professional, practical and theoretical components which together formed the ideal of the good teacher. It also touched upon the contentious idea that some teaching qualities are innate and natural, not learned or acquired through training. The language of 'power to teach' is prevalent in government reports, books on teaching method and individual reports on student teachers' performance during the period under review, and captured the essence of the five principles for effective teaching.

Experimental pedagogy in its infancy

Findlay recognised the potential for professional tension between research and practice but was persuaded that the way forward was the working through of theory in the classroom. The principles of teaching expounded by Findlay and his contemporaries were applied, to some degree, in practice. It was to the training of teachers and the concept of a demonstration or experimental school, exemplified in the Manchester Fielden Demonstration Schools, that Findlay looked for a practical realisation of his educational vision. By exemplifying the whole of school life – its organisation, discipline and the 'social work of the teacher' as well as simple teaching methods – the demonstration school was ideally placed as the living embodiment of the emerging new educational theory. It was envisaged that in the demonstration school the systematic observation and recording of children's learning, demonstration of good practice to students by experienced teachers and opportunities for teaching practice for students would combine to provide a sound scientific basis for a practical pedagogy. Moreover, the demonstration school would bridge the theory of the lecture theatre with the practice of the school. According to Findlay, 'the demonstration school is expressly designed to correlate the lectures on education with the practical exposition of method, to give reality to the study of method and of curricula, to foster the spirit of investigation, to enable the student to come into close contact with individual children for an extended period' (Public Record Office 1911). Students were introduced to practical study in the schools in two ways: the demonstration lesson and the constructive criticism lesson. One or two hours in each week were set apart for a demonstration lesson, which could be attended by some 30 students at a time. The lesson was selected from the regular programme of a class, to exemplify certain principles of curriculum and method, and would be preceded by an account in the lecture-room of the aims underlying the work and followed at a subsequent lecture by a discussion of results. The student was required to record the lesson and to seek an interpretation of his observation. At the same time he was encouraged to see the relation of this single lesson to the entire plan of pursuits. A series of such lessons, accompanied by investigation of principles, provided students in further sessions with a practical body of knowledge on the daily work of teaching children in classes. Having gained experience in this way, students proceeded to put this knowledge to use by undertaking charge of a class. A few lessons would be observed to gain knowledge of the class and then the student would be made responsible for teaching the class for a school term, guided and supported by a demonstrator or class teacher. All preparation of lessons would be recorded and evaluated. The oversight and examination into methods was completed in the work of the pedagogical seminar, which was an idea borrowed from the German model introduced by Rein, a follower of Herbart at the University of Jena. A student was expected, as soon as he had his class of scholars well in hand, to give an open lesson in the presence of a large body of third year or of diploma students, and thereafter, at a separate meeting, to explain, and if need be to defend, his plan of teaching. A well-conducted seminar served to bring into relief the main ideas underlying the plan of teaching, and as, week by week, the work of different parts of a school were brought under review, the students were encouraged to make a comprehensive survey of the various groups of school pursuits and of the methods employed to achieve the ends proposed. The ethos of the model emphasised collaboration between children, teachers, lecturers and demonstrators.

Detailed records were logged of the physical and mental development of the children. As well as providing a valuable database for the study of child development and children's learning, they were also an integral part of a child development course taken by students. This course, for example, was planned to provide a practical knowledge of the mental and physical development of children. Selected problems of school life, such as the development of speech, the growth of number ideas, self-expression in drawing, were dealt with in some detail. Students would undertake detailed observations of, for example, a child's speech, recording what was said and the conditions under which the observation took place. Results would then be discussed, classified and examined in seminars. A government inspection of the school in 1908 found that: 'Students there see the whole question of practical education approached in a systematic and scientific manner; they learn the problems involved are more complex and closely related to individual difference than they would find in the ordinary course of practice; in particular they are made to realise the human (or humanistic) side of their work' (Public Record Office 1908).

In contributing to professional debate about the nature of effective teaching, the TCA through the *Journal of Experimental Pedagogy* and such educationists as Findlay, Raymont and Welton were beginning to formulate a particular model of teaching which pulled together elements of received professional wisdom but which also sought a scientific, rational basis. The development of ideas around the rudiments of good teaching during the first two decades of the twentieth century, however, only went so far. They were generated as principles based on the experience of practice and to some extent were grounded in scientific research and analysis. But it was clear that more systematic research based on observation of classroom life was needed to underpin and validate knowledge and understanding about the relationship between teaching and learning. The broad propositions for effective teaching outlined did not, for example, satisfactorily penetrate the vexed question of balancing the needs of the individual against a whole class in mass schooling. Neither did they engage with questions about the relationship between curriculum development and teaching nor systematic assessment of pupil learning as we would know it today.

Nevertheless, for a few decades at the turn of the twentieth century, there were the beginnings of a movement among educationists and teacher trainers which was pregnant with the possibility of a new world of teacher-based research, observation, training and debate around the nature of teaching and learning. There was an embryonic form of 'sane' educational theory which envisioned a teaching profession responsible for the development of a practical pedagogy. There was a call for fundamental pedagogical questions to be solved by observation and experiment conducted under scientific principles. Findlay, somewhat prophetically in view of the English government's prescription around the teaching of the literacy and numeracy strategies in English primary schools, argued that if teachers did not take upon themselves the responsibility for finding out how best to teach then agencies external to the profession would take over. He wrote, 'if such claims to usurp the teachers' function by prescribing text books, by rigid limitation as to time and manner and method, it should be resisted' (Findlay 1902: 11).

Historical and current resonance

At the beginning of this chapter Compayre's call, in 1886, for the seeking out of permanent truths in educational theory was put forward. Even early twentieth-century educationists were anxious to dispel uncritical, unthinking, mechanical, craft and imitative models of the business of teaching and learning. The idea of a historical continuum is largely absent from current analysis of pedagogy, yet many of the ideas and principles for effective teaching forwarded by Findlay,

Raymont and Welton clearly anticipated current models of practice. The five core principles identified in this chapter, though they refer to a different set of contexts and climates than those of today, do clearly resonate with recent research and recommendations for good practice, found for example in the work of Muijs and Reynolds (2001a) and the Hay McBer report, commissioned by the Department for Education and Employment in 2000 (DfEE 2000). The current model of effective teaching focuses on the combined interaction of core teaching skills, professional characteristics and classroom climate and this is examined in some detail in Chapter 9. The historical model advocated thorough planning and sharing of objectives with the structuring of lessons in clear parts, with an introduction, main activity and plenary within a safe climate. Effective teaching skills included appropriate questioning and exposition, formative evaluation, differentiation and interactive whole-class teaching as well as good classroom and behaviour management. These effective teaching practices are not novel.

Aside from the rather obvious observation that current research on effective pedagogy is overly presentist and fails to consider its historical antecedents, what else can this historical analysis offer? By seeking to clarify and define principles of teaching which rest on a clear understanding of the relationship between teaching and learning and the complexities of classroom interaction, this historical perspective can inform and enrich new departures. In particular, the historical notion of power to teach which incorporated a more holistic approach to effective teaching than is currently conceived, by emphasising the difficult area of personal qualities, might offer a further dimension to the construction of a more refined model of differentiated effective teaching as it is explored in this book.

4 Review of current research in teacher effectiveness

Current research on teacher effectiveness is usually considered to have gone through a number of discrete phases, from presage–product studies up to the new paradigms focusing on teacher beliefs, efficacy and constructivist teaching strategies, and these phases will be reviewed in this chapter.

It has to be pointed out, however, that this chronological ordering is in many ways simplistic as phases overlap, and research on some of the 'older' factors is still continuing. For example, studies of teacher behaviours, supposedly the 'last but one' phase of teacher effectiveness research, are ongoing (e.g. Muijs and Reynolds 2002, Teddlie and Stringfield 1993). Indeed, elements of prior phases can regain popularity and research interest at later dates, as is the case with teacher personality, a key characteristic of the Hay McBer model, which has recently come to the fore through their teacher effectiveness study for the Department for Education and Skills (Hay McBer 2000).

As we will see, the 'received wisdom' view of this chronology, which states that presage–product and teaching styles studies failed to produce useful findings, is not entirely correct, there being some merit in all phases of research.

Presage–product studies

Presage–product studies attempted to identify the psychological characteristics of an effective teacher by looking at personality characteristics such as authoritarianism and flexibility, attitudes such as motivation to teach, and experience and background.

Personality characteristics have been studied using a variety of psychological tests which have attempted to uncover a wide range of personality traits. Generally, no direct relationship between personality and achievement of pupils has been found (Borich 1996). This does not mean, however, that this avenue of research was entirely fruitless, as there is some evidence of an indirect effect through the effect of personality on classroom behaviour of teachers. For example, in a study of 36 science teachers using a battery of personality tests, some correlations were found with classroom climate, teachers with needs for dependence and power having formal, subservient classes with little conflict between class members, teachers with need for interaction (aggressive and affiliative) having controlled, goal-oriented classes, while one self-centred teacher had a disorganised, undisciplined class (Walberg and Welch 1967). In their study, Bemis and Cooper (1967) found a relationship between teachers' self-rating on factors such as needs for achievement, affiliation and abasement, dominance, change, order and heterosexuality and teacher behaviours, which were in turn related to achievement in reading, although the correspondence between effective behaviours and personality characteristics was complex. Costin and Grush (1973) found a relationship between students' ratings of teachers' personality and their perception of teachers' effectiveness. However, there was a low correlation between teacher self-rated personality and students' rating of their personality, which seemed mainly determined by teachers' classroom behaviours. Leverne's (1991) more recent study likewise found a relationship between personality characteristics and effective teaching behaviours. A study of the relationship between teachers' scores on the 16 personality factors scale or locus of control and their views on classroom management, however, did not find any significant relationships (Martin 1995).

Therefore, while no direct effect was found, there is some evidence that supports an indirect effect of teachers' personality on achievement. The often experimental nature of the studies, the wide variety of psychological factors tested, and the relative immutability of personality characteristics make this knowledge difficult to translate into advice on improvement of classroom practice, however.

Teacher attitudes towards teaching, whether their pupils or a particular task, were also studied in an attempt to link them to outcomes. Most of these studies did not find strong effects on achievement. Young (1973), for example, found that teacher enthusiasm did not affect achievement in business studies, while Keane (1968) found no effect of teacher attitudes on student achievement in his study of 32 maths teachers. Rossmiller (1982), in his longitudinal study of Wisconsin teachers, found no consistent effects of attitudes on achievement. All this left Walberg (1986) to conclude, in his overview of research, that there was little evidence of a relationship between teacher attitudes and achievement, although the hypothesis of a relationship between attitudes and behaviours remains underexplored.

As regards teacher experience, evidence is again weak, a fact that Borich (1996) attributes to the broadness of definitions of experience (e.g. years of experience, graduate credits earned) used in most studies, which he sees as insufficiently relevant to teachers' day-to-day teaching tasks. Examples of this can be found in Anderson and Dorsett's (1981) study, in which teacher experience was only occasionally a predictor of student outcomes, and Heim and Perl's (1974) educational production function study of New York State, in which teachers' experience was likewise not a predictor of student achievement. Levin (1970) similarly reported that recruiting experienced teachers was economically inefficient due to the limited effect of this factor on achievement. One recent study in the very different cultural context of Nigeria did find a relationship between teachers' experience and pupil achievement (Chidolue 1996).

Teaching styles

Following the relative, although far from total, failure of the presage–product studies to produce clear findings on teacher factors that could improve pupil outcomes, researchers looked at teaching styles. Most of the initial studies on teaching styles developed dichotomies along the 'non-directive versus directive' or 'progressive versus traditional' lines, the former usually using more student-centred methods, the latter being more teacher-directed and disciplinarian, although the exact content of the styles varies from study to study.

Tuckman's (1968) study, for example, looked at the effects of 'directive' and 'non-directive' teaching styles, hypothesising that their effect would interact with students' personality characteristics in determining effectiveness, a directive teaching style being more effective with concrete authoritarian students and a non-directive teaching style being more effective with abstract, non-authoritarian students. Findings did not support this, showing that all students earned higher grades from, and were more satisfied with, non-directive teachers. Similar results were found by Souster (1982), students taught by teachers using an indirect instructional style doing significantly better on the CTBS language, reading, and mathematics subtests in his study of 504 students. However, teachers who used a combination of direct and indirect teaching styles had higher group mean scores than either the direct or indirect styles in this study.

A further development was the use of experimental studies attempting to investigate the impact of specific teaching methods on student achievement. However, the majority of these studies produced inconclusive results because the differences between teaching methods were not significant enough to produce meaningful differences in student achievement (Medley and Crook 1980). Furthermore, the significant differences that did appear tended to contradict one another (Borich 1996).

The first major teaching styles study in Britain was conducted by Bennett (1976). On the basis of the responses to the questionnaire teachers were categorised into a continuum of 12 'teaching styles' ranging from the most 'progressive' style, focusing on pupils organising their work individually, integrating individual subjects into projects, and low use of formal testing methods, to the most 'traditional' style, in which the whole class was taught, subjects were taught separately and formal testing and assessment were widely used. Most teachers fell in the ten middle groups.

Bennett (1976) found that both English and math students in the more formal classrooms made more progress over time than students in the more 'progressive' classrooms. Results were not entirely clear-cut, however, in that some of the highest rates of progress were achieved by informal teachers. This study was the subject of fierce methodological criticism, the clustering of teachers, for example changing over time (Goldstein 1976).

A British study that employed individual teacher behaviours but used them to form teaching styles was the ORACLE study, conducted by a team of researchers led by Maurice Galton in the late 1970s (Galton *et al.* 1980). Using cluster analysis, teachers in the original study were grouped into four main groups: *individual monitors*, who mainly let pupils work on their own and interacted with individual pupils; *class enquirers*, who spent an above-average time teaching the whole class (although this was still less than half of the lesson); *group enquirers*, who favoured group work and spent little time teaching the whole class, and *style changers*, who tended to move between these teaching styles. Relationships of these groups with achievement were limited, but in a reanalysis of the 1976 data set, Croll (1996) correlated the academic gain made by different classes with different patterns of class–teacher interactions, finding a moderate statistically significant positive (0.29) correlation between whole-class and small-group interaction and children's progress.

In the late 1990s a replication study was conducted with 29 teachers in many of the same schools used in the 1976 study. This showed a number of changes in primary school teaching in England. There was a significant rise in behaviours associated with the class enquirers and style changers styles and a decrease in behaviours associated with the individual monitor style. There were also changes within teaching styles, the 1996 class enquirers for example, using far more open questions and praise than their counterparts in 1976. This could be a result of changes in teaching over time, but likewise could result from methodological artefacts in developing teaching styles through cluster analysis, which might not be particularly stable.

This classification of teachers by styles is open to criticism. Mortimore *et al.* (1988) point out that even within the ORCALE study, variance within styles was far greater than variance between styles. Also, we would argue that looking at actual behaviours that can make a difference could be more useful to practice than advocating global teaching styles. Further criticism receives support from the finding in the Bennett study that notwithstanding the overall support for traditional teaching, the single most effective teacher was characterised as progressive. A further problem is the profusion of possible teaching styles one could study. The progressive/traditional dichotomy identified by Bennett would now clearly be seen as simplistic, but the replicability of the ORACLE styles identified through cluster analysis is questionable.

Process–product studies

As a result of this relative failure of previous paradigms to produce robust findings on factors that could affect student outcomes, researchers turned to looking at specific teacher behaviours as a possible cause of pupil achievement. In this they were influenced by behaviourist learning theory, which was developed by psychologists such as Ivan Pavlov, B. F. Skinner and A. Bandura from the 1920s onwards, and was highly influential in the 1960s. This theory emphasises change in behaviour as the main outcome of the learning process. Behavioural theorists concentrate on directly observable phenomena using a strict positivistic scientific method borrowed from the natural sciences. The most radical behaviourists, such as B. F. Skinner, considered all study of non-observable behaviour ('mentalism', according to pioneering behaviourist John B. Watson) to be unscientific. In recent years, however, most researchers and psychologists in the behaviourist tradition, such as Bandura (1986), have expanded their view of learning to include expectations, thoughts, motivation and beliefs. This notwithstanding, it is now clear that behaviourism offers a limited and partial view of learning that has been substantially altered by developments in cognitive and brain sciences. This obviously does not mean that teacher effectiveness findings based on this paradigm are no longer useful, but it does raise the question of to what extent they are in need of expanding, and how the new psychological findings can inform teaching research (Muijs and Reynolds 2000).

Generally, the methodology used in process–product research has involved the testing of pupils at the beginning and end of the study using standardised achievement tests (which obviously points to a certain narrowness in the outcomes tested). Teachers are then observed by researchers using structured observation instruments or, alternatively, they fill in questionnaires on their teaching methods. Correlational methods are then used to relate the teaching factors with the outcome or growth measures.

This type of research started off in the US in the late 1960s, and studies followed by Rosenshine (1979), Good *et al.* (1983), Evertson and Anderson (1980) and others. A large number of studies were undertaken. The main findings can be summarised as follows.

1   *Get the classroom climate right.* Learning occurs when the classroom is an orderly, businesslike environment. Transitions need to be brief, lessons need to start on time, rules for student behaviour need to be established early and be clearly understood by students (these elements could be termed *classroom management*). Student misbehaviour needs to be corrected immediately, accurately (punish the right student) and constructively (no shouting) (*behaviour management*). The effective classroom is warm and supportive, characterised by high expectations and teacher enthusiasm (a factor one could term *classroom climate*) (Doyle 1986, Brophy and Good 1986, Brophy 1986, Creemers 1994, Mortimore *et al.* 1988, Reynolds *et al.* 1996, Muijs and Reynolds 2000, Reynolds and Muijs 1999).

2   *Get the teaching right.* Mathematics achievement has been found to increase when most of the lesson is spent teaching the whole class rather than letting students work through worksheets or schedules on their own. This whole-class (*direct*) teaching needs to be highly structured, setting out objectives of the lesson, stressing key points of the lesson, making clear and structured explanations and summarising the lesson at the end. Whole-class teaching needs to be *interactive*; lecture-style lessons are to be avoided. Teachers need to involve students in the lesson by asking a high

number of questions, mixing higher and lower cognitive order questions according to the topic (but always using higher order questions, including open questions), using an appropriate wait-time, which is short (but still at least three seconds) for lower order questions and longer for higher order questions. Students must receive immediate feedback when they have answered a question. This feedback must be businesslike but positive, acknowledging correct answers and prompting when incorrect answers are given before going over to the next student. While whole-class teaching is important, students also need to have the opportunity to practise what they have learnt during *seatwork* sessions which should include cooperative small-group work. During seatwork the teacher again needs to take an active role, going round the class to help students and being open to student questions rather than remaining behind her/his desk (Borich 1996, Brophy 1986, Brophy and Good 1986, Creemers 1994, Croll 1996, Evertson *et al.* 1980, Galton 1989, Galton and Croll 1980, Mortimore *et al.* 1988, Muijs and Reynolds 2000, 2003, Reynolds and Muijs 1999).

3   Effective mathematics teaching, however, is not rigid. Teachers need to use a *variety of teaching strategies* aimed at students with different learning needs. They need to vary the difficulty of questions and explanations to match students' levels, and need to use a variety of manipulatives and materials to engage students, address different learning styles and allow easier transferability of knowledge (Borich 1996, Brophy and Good 1986, Reynolds and Muijs 1999, Muijs and Reynolds 2003).

Generally, the findings do not indicate that any particular behaviour would lead to higher levels of teacher effectiveness. Rather, a combination of significant but modest or weak relationships emerged, which together formed a relatively coherent whole that has become known as 'direct instruction', 'active teaching' or, more recently, 'whole-class interactive teaching'.

The first British study explicitly to link school and teacher effectiveness was the Junior School Project, a study into school and teacher effectiveness in 50 primary schools conducted by Mortimore *et al.* (1988). The study involved collection of a considerable volume of data on children and their family backgrounds ('intakes'), school and classroom 'processes' and 'outcomes' in academic (reading, mathematics) and affective (e.g. self-conception, attendance, behaviour) areas. The researchers used the ORACLE study instruments in their classroom observations. Sophisticated multi-level modelling techniques were used to analyse the data. This study reported 12 school and teacher effectiveness factors that were associated with effectiveness across outcome areas. These were:

- purposeful leadership of the staff by the Head Teacher
- the involvement of the Deputy Head in policy decisions
- the involvement of teachers in curriculum planning and decision-making
- consistency among teachers in their approach to teaching
- structured sessions
- intellectually challenging teaching
- a work-centred environment characterised by a high level of student industry with children enjoying their work and being eager to start new tasks
- a limited focus within sessions
- maximum communication between teachers and students
- record-keeping
- parental involvement
- a positive climate.

An ongoing teacher effectiveness study in the UK is being conducted as part of the evaluation of the Gatsby Mathematics Enhancement Project Primary, a project designed to improve the teaching of mathematics in primary schools using whole-class interactive methods. A team from the University of Exeter led by David Reynolds and Daniel Muijs was appointed to evaluate the project. As part of this evaluation, the researchers decided to look at the effectiveness of teaching in both the project and the control schools. In order to do this, pupils were tested twice yearly using a standardised numeracy test that contained both a mental and a written part. The written part was made up of open questions, usually asking students to provide their working out as well as the answer. Teachers in the project were observed twice yearly, using an observation instrument (MECORS, Schaffer *et al.* 1998) adapted for an English context from the SSOS and Vergilio instruments developed in the US. A questionnaire probing teachers' beliefs and attitudes about teaching and maths was also administered.

This longitudinal project has provided detailed findings on teacher effectiveness in mathematics, which largely support the findings of the abovementioned studies as well as American teacher effectiveness research. Most of the behaviours observed were related to gains in pupil progress, with correlations ranging from .1 to .4. While these correlations are weak to modest, it was found that all the observed behaviours were positively related to one another, with correlations ranging from .5 to .8. In all three years, confirmatory factor analyses supported a hierarchical structure, one higher order ('effective teaching') factor underlying nine first order factors (classroom management, behaviour management, direct instruction, interactive teaching, varied teaching, classroom climate, individual review and practice, connectionist methods and mathematical language). The aggregate factors were related moderately to gains in all three years analysed so far, with direct instruction, interactive teaching and varied teaching showing the strongest relationships (around .4).

Using multi-level modelling techniques, it was possible to establish the contribution of teacher behaviours in explaining achievement gains in maths over the year. The percentage of variance in achievement explained at the classroom level varied around 15% in all three years, being highest in year 1 and lowest in year 3 of the project. The effective teaching factor was able to explain three-quarters of this classroom variance. This percentage is highly practically significant. We were able to predict that, all else being equal (free meal eligibility, special needs status, gender achievement at the beginning of the year), a pupil taught by the most effective teacher would achieve an end of year test score 20% higher than a pupil taught by the least effective teacher. As in the American studies, rather than any particular behaviour or group of behaviours impacting on gains, it would seem that effective teachers are effective in a number of ways. If supported further, this kind of finding might raise questions about the extent to which effectiveness in teaching is differentiated, as we are exploring in this book.

The emphasis on teacher behaviours has been criticised among other things for the lack of attention given to teachers' own beliefs about, and attitudes to, teaching and the subjects they teach, arguing that these deeper structures are more important to teaching quality than immediately observable behaviours (De Corte and Greer 1996, Fennema and Loef-Franke 1992, Thompson 1992, Askew *et al.* 1997). Furthermore, research in psychology has seen a move away from traditional behaviourist models towards models stressing individuals' complex information processing strategies, metacognition and knowledge construction. The various models emerging (constructivism and information processing theory, for example) share an emphasis on pupils' active construction of learning, a view that differs from the 'stimulus–response' behaviourist models that underlie traditional teacher effectiveness research. Coupled with this has been an increasing emphasis in society on higher order thinking and processing, seen as necessary for societies to function competitively in an increasingly complex and knowledge-based economic order. As is argued in Chapter 9, the latter has also led to an increasing emphasis on adaptability and lifelong learning, as individuals are expected to adapt to changing technology and demands over time. As a result of this, education will need to focus on developing students equipped with a 'learning disposition' that incorporates positive affect towards learning, metacognitive skills and cognitive strategies as well as domain-specific knowledge (Muijs and Reynolds 2000).

Knowledge, beliefs, constructivism

As a result of these criticisms, attention has shifted from teacher behaviours to teacher subject knowledge and pedagogical knowledge and their beliefs and self-efficacy have been examined in order to identify the role such factors have in teacher effectiveness. New ways of teaching, seen as more congruent with developments in psychology, have been proposed.

Teacher beliefs

Belief systems are dynamic and permeable mental structures, susceptible to change in light of experience. The relationship between beliefs and practice is not a simple one-way relationship from belief to practice, but a dynamic two-way relationship in which beliefs are influenced by practical experience (Thompson 1992).

A difference from the behaviourist research is that most behaviourist researchers have focused on a similar set of behaviours, while the belief structures that have been studied are wide-ranging, as the universe of teacher beliefs is larger than the universe of in-class behaviours. This means that any study needs to restrict itself to hypothesising one or a limited belief system as the object of study. One of the belief structures that have been found to underlie teacher attitudes was described by Askew *et al.* (1997) as a distinction between connectionist, transmission and discovery orientations. These ideal types can be distinguished on the basis of teachers' beliefs about what it means to be a numerate student, their beliefs about how best to teach numeracy and their beliefs about students and how they learn to be numerate. We will discuss these three aspects in turn.

According to Askew *et al.* (1997), *connectionist* teachers believe that being numerate involves being both efficient and effective, being able to choose an appropriate problem-solving or calculation method and being able to make links between different parts of the curriculum. Connectionist teachers stress the importance of the application of number to new situations by encouraging students to use realistic problems. *Transmission*-oriented teachers believe in the importance of students obtaining fluency in a number of standard procedures and routines which apply to a particular type of calculation, and they believe that students need to learn to do routine calculations or procedures before applying them to word problems. The *discovery*-oriented teacher believes that all methods of calculation are equally acceptable as long as the answer is obtained, whether or not the method is efficient. They emphasise students' creation of their own methods, and believe that using and applying mathematics is based on the use of practical equipment.

When the researchers looked at teacher beliefs about students and how they learn to become numerate, they found the following differences. *Connectionist* teachers believe that most students are able to learn math given effective teaching, and that students come to school already possessing mental calculation strategies. The teacher's role is then to work with the students to introduce more efficient strategies. Misconceptions are seen as important teaching tools. For *transmission*-oriented teachers, who emphasise set rules and methods, what students already know before they come to class is less important. Students' own methods do not form the basis of teaching. Students are believed to differ in ability, failure to learn once the teacher has explained the procedures to students resulting from lack of ability. *Discovery*-oriented teachers believe that learning is an individual activity, which happens once students are 'ready' to learn a certain concept. Learning takes precedence over teaching, and students' own strategies are paramount.

Finally, teachers were found to differ in their beliefs about how best to teach students to become numerate. *Connectionist* teachers believe that teaching maths is based upon dialogue between teacher and students. This helps teachers to better understand their students and allows students to gain access to teachers' mathematical knowledge. This leads to interactive teaching, with an extensive focus on discussion to help students explore more efficient strategies. *Transmission*-oriented teachers emphasise teaching over learning, and introducing students to routines through clear verbal explanations. Interaction consists largely of the teacher checking whether the student can reproduce the taught procedure using mainly closed questions. *Discovery*-oriented teachers believe in letting students discover methods for themselves, through extensive use of practical experience.

In their study of 90 teachers, Askew *et al.* (1997) found that highly effective teachers were characterised by connectionist beliefs, while transmission and discovery orientations tended to characterise some of the less effective teachers.

In their study, Muijs and Reynolds (2002) used a questionnaire based on the Askew *et al.* (1997) model to test teacher beliefs. They did not find a direct relationship between beliefs and outcomes, but, testing a proximity model in which factors closest to pupils' actual experience (e.g. teacher behaviours) are hypothesised to affect their outcomes more strongly than factors which are less directly related to their experience (e.g. teacher beliefs), they found that teachers who held connectionist beliefs were more likely to engage in effective teaching behaviours than those holding discovery and transmission beliefs, while those teachers holding transmission beliefs were found to engage in more effective behaviours than those holding discovery beliefs.

Another aspect which has recently received increased attention from the research community is that of teachers' philosophical beliefs. Teachers' philosophical beliefs (PBs) are considered as the cornerstone of their teaching practices and their beliefs concerning teaching and learning. Thompson (1992) defines PBs as 'teachers' conscious or subconscious beliefs, concepts, meanings, rules, mental images, and preferences concerning the discipline of mathematics' (p. 132). Research into teachers' PBs was mainly concerned with the subject of mathematics. More specifically, Hersh (1990) asserts that these beliefs affect teachers' conception of how mathematics should be presented, since 'the issue is not what is the best way to teach mathematics but what is mathematics really all about' (p. 13). Ernest (1999) concludes that the research literature indicates that mathematics teaching depends fundamentally on the teacher's belief system and particularly on his/her conceptions of the nature and meaning of mathematics. Teachers' beliefs may develop into a coherent philosophical system that directly influences their overall classroom behaviour. A teacher's own philosophy is thought to function as a filter influencing decisions and actions made before, during and after instruction (Philippou and Christou 1997). Class organisation, the choice of learning activities, the questions posed by teachers, and the homework that teachers assign to students are likely to be influenced by teachers' PBs (Stipek *et al.* 2001). PBs were found to have impact on students' achievement, teachers' attitudes about the effectiveness of various teaching methods, innovations, curricula, textbooks and software material (Ernest 1999, Philippou and Christou 1997, Roulet 2000). A number of studies, however, point out that there are inconsistencies between expressed PBs and actual teaching practices (Raymond 1997, Thompson 1992, Charalambous *et al.* 2002). The subconscious character of PBs and the influence of school environment on the development of these beliefs can justify these inconsistencies (Ernest 1999).

Overall, though, it is clear that the area of beliefs is under-conceptualised and needs new methodological and explanatory frames.

Subject knowledge

As well as behaviours and beliefs, teacher subject knowledge is widely believed to influence teacher effectiveness. The research findings on the effect of subject knowledge on teacher effectiveness and student achievement are mixed, however.

In Askew *et al.*'s (1997) study, in which informal 'concept mapping' interviews with teachers were used to guage their subject knowledge, it was found that the connectionist teachers, who were the most effective, had a wider knowledge of practical and formal methods of representation and of students' mental strategies than transmission- or discovery-oriented teachers. Teachers who made few conceptual links showed fewer student gains in math achievement, although the relationship was weak. There was no relationship between gains and other content knowledge variables, such as fluency, scope explanation or understanding. Teachers did not differ in their understanding of mathematical concepts, although connectionist teachers seemed more inclined to link different numeracy concepts. Formal mathematics qualifications were likewise not linked to student gains.

In their review of research, Fennema and Loef-Franke (1992) make a distinction between teachers' knowledge of mathematics, teachers' knowledge of mathematical representations, teachers' knowledge of students and teachers' general knowledge of teaching and decision-making. Studies suggest that teachers' mathematical content knowledge is linked to both teacher behaviour in the classroom and student outcomes. Teachers' knowledge of mathematical representations refers to how mathematics should be represented in instruction. If teachers do not have this understanding, it will be hard for them to teach students to understand mathematics. In a study of British early years (infant) teachers, Aubrey (1993) found that teachers' lack of deep subject knowledge impeded their bringing into practice their knowledge of how children learn.

Mandeville and Liu (1997) studied the effect of teacher certification (partly based on subject knowledge) on US seventh grade students' mathematics achievement by matching 33 schools in which teachers had secondary mathematics certification with schools where this was not the case. They found that students from schools with higher levels of teacher certification performed better on thinking skills than their peers in lower level certification schools, but that there was no significant difference in performance on understanding and knowledge and competence in mathematics. Teacher certification was also found to be significant in Darling-Hammond's (2000) study of US State policies; teacher preparation and certification were the strongest predictor of relative achievement compared to other states, even after controlling for student poverty and number of students with English as their second language.

Not all studies have shown that teacher subject knowledge affects achievement, however. A number of American studies on the relationship between teachers' scores on the National Teacher Examinations and the performance of their students have found little or no effect (Darling-Hammond 2000). In her review of research, Byrne (1983) reported mixed results, some studies reporting positive effects, but others showing no effect. However, she pointed out that in many of the no-effect studies there was little variation in teacher subject knowledge, attenuating possible relationships.

In a study of over 2,800 students using data from the Longitudinal Study of American Youth, Monk (1994) found a positive but curvilinear relationship between teacher's subject knowledge as measured by courses taken and student achievement. This suggests that a threshold effect may be operating, in that a minimal level of subject knowledge is necessary for teachers to be effective, but that beyond a certain point a law of diminishing returns may operate, which may explain the mixed findings in other studies.

Teacher self-efficacy beliefs

With respect to teachers, two main areas of self-belief have been studied: teachers' self-concept, and teachers' self-efficacy. Self-concept can be defined as 'a person's perceptions of him/herself, formed through interaction with the environment, interactions with significant others and attributions of behaviors' (Shavelson *et al.* 1976). The self-concept is multidimensional, which means that one can have different self-concepts about different life-areas. For example, a primary teacher could have a self-concept of herself as a mathematics teacher, and a different self-concept of herself as a PE instructor. Bandura (1986) defined perceived self-efficacy as 'beliefs in one's capabilities to organise and execute the courses of action required to produce given attainment' (p. 3). In the same sense, teaching efficacy can be defined as 'a teacher's judgement of his or her capabilities to bring about desired outcomes of student engagement and learning, even among those students who may be difficult or unmotivated' (Henson 2001). Soodak and Podell (1996) found that teacher efficacy is composed of three factors: personal efficacy (PE), outcome efficacy (OE) and teaching efficacy (TE). It is clear that the concept of self-concept overlaps to a certain extent with the concept of self-efficacy.

Teacher self-efficacy has been linked to student outcomes in a number of studies. A variety of studies have found that students with teachers who score highly on self-efficacy did better on standardised tests of achievement than their peers who are taught by teachers with low self-efficacy beliefs (Moore and Esselman 1992, Anderson *et al.* 1988, Watson 1991 (cited in Henson 2001)). Low teacher self-efficacy beliefs have also been linked to low expectations of students, an important factor in student achievement as mentioned above (Bamburg 1994). Teacher self-efficacy was found to be related to student self-efficacy in a study by Anderson *et al.* (1988). Self-efficacy has been found to influence several aspects of behaviour that are important to teaching and learning. For example, Schunk and Rice (1991) revealed that self-efficacy beliefs were positively associated with their students' achievement in mathematics and language. It was also found that students with teachers who scored high on self-efficacy did better on standardised tests of achievement (Anderson *et al.* 1988, Dempo and Gibson 1985). Moreover, low teacher efficacy beliefs have been linked to low expectations of students which is a significant factor predicting student achievement. Finally, teacher self-efficacy was found to be related to student self-efficacy and student motivation (Philippou and Christou 1999).

The self-concept of 16 male and female primary and secondary teachers was measured to study the possible influence of teachers' self-concepts on how they perceive the nature of mathematics and their attitudes to teaching and learning mathematics (measured through individual teacher interviews). It was found that the low mathematical self-concept of some teachers was related to their negative experiences with mathematics as a student. High self-concept teachers were more motivated, more inventive and more creative about how to conduct math lessons, while low self-concept teachers were more likely to be negative and to complain about lack of resources to implement what they considered to be effective ways of teaching mathematics (Relich 1996).

A study of 132 primary school teachers and their 4,535 primary year five and six students in Hong Kong showed that teachers' social self, pedagogical self and personal self were predictors of teacher behaviours, which in turn predicted student achievement (Chan *et al.* 1992).

Constructivist teaching models

The development of constructivism in psychology has led to the development of constructivist teaching methods by a variety of authors, which, though varied and often subject-specific, have many common elements, usually incorporating methods such as:

- modelling – the teacher carries out a complex task and shows students the processes needed to carry out that task
- coaching – help offered to students by the teachers
- scaffolding and fading – the teacher gives assistance to students to achieve tasks that they cannot yet master on their own, and then gradually withdraws her support
- articulation – students articulate their ideas, thoughts and solutions
- reflection – students compare their solutions to those of 'experts' or other students
- collaboration – with other students and the teacher
- connecting new ideas to prior knowledge
- goal orientation – clear learning goals, wherever possible articulated by students themselves
- exploration and problem-solving activities (De Jager 2002).

Constructivist classrooms tend to be more student-centred and open-ended than in the direct instruction model.

Until recently, the effectiveness of these methods has been under-researched, constructivism to many authors being close to a 'belief system' that is *a priori* 'right' and not particularly in need of empirical verification (see e.g. Von Glasersfeldt 1989 and Ernest 1999), while those studies that do exist tend to be small-scale qualitative studies that give a useful insight into constructivist teaching as it occurs in the classroom but have not usually incorporated rigorous methodology using comparator groups or measurement of student learning, leading to scepticism on the validity of these findings, not least by proponents of the direct instruction model.

A recent Dutch study has attempted to remedy this by comparing constructivist approaches to direct instruction using quasi-experimental methods. Teachers were trained in either the direct instruction or a cognitive apprenticeship model based on the principles mentioned above, with a control group of teachers remaining untrained. Pupils were tested on reading comprehension, metacognition and attitudes towards school and learning pre- and post-implementation, while follow-up tests were also administered. Compared to the control group, the pupils taught under the direct instruction model scored better on metacognition on the post-test, but not the follow-up, while pupils taught using cognitive apprenticeship scored better on some aspects of reading comprehension, metacognition and focus on learning (part of the attitudes battery) on the post-test when compared to the comparison group. Only the effect on metacognition was sustained in the follow-up, however. When compared directly to one another, students receiving the cognitive apprenticeship model did better than those taught under the direct instruction model on aspects of reading comprehension (including in one instance the follow-up), the follow-up test of metacognitive skills, and the follow-up tests of perception of skills and focus on learning (attitudes). While these results are somewhat patchy, they are clearly suggestive of the possible strength of the cognitive apprenticeship model and constructivist strategies (De Jager 2002).

Notwithstanding the criticism of 'traditional' teacher effectiveness research as discussed earlier, these findings to date still provide the most robust knowledge base on effective teaching. However, as we shall see in Chapter 5, this knowledge base contains some serious weaknesses which will need to be addressed if teacher effectiveness research is both to elucidate and to transform teaching in the 21st century.

Table 4.1 The main factors associated with effective teaching examined by each phase of research into teacher effectiveness

Studies on teacher effectiveness	Factors examined
Presage–product studies	*Psychological characteristics* (a) Personality characteristics (b) Attitude (c) Experience (d) Aptitude/Achievement
Process–product model	*Teacher behaviour* (a) Quantity of academic activity • *Quantity and pacing of instruction*: Effective teachers prioritise academic instruction and maximise amount of curriculum covered but at the same time move in such steps that each new objective is learnt readily and without frustration. • *Classroom management*: Effective teachers organise and manage classroom environment as an efficient learning environment and thereby engagement rates are maximised. • *Actual teaching process*: Students should spend most of their time being taught or supervised by their teachers rather than working on their own and most of teacher talk should be academic rather than managerial or procedural. (b) Quality of teacher's organised lessons • *Giving information*: The variables which were examined referred to structuring and clarity of presentation. • *Asking questions*: The variables which were examined referred to the cognitive level of question, the type of question (i.e. product vs process questions), the clarity of question, and the length of pause following questions. • *Providing feedback*: The variables which were examined referred to the way teachers monitor students' responses and how they react to correct, partly correct, or incorrect answers. • *Practice and application opportunities* (c) Classroom climate • Businesslike and supportive environment
Beyond classroom behaviour model	(a) Subject knowledge (b) Knowledge of pedagogy (c) Teacher's beliefs (d) Teacher's self-efficacy

Part II

Towards a differentiated model

5 A critique of teacher effectiveness research

The purpose of this chapter is to raise conceptual and methodological issues dealing with the way that teacher effectiveness was studied during the various phases of teacher effectiveness research (TER) presented in Chapter 4.

Conceptual issues

The narrow conception of teacher effectiveness

The conceptualisation of teacher effectiveness and its operationalisation in investigations have been narrow. The description of the various phases of TER presented in the previous chapter has shown that TER has been mainly concerned with the identification of different kinds of variable (e.g. teacher behaviour, teacher knowledge) which are related to students' achievement. This approach implies that the main criterion of an effective teacher is the extent to which his/her students achieve specific educational goals. Thus, most studies of teacher effectiveness adopt a goal-oriented model for measuring effectiveness (Stufflebeam and Shinkfield 1990). This model assumes that a teacher is effective if she/he can accomplish the planned goals and assigned tasks in compliance with school goals. Thus, the extent to which the goals and tasks have been accomplished was seen as the measure of teacher effectiveness (Walberg 1986) and typical indicators of teacher effectiveness include student learning outcomes and performance standards. The advantage of this model is that it enables researchers, policy-makers, school administrators, and teachers to focus their attention on measurable teacher performance in tasks that can directly or indirectly contribute to educational outcomes (Wang and Walberg 1991). However, following Cheng and Tsui (1996), we would argue that within the limitation of resources and support, teachers may not be able to accomplish successfully all the assigned tasks at one time, especially if the goals and tasks assigned to them are demanding, diverse, or conflicting in nature.

The conception of effectiveness is narrow in two senses. First, the measures of outcome are typically performance on standardised or other tests, usually in the national language or mathematics. Although this is justified in terms of validity and reliability, it means that effectiveness in other subjects, or in aspects of the subject not included in the tests (for example speaking and listening, or practical applications in mathematics or ICT use) are excluded. Effective teaching of art, say, or physical education, or laboratory science, might require different skills or behaviours from those identified in mathematics and language. Second, as has been argued in Chapter 2, this conception of effectiveness can no longer meet the needs of the changing school environment. Clearly effective instruction is a major dimension of teaching, but the work of teachers is substantially broader than classroom performance. Teaching in modern societies has been analysed by a variety of supra-governmental agencies (e.g. OECD 1990, ILO 1991). These show that under modernising tendencies and as societies become more secular, schools become the main site of moral and social value formation. Under these trends teachers in the 21st century are expected to adopt expanded roles and responsibilities such as curriculum developers, action researchers, team leaders and staff development facilitators. All those roles suggest that the traditional conception of teacher effectiveness which is focused exclusively on the teaching performance of individual teachers in the classrooms has been rendered anachronistic. The consequence is that we need a broader and multidimensional conception of teacher effectiveness to incorporate measures of effectiveness across these different roles rather than, as now, being limited to aspects of classroom instruction, important though that is.

Recently some educators have attempted to develop models of teacher effectiveness based on the organisational theory literature (e.g. Cheng and Tsui 1999, Johnson 1997). Each proposed model emphasises certain factors that are closely related to teachers' performance within the school's organisational context. It is not our intention to present them in detail or to deal with the contextual constraints on the usefulness of each model. Our point here is that the basic characteristics of each model might be very different and that each of them has its own strengths and weaknesses. A brief description of three typical models follows, which we would argue illustrates that the adoption of one of them alone is not sufficient and is as problematic as the traditional model focused only on the classroom level.

The 'resource utilisation' model (Cheng and Tsui 1999) considers resources and support as critical factors in accomplishing the assigned tasks and meeting diverse goals and expectations. For this reason, teachers are deemed effective if they can maximise the use of allocated resources in their work and procure the needed support to overcome difficulties and accomplish tasks and competing goals. However, this model is useful only when the relationship of the efficiency of resource utilisation to work process and outcomes is clear, and lack of the resources can be shown to limit the ability of teachers to achieve stated goals and assigned tasks.

The 'continuous learning' model (Cheng and Tsui 1999) is based on the fact that the changing education environment affects every teacher and therefore effective teachers are expected to be able to adapt to external and internal changes, cope with the different challenges, meet the diverse expectations and develop themselves through continuous learning. The continuous learning model assumes that environmental changes are inevitable and, therefore, a teacher is effective if he/she can adapt to and improve his/her learning environment. The model is useful only when teachers are working in a changing education environment and need to adapt to changes and face internal and external challenges. This may apply especially in post-modernised societies where lifelong learning is seen as a prerequisite for effectiveness but less so in more stable education systems. Another problem with this model is that it assumes that all change is positive, and therefore that effective teachers should always adopt and never resist policies on educational changes. Yet it is clearly possible to imagine circumstances where some government initiatives could harm rather than help pupils, and teacher resistance could therefore be a more effective response.

The third model is based on the Cameron's (1984) argument that it is easier to identify the weaknesses and defects (i.e. the indicators of ineffectiveness) of a teacher than his/her strengths (i.e. the indicators of effectiveness). Hence, if a teacher can meet the minimal requirements and display no apparent problems and ineffectiveness in daily work and teaching, one can assume that he/she is working smoothly and performing effectively due to the fact that he/she is able to solve the problems in his/her school environment. Although the specific criteria of teacher effectiveness which might emerge from this model are not very clear, this model may be important in schools in difficult circumstances. Moreover, this model is clearly limited by the fact that it is unable to distinguish highly effective from average teachers, and therefore would promote adequacy rather than excellence. Thus, this model is focused on minimum performance indicators and does not address effectiveness in teaching higher order learning skills or creativity.

Thus we would argue that the above three models of teacher effectiveness emphasise different aspects of teacher's work and performance, and that they illustrate the difficulty of adopting a single model. A single-model approach is not sufficient to understand the multifaceted conception of teacher effectiveness required for the educational context of the 21st century. Similar conclusions could be drawn, we believe, from any of the models developed during the past decade on teacher effectiveness (such as the accountability model or the school constituencies satisfaction model). What is needed is a multi-dimensional conception of teacher effectiveness in order to deepen the understanding of teacher effectiveness and improve its relevance to the context in which teachers work.

The disconnection of TER from teachers' professional development

A constraint of the existing approaches of TER is that the process does not contribute significantly to teachers' professional development or to improving teachers' effectiveness. The widely cited meta-analysis by Gipps (1996), *What We Know about Effective Primary Teaching*, is succinct and analytical, but does not show how a teacher could move from ineffective to effective practice. From this and most of the other research the best that could be inferred was a set of characteristics about the effective teacher, but a teacher thought to be ineffective on the criteria used to define effectiveness would not be helped to identify ways of improving. The explanation for this does not lie in researchers' lack of interest in improvement so much as in the research methodologies. These involve correlational research findings which are based on variation in existing practices. Even most of the experimental studies involved practices previously observed (Griffin and Barnes 1986). Thus, where there were attempts to transfer findings to classroom practice (Brophy and Good 1986) or to professional development programmes such as the Active Mathematics Teaching (Good *et al.* 1983) or the Teacher Effectiveness Enhancement Project (Muijs and Reynolds 2000), prescriptions for applications usually remained within the ranges of teacher behaviour observed. Since the variables associated with teacher effectiveness were primarily generated by the researchers through naturalistic classroom observation, specific needs for real professional development which takes into account teachers' needs, skills and involvement were not identified (Walker and Cheng 1996). For this reason, TER has been criticised as an isolated academic exercise attempting to describe effectiveness characteristics which has had a limited application to improvement of teaching (Campbell *et al.* 2003).

However, new paradigms are beginning to emerge. Some moves to connect training with research findings are under way. For example, the text by Muijs and Reynolds (2001a) for student teachers uses teacher effectiveness research to draw implications for practice, and Gipps *et al.* (2001) have produced a text drawing implications from the research for primary teaching. Also, the Hay McBer model of teacher effectiveness (DfEE 2000) identifies criteria for effective practice and links them with the professional values and characteristics needed to develop effectiveness. In addition, the model claims to be based on research and shows 'three factors within teachers' control' that significantly influence student progress: teaching skills, professional characteristics, and classroom climate. The first two are seen as input that teachers bring to teaching, while the third is an output measure. Within each factor several sub-factors are identified. For example, teaching skills comprise 35 behaviours clustered into seven sub-factors, namely, high expectations, planning, methods and strategies, pupil management/discipline, time and resource management, assessment, and homework. Professional characteristics have to do with self-image and values, traits and motivation. Sixteen characteristics under this factor are clustered into five sub-factors: professionalism, thinking, planning and setting expectations, relating to others, and leading. Classroom climate is defined by reference to how pupils feel in the classroom. Nine dimensions are identified: clarity, order, standards, fairness, participation, support, safety, interest, and environment.

The model claims that its findings are consonant with those of established researchers. For example, it cites Creemers and Reezigt's (1999) study of classroom climate factors as having similar findings to those in the model. There are substantial methodological problems with the Hay McBer model, as Bassey and Mortimore (2001) argue. However, it provides the basis for enabling teachers, school leaders or policy-makers to know how to advise a teacher considered ineffective on the effectiveness criteria to become effective. We also have independent evidence that research into teacher effectiveness can incorporate a concern for teaching improvement (Kyriakides *et al.* 2002).

The exclusion of school-wide factors

Teddlie (1994) argues that most TER has been concerned with classroom processes to the exclusion of school-wide factors. On the other hand, most school effectiveness studies have involved phenomena that occur throughout the school, with, until recently, little concern for teaching and learning in classrooms (Teddlie and Reynolds 2000). This polarisation has been unproductive, since effective change in schools probably has to be managed at the level of both the school and the class, and, indeed, in secondary schools, as Harris (2000) argues, at intermediate levels such as the department. No level can be adequately studied without considering the others. Virgilio *et al.* (1991) showed that there were mean and variance differences in the behaviours of teachers from effective and less effective schools. It can therefore be claimed that the fact that TER has been concerned with classroom processes to the exclusion of school-wide factors might also lead to a restricted list of variables associated with teacher effectiveness. Thus, combined research into school and teacher effects could yield results leading to the generation of more probing questions about the processes underlying these effects (Kyriakides *et al.* 2000).

This argument implies that TER should be seen in terms of three main theoretical models of schooling which have been developed (Scheerens and Bosker 1997) and which are briefly presented below. The first method, perhaps the most commonly held belief regarding schooling effects, assumes that organisational features influence instructional practices, which subsequently influence student achievement (Bidwell and Kasarda 1980). This approach postulates that effective school-level policies will increase the degree to which teachers employ effective instructional practices. The second model, the environmental model, assumed that school effects would 'add to' or supplement the classroom level. In a sense, the original effective school models were examples of this approach because they did not distinguish between school levels (e.g. the Edmonds (1979) five factor model). It was assumed that school environmental effects were independent of classroom determinants and therefore teacher effectiveness could be measured without taking into account school environmental factors. Finally, the interactive model specifies that classroom practices function within the context of the school environment. Higher-level conditions therefore can either foster or impinge on the relationship between classroom procedures and student achievement. Classroom variable influences are assumed to depend on the presence or absence of certain school variables. This model stresses the cross-level interactions between school features at different levels. We conclude from the above outline of the three models of educational effectiveness that the development of joint teacher/school effectiveness research is required since it will enable researchers to compare empirically the three models and determine which model best represents the relationship between variables defining school effectiveness and variables defining teacher effectiveness, and the strengths and problems associated with each.

The development of the concept of teacher effectiveness in a generic way

The final, and possibly the most important, conceptual problem of TER is that the concept of teacher effectiveness has been developed in a generic way, drawing up a 'one size fits all' model, in which the assumption is that effective teachers are effective with all students, in all contexts, in all aspects of their subjects and so on. This is reflected in the fact that much of the earlier research (e.g. Brophy and Everston 1976, Everston *et al.* 1980, Rosenshine 1971, Rosenshine and Furst 1973), and the policies for teacher appraisal that claim to be connected to it, have tended to identify a general set of characteristics that define the effective teacher; they provide a profile of teacher behaviour, knowledge and beliefs assumed to be generic, irrespective of age of student, ability of pupil groups, social and organisational context, or even the subject being taught. Such conceptualisation of effectiveness has led to a simplistic dichotomy between effective and ineffective teachers and has eschewed the possibility that teachers may have strengths and weaknesses in their professional practice. One consequence is that it becomes difficult to use findings of TER for measuring such strengths and weaknesses and therefore to become a source for conducting formative teacher evaluation (Kyriakides and Campbell 2003). We believe that the field is now ready for a challenge to and development of this base, to explore differentiated teacher effectiveness and to examine how far it is possible to build a theory incorporating it.

Methodological issues

The approaches used to examine teacher effectiveness face several methodological limitations (Shavelson *et al.* 1986). This section of this chapter deals with three principal ones.

The methods used to measure the outcomes of teaching

The problem of outcome measurement arises from the assumption that a teacher was considered effective if, within the time period studied, students, averaged over the whole class, answered more questions correctly, usually on a standardised test, than expected, based on their pre-test performance (Good 1979). That is to say, the operationalisation of effectiveness was based on three further assumptions: (a) that there is communality of curriculum goals, objectives, and content coverage across classrooms, since a single test is used to judge effectiveness; (b) that effectiveness is strictly summative in its measurement of subject matter knowledge; and (c) that effectiveness is strictly aggregative across students within a classroom, since regardless of how student performance is distributed within the classroom, the class average is taken as a representative measure of the teacher's performance. These assumptions are examined below.

Standardised tests were usually used to measure outcomes (especially during the process–product phase of TER) based on the fact that standardised tests are designed to reflect curriculum over a broad array of schools and districts and the scores they typically generate cover a variety of objectives within a content area. But given the evidence that curriculum coverage affects student performance on standardised achievement tests (Carroll 1963, Creemers 1994), it is somewhat surprising that so few of the major studies of TER actually controlled for curriculum variation. The virtual absence of information about 'opportunity to learn' aspects of the instructional environment and curriculum content from TER provides an inadequate basis for judgement about the plausible sources of performance gain that may be associated with teaching practices (Cooley 1981, Linn 1986). Therefore, there seems to be no sound basis for TER to ignore subject matter and its interactions with the processes and outcomes of instructions.

As far as the adequacy of summative evidence about student knowledge and skills is concerned, we would argue that an important aspect of students' learning is missed when summary scores alone are considered. In a classroom where most students cover the same topic (although pacing and depth might vary), the typical change in the pattern of responses from incorrect to correct answers and the type of incorrect answers that persist from pre-test to post-test can reflect the consequences of teaching and may be particularly informative about effective teaching practice (Kyriakides and Telemachou 2002). There is also evidence that student attributes such as ability, personality and motivation interact with instruction to yield differential gains (Kyriakides 2003a, Demetriou *et al.* 2003, Peterson 1977). For example, Peterson (1977) shows that some students learn more effectively under highly structured conditions while others benefit from less structure. This evidence of a teacher's differentiated effectiveness is missed when concentrating on class means to measure factors associated with teacher effectiveness. Similarly, American research has drawn attention to the different behaviours or characteristics needed for effectiveness in different contexts (e.g. Teddlie and Stringfield 1993, Borich 1996). We believe that 'context specificity' (Hopkins and Reynolds 2001) can be addressed if researchers use multi-level modelling techniques to examine effectiveness, since class means can be eschewed in favour of achievement data at the level of the individual pupil linked to teacher factors at the classroom level. Thus, the methodology exists for a more differentiated model of teacher effectiveness.

The reliability of the measures of variables examined through TER

In the first and second *Handbooks of Research on Teaching*, concerns about the reliability of measures of teacher behaviour under the process–product were expressed (Medley and Mitzel 1963, Rosenshine and Furst 1973). Similar concerns are expressed in the current fourth edition of the handbook (e.g. Crawford and Impara 2001, p. 145). We would argue that researchers in the area of teacher effectiveness could use generalisability theory (Cronbach *et al.* 1972, Brennan 1983, Shavelson and Webb 1981) in order to assess multiple sources of variation in measurements of variables associated with teacher effectiveness and thereby examine the reliability of their measures. Generalisability theory is a theory of the multifaceted errors of measurement. The concept of a *universe score* is at the heart of generalisability theory and can be viewed as the mean score for an object of measurement (usually an individual) over all conditions in the universe of generalisation. The universe of generalisation is defined in terms of those aspects (called *facets*) of the observations that determine the conditions under which an acceptable score can be obtained. According to Cronbach *et al.* (1972), the conceptual framework underlying generalisability theory is that 'an investigator asks about the precision or reliability of a measure because he wishes to generalize from the observation in hand to some class of observations to which it belongs' (p. 15). Thus, generalisability theory asks 'how accurately observed scores permit us to generalize about persons' behaviour in a defined universe' (Shavelson *et al.* 1989). Ideally, a measurement procedure should provide information about an individual's universe score over all combinations of facets, but in reality investigators are limited in their choice of particular facets. The need to sample facets inevitably introduces error into a measurement procedure and limits one to estimating rather than actually measuring the universe score. Thus, a universe score is really an 'ideal' score for an individual given a universe of generalisation (Marcoulides and Kyriakides 2002). Besides providing extensive methods for estimating the precision or reliability of a measurement procedure, Cronbach *et al.* (1972) suggested various ways to compute the universe score. Comparable methods for estimating universe scores were also introduced by Jarjoura (1982) and Searle (1974).

Thus, the first task in a generalisability study is to conceptualise the measurement under consideration by defining the objects of measurement and the conditions that are acceptable to the researcher as ways to take observations of the objects of measurement. The set of these conditions constitutes the universe of admissible observations. Researchers of teacher effectiveness wishing to partition, for instance, sources of variation in teacher behavioural measurement could apply the same framework. In this case, the results of a generalisability study are able to show the relative influence of (say) observers, occasions and settings on a measure of teacher behaviour and can be used to determine the number of observations needed to attain maximum generalisability in prespecified varieties of teaching situations. The use of generalisability theory can therefore help us examine the extent to which there are limitations on the three assumptions upon which the operationalisation of effectiveness is based, and could also raise questions about the existence of a generic concept of teacher effectiveness.

A limited perspective of the function of teaching has been adopted

As far as the perspective on the function of teaching is concerned, we would argue that in much previous research, factors contributing to teacher effectiveness have tended to be presented as being in opposition to one another, instead of being combined in order to investigate the relationship between student achievement and all the factors examined in each phase of TER taken together. It can be argued that because of this limited perspective of teaching, the studies which were conducted during the past three decades are focused on a limited range of traits of the effective teacher concerning mainly their behaviour, whereas a number of other traits (e.g. personal characteristics of teachers and their value systems) are given less attention since they were found not to be related with student achievement gains. Thus, researchers should attempt to investigate the relationship between teacher effectiveness and all the factors examined during the various phases of TER. Such studies may contribute to the development and empirical testing of a theoretical model reflecting the interrelations among these variables and student achievement.

Strengths and limitations of recent developments in quantitative research methods

At the end of this chapter, we explore the limitations and strengths of recent statistical methods and models, including multi-level models and structural equation modelling (SEM), which have been critical to recent developments in research into educational effectiveness. SEM models represent translations of hypothesised cause–effect relationships between variables into a composite hypothesis concerning patterns of statistical dependencies. The relationships are described by parameters that indicate the magnitude of the effect (direct or indirect) that independent variables (observed or latent) have on dependent variables (observed or latent) (Raykov and Marcoulides 2000). It can therefore be claimed that by enabling the translation of hypothesised relationships into testable mathematical models, SEM offers researchers a comprehensive method for studying theoretical models (Kline 1998). Thus, it is now possible to test a comprehensive and differentiated model of teacher effectiveness against empirical data.

We also argue that researchers should attempt to consider the multi-level structure of the data collected in order to examine both school and teacher effects. Therefore, multi-level modelling should be used as the method of analysis in joint teacher and school effectiveness studies (Goldstein 1995). In its detail, multi-level modelling is a relatively new approach to the analysis of hierarchically structured data (e.g. students within classrooms within schools), but in broad terms it is an elaboration of multiple regression to incorporate the hierarchical structure of data (see Paterson and Goldstein 1991). The advantage of multi-level modelling is that it explicitly models the hierarchical structure of the data, and also, like multiple regression, it can be used to investigate differences such as those between the performance of boys and girls, having taken into account their attainment on entry.

However, the multi-level modelling cannot allow for investigating cross-level interactions among variables associated with effectiveness at the pupil, teacher and school level. Therefore, the development and testing of comprehensive models of educational effectiveness looking at both the teacher and school level requires the development of appropriate complex multi-level structural equation models. Although Heck (2002) provides an overview of two-level or disaggregated modelling with SEM techniques, and argues that this approach can be used to examine data obtained from cluster sampling, the use of SEM with more than two levels is still problematic (Hoyle 1995, Kline 1998). For instance, the use of LISREL would confront us with aggregation problems and therefore researchers conducting joint teacher/ school effectiveness studies could not use it for SEM analyses since its use neglects the multi-level structure of the data. This, as Opdenakker and Van Damme (2000) have shown, might lead to research conclusions different from those of analyses which do not ignore the multi-level structure of the data. Therefore, further research into the development of SEM and multi-level analyses would be critical for the attempt of researchers to solve most of the methodological limitations of TER. Regarding the conceptual problems, we argue in the next chapter that a solution to these problems can be found through the establishment of a theory from studies investigating differentiated teacher effectiveness. Although our focus on quantitative studies of effective teachers can be attributed to the fact that the field is dominated by studies using quantitative approaches, one of the critiques on TER has long been what is seen as a preoccupation with quantitative at the expense of qualitative methods. This critique is justified in so far as an exclusive preoccupation with quantitative methods will not enable us to access fully the complexity and depth of classroom situations and interpersonal dimensions of effective teaching.

One major problem with quantitative studies is that they are unable to study the crucial aspect of meaning. This is an important aspect of effective teaching, as why teachers are doing what they do, the meanings they themselves attach to teaching, and their value orientation are all hard, if not impossible, to study using quantitative methods. Yet studies of highly effective teachers clearly show that these teachers themselves see these aspects as crucial to their own effectiveness (e.g. Ponticell and Zepeda 2003). Therefore, in-depth qualitative exploration is needed both to distinguish the highly effective from the effective teachers (as we have seen, traditional teacher effectiveness research finds this hard to do) through the values and meanings they attach to their actions, and to help fill in the 'black box' and explain the relationship between teacher actions and student learning. Qualitative research that looks at students' perspectives is also long overdue in this area – how they perceive their own learning from highly effective teachers is another question that is hard to answer using traditional quantitative methods. Various qualitative methods are appropriate for research into effective teaching. First, ethnographic research explores the way teachers and pupils interact (Hammersley 1991, Hammersley and Atkinson 1983). Secondly, qualitative interview methods could help us to interrogate the views of key stakeholders (not just teachers themselves, but pupils, parents and management) more thoroughly than questionnaires (Brown and McIntyre 1993). Third, case studies of highly effective teachers will allow us to produce a more rounded and informative picture of what these teachers do than is possible using correlational quantitative methods (Yin 1994, Seidman 1998, Merriam 2001). Finally, as has been demonstrated in Chapter 3, historical approaches can help us contextualise current theories.

6 Developing a model of differentiated teacher effectiveness

The purpose of this chapter is to develop a concept of differentiated teacher effectiveness in ways that attempt to overcome the problems identified in the previous chapter. Thus, the various dimensions of the capacity of teachers to perform effectively with different groups of pupils and under different conditions are examined.

Consistency and stability of teacher effects on students' achievement

We take the view that the consistency and stability of teacher effects are two fundamental challenges for teacher effectiveness research. Consistency refers to different criterion variables whereas stability has to do with different time points, and both of them can be seen as dimensions of differentiated teacher effectiveness. So, for example, one might rank order primary teachers on the basis of an output measure, such as their pupils' achievement in mathematics, and correlate this with the rank order based on language achievement (i.e. a subject consistency measure). Evidence from inspections conducted by the Office for Standards in Education (Ofsted) in England at primary school level is beginning to demonstrate that the same teacher can be judged to be outstanding at, say, teaching mathematics, but only adequate at, say, teaching history or physical education. This is because the inspections now provide a profile of teacher performance in relation to each lesson observed (typically up to four lessons in an inspection). The lessons are commonly of different subjects. The data are logged onto a national database and may be made available to researchers, while data at the level of the individual school are made available to governing bodies of the school. This analysis is probably not restricted to primary schools; secondary and middle school teachers in some countries teach subjects other than their specialist subject, especially to the younger classes. In England, for example, according to Her Majesty's Chief Inspector for Schools, a substantial amount of teaching in Key Stage 3 (11–14 year olds) is provided by teachers without a specialisation in the subject being taught.

There is a similar issue within a subject. One might rank order secondary school teachers in mathematics on the basis of their pupils' achievement in geometry and correlate this with the rank order based on arithmetic (or algebra) achievement (i.e. a subject component consistency measure). Obviously, the argument about subject components applies equally to secondary teachers and their primary colleagues. However, as far as we are aware, there is as yet little evidence about different performance by teachers in different subject components, because the inspection data are not presented at that level of detail either in England or in any other country. (The international comparisons provided by the Second International Mathematics Study (SIMS) and the Third International Mathematics and Science Study (TIMSS) do provide subject component breakdowns.) On balance, therefore, it is reasonable to believe that a teacher can perform differently in different subject components.

Therefore, research into the consistency of teacher effects could help identify the most appropriate criteria for evaluating teachers, especially in cases where the evaluation is designed to contribute to decisions concerning selection of the most effective teachers in specific subjects (e.g. selection of a curriculum coordinator). Where the evaluation has a formative purpose for the individual teacher it might help identify professional development needs in relation to specific subjects and/or subject components.

Stability over time is a different, but equally important, form of consistency. A time stability measure can be obtained if we, for example, rank order teachers on the basis of their output this year and then compare this with the rank order for the preceding year. The issue of teacher effect size might become more meaningful when teachers produce similar positive effects year after year. Where this can be shown, we would argue that even a small teacher effect is meaningful; these teachers produce better than average output each year, so hundreds of pupils will benefit over time. In the outlier tradition of teacher effectiveness research the stability question is crucial, since if the selected excellent teachers are not excellent the next year, it would be hazardous to translate teachers' behaviours that are seen as the causes of achievement differences into policy measures, such as teacher-improvement programmes. It can therefore be claimed that answers to the stability question are closely related to the reliability of studies measuring teacher effects.

It has been argued in Chapter 5 that researchers in the field of effectiveness would benefit from making use of generalisability theory. Thus, investigations into time stability could take the form of a generalisability study in which one of the levels by which the data of the study on measuring teacher effectiveness will be categorised is the measurement occasion (i.e. the different time periods at which teacher effect was measured). Moreover, the stability issue could play a role in studies attempting to evaluate local or national professional development programmes, since the extent to which teachers manage to improve their effectiveness in the period they were attending the programme might be seen as an indicator of the value of the programme. Information on such stability measures might be useful for evidence-based policy-making.

The stability over time assumption is important in another way. Since most of the variables associated with teacher effectiveness (i.e. personality, knowledge, behaviour, beliefs) are assumed to be relatively stable over time, at least for experienced teachers, it is important to know whether the rank order of teachers on output remains the same regardless of the point at which the effect is measured. If the rank order does not remain the same, the explanation must be that some other variables, which do change over time, are the causes of achievement differences, or that the measures of teacher effectiveness are defective, or that the stability of the variables is weaker than has been assumed.

Teacher effectiveness with different groups of pupils: students' background factors

As has been explained in Chapter 5, teacher effectiveness research (TER) was based on the assumption that a teacher could be considered effective if, within the time period studied, students, averaged over the whole class, answered more questions correctly, usually on a standardised test, than expected based on their pre-test performance. Therefore, TER was based on the assumption that the effectiveness of a teacher is effectiveness for the average student, i.e. average with respect to aptitude, socio-economic status, etc. As a consequence, despite the fact that a large number of TER studies have been conducted in many countries, very little attention has been paid to the extent to which teachers perform consistently across differing groups of pupils.

There have been some studies investigating differentiated school effectiveness in several countries. Bryk and Raudenbush (1992) discovered that public and private secondary schools in the USA differed with respect to their relationship between the socio-economic status of students and their achievement level. It was demonstrated that the differences between the public and private schools were twice as large for low socio-economic status students as for students from middle-class families. Moreover, there were hardly any differences between the schools with respect to upper-class families. In England, Sammons *et al.* (1993) showed that for primary schools differential effects could only be demonstrated for the prior attainment of students and not with respect to their gender, socio-economic status or ethnicity. The evidence about differentiated effectiveness related to pupil gender and for ethnic differences shows little overall consensus across the various countries where such studies have been conducted (Nuttall *et al.* 1989, Kyriakides 2003b). If supported further, this would raise questions, as with the Muijs and Reynolds study reported in Chapter 4, about the extent to which teacher effectiveness is differentiated along pupil background factors.

Although there is not a substantial and consistent evidence base (though see Chapter 7) concerning differentiated teacher effectiveness for particular groups of pupils and for different levels of prior attainment, this dimension of teacher effectiveness is clearly of importance. We would argue that research in this area may provide a new perspective on educational equality, and might be the basis for a response to the critics of educational effectiveness research who argue that it has not given consideration to equity and social justice (Slee *et al.* 1998). Currently, findings concerning differential school effects from studies conducted in the USA support the conclusion that schools have the biggest effect on underprivileged and/or initially low-achieving students (Scheerens and Bosker 1997). This implies that school choice, or at least school attended, is a critical issue for pupils from disadvantaged backgrounds, and we would argue that, as a hypothesis, it is in the interests of such pupils that differentiated performance data become available. For example, it might be found that some teachers are extremely effective in promoting the learning of pupils with special educational needs but less so with very able pupils, and vice versa. Likewise, there may be teachers who are able to reduce gender and socio-economic differences. Any model of differentiated effectiveness would need to be able to identify such strengths and enable the identification of significant variables associated with different outcomes.

Teacher effectiveness with different groups of pupils: students' personal characteristics

The fourth dimension of differentiated effectiveness is also focused on the capacity of a teacher to perform effectively with different groups of pupils. This dimension is, however, focused on pupils in relation to their personal characteristics. More specifically, we explore whether teachers are differentially effective in promoting the learning of pupils according to their personal characteristics such as their personality, thinking style, extent of motivation and self-esteem. This follows from the argument that the research agenda of educational effectiveness should focus on individual differences as well as social and administrative issues (Kyriakides 2003b).

In the literature, variables such as personality, thinking style, motivation and self-esteem are seen as related with intelligence. For example, the work of Ackerman (1996, 1997; Ackerman and Heggestad 1997) is exemplary in investigating the intelligence–personality relations. Based on the meta-analysis of a large number of studies that investigated the intelligence–personality relations, Ackerman and Heggestad (1997) found that, overall, there was a correlation between intellectual ability and personality such that the higher the intellectual ability, the more self-confident, satisfied, achievement-oriented, and open to others and to experience the individual is. That is, it was found that, on the one hand, various measures of intellectual ability, such as general intelligence, fluid intelligence, crystallised intelligence, or more specialised measures (e.g. mathematical or spatial ability) were positively related with personality characteristics such as extroversion, social potency, achievement, openness to experience and positive emotionality. On the other hand, intellectual ability was negatively related with personality traits such as neuroticism and psychoticism and negative emotionality in general (e.g. stress reaction and test anxiety). Moreover, further research (Ackerman 1996, 1997) suggests that trait complexes are formed so that intellectual profiles get intertwined with personality and interests profiles, which are compatible with each other in terms of the needs and demands they pose on the individual. For instance, persons high in mathematical and spatial reasoning tend to be investigative and have engineering and mechanical interests. Persons high in crystallised intelligence (i.e. on general knowledge) tend to be investigative, open to experience, and to have artistic interests. Persons fast in processing speed, who are self-restrained and conscientious, tend to have conventional and conforming interests. That is, they prefer to operate in contexts where there are well-defined rules that make fast routine activity possible. The meta-analyses show that students' thinking style is related to achievement both directly and indirectly (i.e. through its relation with particular types of personality) (Guildford 1980, Ruble and Cosier 1990, Furnham 1995).

Since teacher effectiveness is measured in reference to pupils' achievement, variables which psychologists found to be related to intelligence and achievement (such as type of personality, thinking style, motivation, self-esteem) cannot be ignored by teacher effectiveness researchers (Kyriakides 2003a). As a consequence, studies focused on differentiated teacher effectiveness could also attempt to deal with differences in effectiveness according to their students' personal characteristics. The results of these studies might help researchers to build comprehensive models of educational effectiveness which could contribute to theory building, as part of a reply to those who criticise research into educational effectiveness as being atheoretical (e.g. Thrupp 2001a, 2001b, Slee and Weiner 2001). Theorising in this field might be significantly improved if it were possible to connect teacher effectiveness with well-established concepts in psychology, especially if the empirical research were able to explain some of the variance in pupils' achievement which remains unexplained from the studies conducted so far (Kyriakides 2003a).

Teacher effectiveness and organisational context

The fifth dimension of differentiated teacher effectiveness refers to the various cultural and organisational contexts in which teachers work and which may have an impact on their effectiveness. More specifically, it is assumed that teachers may be differentially effective in response to the various contexts in which they work. For example, effectiveness in a two-teacher rural primary school may be different from in a 2,000-pupil urban school or college; in different departments or faculties in the same school; with several para-professionals to manage as against with none; in homogeneous compared with heterogeneous classroom groups; in schools with strongly framed cultures as against schools with weakly framed cultures. This would require a model in which the interrelationships between school context and teacher effectiveness were reflected and is therefore closely related to the criticism of TER that most studies have been concerned with classroom processes to the exclusion of school-wide factors. The exclusion of school-wide factors from TER has been unproductive, since effective educational change probably has to be managed at the level of both the school and the class. Thus, the joint study of school and teacher effects could yield consistent and predictable results leading to the generation of more probing questions about the processes underlying these effects. At the moment the recognition of this issue has been reflected in the adoption of the term 'educational effectiveness' (Creemers 1994, Scheerens and Bosker 1997) but its use may serve to fudge matters by avoiding the necessity to tease out the interactions, which in many contexts are extremely complex.

This dimension is also closely related to the work of researchers in the 1990s who attempted to develop comprehensive models of educational effectiveness by integrating the findings of school effectiveness research, research on teacher effectiveness and the early input–output studies (Stringfield and Slavin 1992, Scheerens 1992, Creemers 1994). The main characteristics of the resulting models, called *integrated multilevel educational effectiveness models*, are presented in Chapter 8. Thus, researchers who provided empirical support to the main assumptions of these models (e.g. Jong and Westerhof 1998, Kyriakides *et al.* 2000) and revealed that the influences on pupil achievement are multilevel provide, at least indirectly, support for the importance of investigating differentiated teacher effectiveness by looking at differences in their cultural and organisational working contexts. However, the studies cited above revealed that very specific organisational factors at school level, such as school climate, consensus on the mission of the school and assessment policy, influenced effectiveness at the classroom level (Teddlie and Reynolds 2000, Reynolds *et al.* 2002, Kyriakides *et al.* 2000). Therefore, longitudinal studies which make use of purposive sampling techniques should be conducted in order to examine whether there are teachers who might be more effective in some organisational contexts and less effective in others. Obviously, there are many practical difficulties in identifying an appropriate sample of teachers who worked during two consecutive years in different organisational contexts, but the characteristics of their pupils at classroom level or any other variable found to be associated with their effectiveness (such as the content of the curriculum taught) remained the same. The extent to which their effectiveness has changed might be attributed to the fact that they are more effective in one type of school than another, or working in a school with one type of climate or curriculum policy than another. A further complexity is that it is not ethical to use an experimental research design to show that differences in the effectiveness of a group of teachers can be attributed to changes in the organisational context of their work (Miller 1984, Cohen *et al.* 2000). On the other hand, action research projects attempting to improve the effectiveness of teachers through changes in the organisational context of their work might be used to investigate the extent to which there is differentiated effectiveness across this dimension.

The capacity of a teacher to be effective across the range of work activity: a criterion consistency measure

The five dimensions of differentiated effectiveness described above are based on the assumption that effective teachers are those who are able to help their students to achieve specific educational goals. For this reason, it was claimed in Chapter 5 that most studies of teacher effectiveness adopt a goal-oriented model for measuring effectiveness (Stufflebeam and Shinkfield 1990). However, as was also argued in the previous chapter, it should be acknowledged that within the limitation of resources and support, teachers may not be able to accomplish successfully all the assigned tasks at one time, especially if the goals and tasks assigned to them are demanding, diverse, or conflicting in nature (Cheng and Tsui 1996). This is especially true since as has been argued in Chapter 2, the range of activities expected of teachers in modernising education systems is extremely broad. These include social, pastoral, welfare dimensions and management of other adults, in addition to the formal instructional dimension. Accepting that the sampling of these kinds of teacher function is desirable for an appropriate approach to defining teacher effectiveness, what is required is a multidimensional concept of teacher effectiveness. This would include effectiveness in achieving, for example, pastoral goals, in the management of other adults to improve student learning, and so on. It is therefore important to incorporate in the model of differentiated teacher effectiveness, the investigation of the extent to which teachers are able to perform effectively in accomplishing this range of activities. Thus, we would argue that TER should attempt to measure the consistency of teacher effectiveness in terms of the different criteria for measuring effectiveness in the various duties of teachers in the 21st century (Scriven 1994).

There is some evidence that teachers themselves would value the inclusion of this dimension into a model of differentiated teacher effectiveness. A study involving the generation by teachers themselves of criteria for teacher effectiveness found that teachers suggested a range of extra-classroom characteristics concerning the effective teacher, in principle providing a basis for the expansion of the existing theory on the subject (Kyriakides *et al.* 2002). This suggests that for these

Table 6.1 A model of differentiated teacher effectiveness

	DIFFERENTIATED TEACHER EFFECTIVENESS: INSTRUCTIONAL ROLE		
Time stability	*Subject consistency*	*Differentiation*	
1. School year	1. Curriculum subjects	*Different people*	*Working environment*
2. Phase of implementation of an educational policy	2. Areas within a subject	1. Group of students (sex, age, SES, learning needs)	1. School type
3. Teaching periods	3. Difficulty of a teaching unit	2. Colleagues	2. Availability of resources/ support
4. Periods in relation to the assessment of a teacher	4. Type of teaching objectives	3. Parents	3. School culture
			4. Community

DIFFERENTIATED TEACHER EFFECTIVENESS: ACROSS VARIOUS ROLES

teachers at least it is not sufficient to understand teacher effectiveness by reference to classroom behaviour only.

A summary of the model

The five dimensions of differentiation upon which we could design studies investigating differentiated teacher effectiveness are elaborated as a theoretical model in Table 6.1. Specifically, Table 6.1 reveals that the first four dimensions of differentiation can be based on the assumption that teacher effectiveness is measured through his/her ability to achieve learning goals. These four dimensions are also seen as related to the three conceptual issues of educational effectiveness, namely stability, consistency and differentiation. The fifth dimension of our model refers to the importance of investigating differentiated effectiveness in relation to the various tasks that teachers are expected to accomplish. This dimension is shown in the last row of the table.

Finally, the development of a differentiated teacher effectiveness model along the lines indicated above could serve two main functions. The first would be to guide research design in the future, in order to have a more sophisticated and appropriate knowledge base about teacher effectiveness. The second function would be to provide a more equitable and appropriate model for teacher appraisal and for contributing to the development of educational policy. The first of these functions is examined in Chapters 7 and 8; the second is explored in Chapters 10 and 11.

7 Evidence in support of differentiated teacher effectiveness

The purpose of this chapter is to explore the evidence that exists at present for the kind of theoretical model of differentiated teacher effectiveness advanced in Chapter 6. As we argued in Chapters 4 and 5, most research to date has not sufficiently conceptualised or studied these issues. Nevertheless, if we examine the evidence closely, we can find some indication of the need for differential skills associated with the forms of effectiveness we discussed in the previous chapter.

Teachers' differentiated effectiveness in different subjects and curriculum areas

One of the areas where some evidence of differentiated effectiveness exists is that of curriculum and subject areas. While generic teacher behaviours have been developed, these are by no means all equally effective in different subjects, which is testified to by the large number of publications devoted to subject-specific teaching strategies. Many of these texts, however, either are full of generic strategies or do not go beyond practical 'tips for teachers'-type approaches, usually presenting little or no research evidence for the effectiveness of proposed strategies.

Some evidence for differentiated effectiveness can be culled from two parallel projects looking at teacher effectiveness in numeracy and literacy commissioned in England by the Teacher Training Agency. While there were clear similarities between the two studies in that, in both subjects, meaning rather than mechanical application of rules and the making of connections characterised effective teachers, there were also differences. One lay in the fact that effectiveness in numeracy was seen to depend less strongly on subject knowledge than in literacy. Effective teachers of numeracy were also more likely to differentiate tasks by ability than were effective teachers of numeracy (Askew *et al.*

1997, Medwell *et al.* 1999). It can be expected that there are more differences between subjects, which may be related to such factors as the more or less hierarchical nature of the subject, whether it is science, arts or humanities based, and the extent to which the subject is loosely or tightly coupled. It has to be pointed out here that, because these were discrete investigations, it is not possible to establish how the teachers sampled behaved in teaching the two subjects, or if there was any association between the way each teacher behaved in one subject and the way he/she behaved in the other, in these studies.

While broad differences may exist between subjects, within subjects too there is evidence for differentiated effectiveness, as has been suggested in Chapter 6. Reynolds and Muijs (2004) reanalysed data from the Reynolds and Muijs study into teacher effectiveness in mathematics (e.g. Reynolds and Muijs 1999, Muijs and Reynolds 2002, 2003) and found some suggestive differences when comparing three different parts of the English National Curriculum in mathematics: number; calculation; and measures, shape and space. Once the effects of overall differences in effectiveness of the observed teacher were partialled out, the following differences remained:

- varied teaching was less strongly related to gains in achievement in teaching number than in teaching calculation and measures, shape and space
- a high pace during the lesson, varied teaching, immediate feedback and using a variety of materials and manipulatives were more strongly related to gains in achievement in calculation than in measures, shape and space
- clear explanations and presentations, using a sufficiently long wait time after questions, using open-ended questions, asking pupils to explain their answers and guiding pupils through the material were more strongly related to gains in measures, shape and space than in calculation.

One notable finding is that lessons on problem-solving were observed too rarely for the researchers to be able to include them in the analysis.

As well as differences between subjects, an important part of differentiated effectiveness relates to the different goals that can be pursued within subjects. In recent decades there has been an increasing emphasis on higher order thinking skills, as opposed to the basic skills which were emphasised in the past. Many authors have argued, and there is some evidence supporting this, that different teaching methods may be needed to address higher order thinking skills. In particular, direct instruction methods found to be highly effective in teaching basic skills may be insufficient for addressing higher order thinking skills (Muijs and Reynolds 2001a). These views have led to the development of models of teaching that seek explicitly to address higher order thinking.

A number of approaches have been developed aimed at improving pupils' higher order thinking skills, often focusing on the development of metacognition (thinking about thinking, the ability to reflect on one's own thinking), and employing more open-ended and pupil-centred approaches to teaching. Some of these are specific 'thinking skills programmes', such as CASE and the Critical Skills Approach, while others are broader philosophical approaches that simultaneously aim to improve thinking skills, such as the constructivist movement, discussed in Chapter 4.

One approach which has shown some significantly positive effects is that developed in the UK by a team from King's College London, the Cognitive Acceleration Approach. This programme, based on Piagetian and Vygotskian models, was originally developed for science, but has now been extended into other subjects and age groups (Adey and Shayer 1994, Shayer and Adey 2002). This approach has five main elements.

1   Concrete preparation to introduce the necessary vocabulary and clarify the terms in which the problem is to be set. This means that the teacher needs to set the problem in context, and explain the meaning of the vocabulary that the student will need.
2   The teacher needs to introduce 'cognitive conflict'. This occurs when students are introduced to an experience which they find puzzling or which contradicts their prior knowledge or understanding.
3   Students then need to move on to an activity which ensures that they go beyond their current levels of understanding and competencies. This has been facilitated by the cognitive conflict, which has forced students to challenge their own preconceived notions and thought processes.
4   Students need to reflect consciously on their problem-solving (metacognition) in ways similar to those described above.
5   Students then need to 'bridge' their new skills or knowledge, i.e. be able to apply it in different contexts. A number of methods can be used to facilitate this.

Results appear to be positive. The programme developers report that students involved in the project performed significantly better on the age-16 national science examination in the UK (GCSE exams) than a matched control group, not just in science but in other subjects as well. This would suggest that the thinking skills obtained transfer to other subjects (Adey and Shayer 1994). Later studies support this, positive effects being found in many subjects and curriculum areas (Shayer and Adey 2002). Two caveats are needed here, however. One is that none of this research is independent; all appears to have been carried out by the programme developers themselves. Secondly, there is a lack of research that compares the result of this programme to other initiatives and programmes, rather than just to a control group in which no intervention takes place.

Overall, then, there does appear to be some evidence that different teaching skills may be more suited to developing higher order thinking skills than those identified as part of traditional teacher effectiveness research, although there is clearly a lack of research on this subject.

Teachers' differentiated effectiveness in promoting the progress of different groups of pupils according to pupil SES

One of the most directly researched areas of differentiated teacher effectiveness is whether different teacher behaviours and curricula are necessary for pupils of different socio-economic status (SES) backgrounds.

There is some evidence that low- and high-ability pupils respond to different teacher behaviours and styles (Brophy 1992, Walberg 1986b). Generally speaking, low-ability students are more strongly affected by teaching quality than high-ability students, a recent study in the UK finding that relationships between teacher behaviours and student outcomes differed in strength according to school context. In schools with a low proportion of students eligible for free school meals, a low proportion of high-ability students and a high proportion of students with special needs, correlations tended to be weaker than in other schools, suggesting that in general these teacher behaviours are less strongly correlated to outcomes in advantaged schools, possibly due to the greater support students from more privileged backgrounds receive at home (Muijs and Reynolds 2001a). Low- and high-ability and low- and high-SES students tend to respond to somewhat different behaviours. Low-SES students need more structure, more positive reinforcement from the teacher and need to receive the curriculum in smaller packages followed by rapid feedback (Brophy 1992). They will generally need more instruction. While middle- and high-ability students do not benefit from praise unrelated to the task, there is some evidence that low achievers do benefit from non-contingent feedback, due to the low self-esteem many of these students suffer from (Brophy 1992). Pupils from lower SES backgrounds have been found to benefit from a more integrated curriculum across grades and subjects (Connell 1996). Connecting learning to real-life experience and stressing practical applications have been found particularly important to low-SES pupils, as has making the curriculum relevant to their daily lives. This may diminish disaffection as well as promoting learning (Guthrie *et al.* 1989, Henchey 2001, Hopkins and Reynolds 2002, Montgomery *et al.* (1993).

One study looked at students' perceptions of what made for an effective teacher, and found that high-ability students were more likely to mention teachers' subject knowledge, while low-ability pupils were more likely to mention teachers' ability to connect with pupils (Jamieson and Brooks 1980). According to Mortimore (1991) effective teaching in schools with a low-SES intake should be teacher-led and practically focused, but not low-level or undemanding. Creating consistency in teaching approach is important for pupils from low-SES backgrounds, and has been found to be related to improved outcomes (Connell 1996).

These findings mirror findings from research on school effectiveness, which has likewise found differences between schools in low- and high-SES areas with respect to what makes them effective, effective schools in low-SES areas emphasising external rewards and basic skills, while effective schools in high-SES areas downplayed external rewards and offered an expanded curriculum (Teddlie and Stringfield 1993).

There is an ongoing debate as to whether or not teaching should focus more strongly on basic skills where pupils are largely from low-SES backgrounds. In their study of schools in high- and low-SES areas, Teddie and Stringfield (1993) found that in effective low-SES schools there was more emphasis on basic skills, and less on extending the curriculum, than in effective high-SES schools. Likewise, a survey of 366 high-performing schools in high-poverty areas found that they had focused more strongly on maths and English by extending teaching time and changing the curriculum so there was a stronger emphasis on basic skills (Barth *et al.* 1999). A study by the Dutch education inspectorate found that in effective schools with high numbers of underperforming ethnic minority students, there was a strong emphasis on basic skills, and a strongly structured curriculum. However, other authors claim that pupils from low-SES backgrounds are more capable of higher order thinking than is often supposed, and should be exposed to an equally rich curriculum as their disadvantaged counterparts, built around powerful ideas and focusing on metacognitive skills (Guthrie *et al.* 1989, Leithwood and Steinbach 2002). Interestingly, one school improvement project that chose to narrow the curriculum by aligning it to a basic skills test used by the region (the Iowa Test of Basic skills) failed to improve performance after two years (Philips 1996). Further evidence comes from an American project in which the curriculum of a highly selective private school was transplanted to two high-poverty schools in Baltimore (with a large amount of professional development and support through a school-based coordinator), leading to strong improvements in achievement in both schools, as well as improvements in attendance (McHugh and Stringfield 1998). A danger with focusing on basic skills in schools with a low-SES intake is that by offering them an impoverished curriculum social divides could be exacerbated rather than diminished. A study of 26 high-achieving impoverished schools in Texas showed that both direct instruction and constructivist teaching strategies were employed in these schools, neither seeming inherently more effective (Lein *et al.* 1996). Similar findings were reported by Ledoux and Overmaat (2001) in their Dutch study, effective schools using a mix of traditional and constructivist methods. An earlier survey by HM Inspectors in England likewise found that a broad and balanced curriculum was a hallmark of effective primary schools (Department for Education and Skills 1978). Interestingly, in two well-executed studies in the US and UK, improving schools were found to have instigated arts classes in the curriculum, while in a study of schools effective in improving the achievement of white and black working-class boys an emphasis on arts and sports was present in all studied schools (Connell 1996, Maden 2001, Lindsay and Muijs 2003).

Teachers' differentiated effectiveness in promoting the progress of different groups of pupils according to their personal characteristics

A field that is currently somewhat under-researched is the relationship between psychological characteristics of learners and teacher behaviours. One aspect that has recently received attention is research into different learning styles. A large number of classifications of learning styles currently exist. One of the most widely used is Kolb's (1973) four-factor model, which includes *assimilators* who think logically, prefer abstract ideas, and respect the views of experts; *convergers* who take a practical view of knowledge as having to have direct relevance; *divergers* who, by contrast, focus on the meaning and abstraction rather than on practicalities; and *accommodators* who prefer an active learning style, tend to rely on intuition rather than on logic, and like to connect learning to personal meaning and experiences. Some consequences for teaching clearly follow from this classification. Teachers may need to consider how to teach to all these learning styles, or at least those existing in their pupils (these can be identified by having them take a test, such as the Learning Styles Inventory, which will tell the teacher what learning styles they prefer). Different types of learners prefer different activities. Assimilators learn well from case studies in which they can get involved, and through reading texts individually. Convergers like activities where they can apply skills, and peer training approaches. Accommodators learn well from small group work, discussion and peer feedback. Finally, divergers like to have time to reflect and engage in creative activities.

Gardner's (1983, 1993) theory of multiple intelligences has also been widely popularised, and is being used increasingly in education. Gardner proposes seven primary intelligences:

- linguistic intelligence (ability to use language communicatively and expressively)
- musical intelligence (ability to recognise musical pitches, tones and rhythms)
- logical–mathematical intelligence (ability to detect patterns, reason deductively and think logically)
- visual/spatial intelligence (ability to manipulate and create mental images in order to solve problems)
- bodily–kinaesthetic intelligence (ability to use mental abilities to coordinate one's bodily movements)
- intrapersonal intelligence (ability to understand one's own feelings and motivations)
- interpersonal intelligence (ability to understand others' feelings and motivations).

Doing different tasks may involve different combinations of these intelligences, but very rarely involves only one.

According to Gardner (1983, 1993) teaching and learning should focus on the particular intelligence of each individual, who should be encouraged to develop this particular ability. Thus, people with a strong linguistic ability should be given the opportunity to read and see and hear words associated with the topic/skill they need to learn. Logical/mathematical students should be given the opportunity to classify, categorise and work with abstractions and relations of different concepts to one another. Students with a strong visual/spatial intelligence can best be presented with visual information, maps, charts and colours. Musically intelligent learners should be given the opportunity to learn through melodies, musical notation and rhythms, using singing and clapping in delivering new information. Students with a strong bodily–kinaesthetic intelligence should be allowed to interact with their environment while learning, through movement, acting and use of body parts to help information retention. Interpersonally intelligent learners should be given the opportunity to interact with others, to compare and contrast information, to share ideas and to cooperate. Finally, students who are intrapersonally intelligent learn better on their own. Individual, self-paced activities will be most beneficial to these learners.

One issue for teachers here is that they themselves will tend to prefer certain learning styles or intelligences, and will be likely to teach towards those learning styles or intelligences, which may, however, not correspond to those of their students. Being aware of what different learning styles exist among students, what one's own learning style is and how to teach to different learning styles are therefore clearly important skills in this area.

Gardner's theories are sometimes seen as somewhat unscientific, a seemingly random selection of intelligences. This is a misconception, arising mainly from vulgarisation and low-level application of his theories in education. In fact, Gardner uses a number of quite stringent criteria for defining an intelligence, taken from a variety of disciplines such as developmental psychology and cultural anthropology.

1 *Isolation as a brain function.* The revolution in methods of brain measurement and the accompanying growth in cognitive psychology are allowing us to find the actual physiological locations for specific brain functions. A true intelligence will have its function identified in a specific location in the human brain.
2 *Prodigies, idiot savants and exceptional individuals.* In order to qualify as an intelligence, there must be some evidence of specific 'geniuses' in that particular area, such as Diego Maradona (bodily kinaesthetic).
3 *Set of core operations.* Each true intelligence has a set of unique and identifiable procedures.

4   *Developmental history.* A true intelligence is associated with an identifiable set of stages of growth, with a mastery level which exists as an end state in human development.
5   *Evolutionary history.* A true intelligence can have its development traced through the evolution of our species as identified by cultural anthropologists.
6   *Supported psychological tasks.* A true intelligence can be identified by specific tasks which can be carried out, observed and measured by clinical psychologists.
7   *Supported psychometric tasks.* Specifically designed psychometric tests can be used to measure the intelligence.
8   *Encoded into a symbol system.* A true intelligence has its own symbol system which is unique to it and essential to completing its tasks.

While strong claims are made for the importance of learning styles, empirical research on this process is so far inconclusive. Stahl (1999), reviewing a number of studies on the effects of teaching different learning styles, concluded that: 'These five research reviews, published in well-regarded journals found the same thing. One cannot reliably measure children's learning styles and even if one could, matching children to reading programs by learning styles does not improve their learning.' In view of the theoretical validity of these concepts, this is clearly an area where more research on effective teaching is urgently needed.

Teachers' differentiated effectiveness in terms of the range of role activities in their work

It is clear that the roles that teachers are currently fulfilling are far more varied than their traditional classroom role assumed. The roles teachers can fulfil are many and are explored more fully in Chapter 2, but it falls outside the remit of this work to discuss all possible roles. Some examples are the pastoral and management roles that teachers are increasingly asked to take on in their schools, and increased collaboration and liaising with parents and colleagues.

Pastoral care is seen as an increasingly important part of the work of the school. As families have in many cases become less able (through increasing work commitments, family break-up and a decreasing role for the 'extended family') to provide fully for the pastoral needs of their children, and communities have likewise abrogated this role, the school has in many cases become one of the key arenas for pupils' social and moral as well as intellectual development. A demand for the fulfilment of this role is increasingly being placed on school, Freydenberg (1997), for example, stating that schools need to equip pupils to:

- be competent in social skills, including the ability to manage conflict peacefully
- cultivate enquiring problem-solving habits for lifetime learning
- acquire technical and analytical capabilities to participate in a global economy
- become ethical persons
- learn the requirements of responsible citizenship
- respect diversity in a pluralistic society.

Connectedness to the school has also been found to be a predictor of behaviours such as smoking, delinquency and early sexual intercourse (Resnick *et al.* 1993), although one needs to be careful about concluding that causality here is necessarily flowing from the school to the outcomes). Therefore, teachers will increasingly need to possess the skills that allow them to take a strong pastoral role in the school, such as effective communication skills; promotion of self-esteem in and out of the classroom; identifying resilient qualities in their students; skill development in friendship, empathy, support and decision-making; and conflict resolution skills (Cox 2002). Some of these are clearly skills that academically effective teachers in the traditional sense would be expected to possess, such as effective communication. Others, such as developing friendship relationships, are clearly different.

A key characteristic in this respect is the emotional intelligence of the teacher. Emotional intelligence can be defined as 'a type of social intelligence that involves the ability to monitor one's own and others' emotions, to discriminate among them, and to use the information to guide one's thinking and actions' (Mayer and Salovey 1993). Emotional intelligence consists of four main facets: *emotional perception* (the ability to identify emotions in others), *emotional facilitation* of thought (the ability to use emotions in problem-solving), *emotional understanding* (the ability to solve emotional problems) and *emotional management* (understanding the implications of social acts on emotions and the regulation of emotion in self and others). The last of these might be particularly important to the pastoral role of teachers (Mayer and Cobb 2000). These characteristics can in part be trained and developed, through the development of skills such as learning to distinguish between thoughts and feelings, validating others' feeling and learning to become non-judgemental in dealings with others.

An important aspect of pastoral care is the permanent duty to develop pupils' non-cognitive skills and attitudes, such as their self-esteem and self-concept in academic areas. As self-concept and, to a lesser extent, self-esteem are related to achievement, one of the main ways of enhancing these factors should be through improving achievement (Muijs 1997). One problem with this, however, lies in the fact that research shows that self-concept is to a large extent a comparative rather than an absolute phenomenon. Thus, a high-achieving pupil in a class full of very high-performing pupils may well experience lower self-concept than a low-achieving pupil in a class full of low achievers (the so-called 'big fish, little pond' effect). What then can teachers do to improve their pupils' self-concept? One factor is having high expectations of all students, as low expectations expressed by teachers will negatively impact on students' self-concept for that subject and on their global self-esteem, which in turn may lead to lower achievement. Giving students responsibilities helps build up a sense of personal power, which will enhance self-esteem. Students should be given the opportunity to make choices and should be allowed to make an active contribution to lessons. Younger students should be given responsibility over small tasks, such as keeping the classroom tidy and wiping the board, while older students should be actively involved in developing classroom rules. Teachers should be supportive of students and create a climate in which their contributions are valued. Emphasising the positive in all students is important. Specific activities, such as Circle Time (Mosley 1996), have also been posited as improving self-esteem.

It is clear that many of these factors, such as having high expectations, are as important to academic achievement as they are to self-concept, and all of these behaviours can be expected to enhance achievement as well as self-concept due to the relationship between the two. However, a specific focus on this type of outcome clearly does introduce a new dimension to teachers' work inside and out of the classroom.

Like the pastoral dimension, the managerial dimension of teachers' jobs has become ever more important in recent years. Teachers have traditionally taken on formal roles as middle managers or in the senior management team, but increasingly take on informal leadership roles as schools go towards more effective forms of distributed leadership, where teachers take on roles as key change agents within the school. This marks a change from the traditional 'strong man' theories of educational leadership, recent studies of effective leadership showing that authority to lead need not be located in the person of the head but can be dispersed within the school and among people (MacBeath 1998, Day *et al.* 2000, Harris 2002, Muijs and Harris, forthcoming, 2004). In this sense leadership is separated from person, role and status and is primarily concerned with the relationships and the connections among individuals within a school. This model of leadership implies a redistribution of power and a realignment of authority within the organisation.

Evidence would suggest that where such conditions are in place, leadership is a much stronger internal driver for school improvement and change (Hopkins and Reynolds 2001). In practice, this means giving authority to teachers and empowering them to lead. This implies a different power relationship within the school where the distinctions between followers and leaders tend to blur, and also opens up the possibility for all teachers to become leaders at various times and suggests that leadership is a shared and collective endeavour that can engage the many rather than the few.

Katzenmeyer and Moller (2001) define teacher leaders as follows: 'teachers who are leaders lead within and beyond the classroom, identify with and contribute to a community of teacher learners and leaders, and influence others towards improved educational practice'. In contrast to traditional notions of leadership, teacher leadership is characterised by a form of collective leadership in which teachers develop expertise by working collaboratively (Boles and Troen 1994).

A number of different roles have been suggested for teacher leaders that further explain the distinctive nature of the leadership activity. Katzenmeyer and Moller (2001) see teacher leadership as having three main facets:

- leadership of students or other teachers – facilitator, coach, mentor, trainer, curriculum specialist, creating new approaches, leading study groups
- leadership of operational tasks – keeping the school organised and moving towards its goals, through roles as Head of Department, action researcher, member of task forces
- leadership through decision-making or partnership – membership of school improvement teams, membership of committees, instigator of partnerships with business, higher education institutions, LEAs, and parent–teacher associations.

These roles require a different set of skills from the traditional teaching skills. Boles (1992) found that the factors for successful teacher leadership included principal support, strong communicative and administrative skills, an understanding of organisational culture and a reexamination of traditional patterns of power and authority in school systems. Teacher leaders need continuously to improve their teaching skills, be involved in school decision-making and be involved in the professional development of others. Skills such as leading groups and workshops, collaborative work, mentoring, teaching adults and action research are required if teachers are to be effective in these new leadership roles (Katzenmeyer and Moller 2001). The ability of teacher leaders to influence colleagues and to develop productive relations with school management is crucial if teachers are to be effective change agents in their schools (Lieberman 1988, Clemson-Ingram and Fessler 1997). This requires an increased ability to interact with and train adults, as well as good interpersonal and social skills. Lieberman *et al.* (2000) identified six main clusters of skills in their study of teacher leaders, which included building trust and rapport with colleagues, being able to undertake organisational diagnosis through data collection, understanding and managing change processes, being able to utilise resources (people, equipment) in the pursuit of common goals, managing their work and building skills and confidence in others. Similarly, Pellicer and Anderson (1995) identified helping other teachers plan instruction, helping other teachers make curriculum decisions, helping other teachers improve their teaching and peer coaching as being the key skills of teacher leaders.

The specific role of teachers as middle managers has also been found to be important in school improvement. Harris (2001) and Sammons *et al.* (1997), for example, have found departmental effectiveness to be a crucial factor in school effectiveness and school improvement. Departmental level effects explain a larger proportion of the variance in school performance than is explained at the school level. Many successful school reforms have started at departmental level, and implementation of school improvement programmes at this level is a key to their succeeding (Harris 2001).

Effective leadership at the departmental level has a number of key elements. Firstly, effective departmental leaders (much like effective school leaders more generally) are neither authoritarian nor *laissez-faire*, but authoritative. They foster a climate of collaboration and collegiality and, crucially, are educational leaders rather than just implementers or managers of decisions taken at the senior management level (Harris 2001, Harris *et al.* 2004). Harris (2000) identifies four main roles for the head of department:

- bridging – translating senior management policies at the departmental level
- collegiality – create a coherent group with a shared vision
- improving staff and pupil performance, through monitoring staff and pupil performance, mentoring colleagues, and acting as a subject expert
- liaison or representation – representing the department and keeping colleagues in touch with other departments within, and organisations outside, the school.

Clearly, effectively fulfilling these four roles requires enhanced leadership competencies from teachers, which will need to be taken into account in any model of differentiated effectiveness.

Again, there is clearly a need for more research measuring teacher effectiveness in any of these roles teachers are expected to perform, as the evidence here is limited at present. Moreover, studies investigating whether teachers are equally effective in their instructional role and in their pastoral and managerial role have not been conducted so far and relevant theories have not yet been established.

Teachers' effectiveness according to the various contexts in which they work

Very little research appears to exist on the effectiveness of teachers dependent on context factors such as class size and school size.

Organisational climate of the school has been found to affect the effectiveness of the organisation, and in schools this is often seen to mean the promotion of effective teaching. Creemers' (1994) influential model of educational effectiveness, for example, clearly posits that it is school factors that create the conditions in which effective teaching and learning can occur, and therefore teacher behaviours may well be affected by school factors, as mentioned in Chapter 5. Recent research has added empirical support to Creemers' model, suggesting that this is a useful way forward in studying these factors (De Jong and Westerhof 1998, Kyriakides *et al.* 2000).

Some research suggests that one of the main differences between more and less effective schools lies in the fact that in the former there is less heterogeneity with respect to teacher effectiveness than in the latter. That is, in both more and less effective schools there are effective teachers, but in more effective schools there are fewer ineffective teachers (Teddlie and Stringfield 1993).

Conclusion

It is clear that there is existing evidence that different skills are needed for teachers to be effective in different domains. In some areas our knowledge base is quite strong, in others very weak, and in general no connection has been made between effectiveness in the five different areas mentioned here.

Evidence is strongest in the area of differentiated effectiveness with respect to different curriculum areas and SES, although in both cases evidence is limited either through a lack of direct comparisons (between curriculum areas) or through the fact that the limited number of studies reach conflicting findings (e.g. in the area of pupil SES). The study of learning styles seems promising, but at present is hindered by a lack of strong empirical research, and a tendency to favour rhetoric and theorising over research. It is clear that teachers are fulfilling increased responsibilities in school, such as pastoral and managerial roles, and it is evident that these require different skills from teachers. The area of school context has hardly been researched in relation to teacher effectiveness.

Overall we take the view that there is an urgent need for research that goes beyond 'one size fits all' teacher behaviour studies, and looks at teaching as a multidimensional role. The question of what exactly makes teachers effective in different areas, and whether there are teachers who are effective in all, or who are more or less effective in different factors, needs exploring both from a research and a professional development/appraisal point of view.

8 Building theory and methodology

The purpose of this chapter is to evaluate current theoretical models of educational effectiveness. We identify benefits of testing the existing models of effectiveness through research into differentiated teacher effectiveness, and explore how these models might be built on to develop theory and methodology. We thereby attempt to extend the ideas in Chapter 6.

Three models of educational effectiveness

It is possible to discern three basic models of educational effectiveness in the literature.

Economic production functions model

Research in this model is generally focused on estimating 'the relationships between the supply of selected purchased schooling inputs and educational outcomes, controlling for the influence of various background characteristics' (Monk 1992: 380). Such research is focused on producing a function which could explain each pupil outcome at a given time, and which according to Hanushek (1979) has the following form:

$$A_{it} = f(B_{it}, P_{it}, S_{it}, I_i)$$

where A_{it} is the outcome of the ith student at time t, B_{it} is the vector of family background influences of the ith student cumulative at time t, P_{it} is the vector of influence of peers of the ith student cumulative at time t, S_{it} is the vector of school inputs of the ith student cumulative at time t, and I_i is the vector of innate abilities of the ith student.

The function may be linear, consisting of main effects and inter-action terms, or non-linear (Brown and Saks 1986). Therefore, the economic functions models are based on the following assumptions:

1 selection of resource inputs is the major type of antecedent condition
2 it is important to measure direct, rather than causally mediated, effects
3 it is possible to use data at only one level of aggregation, either micro (pupil) level data or aggregated (school or national) level data.

The overall rationale behind these models is the assumption that increased input will lead to increments in outcomes. We have seen in Chapter 1 how an early version of such modelling was influential in America (Carnoy 1976) in the debates over the apparent failure of school reform. It is important to note that these 'education produc-tion function' models are static rather than dynamic. However, Monk (1992) discusses the elaboration of the basic production func-tion equation, which produces two other types of conceptual model, discussed below. More specifically, under the designation 'relations between configurations of inputs and outputs', Monk refers to studies investigating school organisational conditions and teachers' percep-tions, which suggest a blending of approaches in the field of educa-tional effectiveness. Monk proposes studies drawing on economic process studies, but which focus at classroom level and are therefore closely related to TER. He discusses various hypothetical con-figurations, which are based on either 'engaged' or 'accommodating' behaviour of teachers. 'Engagement' refers to an active teacher who enjoys the challenge of teaching a particular group of pupils, whereas the term 'accommodation' is used when a teacher protects himself/ herself in order to be able to cope with a difficult class.

Educational/psychological models

The most important difference of educational psychological models from the economic production function models arises from a different choice of antecedent conditions. In addition to 'time', which is a vari-able used in education production function models, variables such as 'content covered' and 'quality of instruction', as well as psychological variables such as learning aptitudes and motivation, are included

(Walberg 1984). These models use only micro-level data (i.e. data collected at the classroom level).

The Carroll model

The Carroll model (Carroll 1963) is usually considered as the starting model and states that the degree of mastery is a function of the ratio of amount of time students actually spend on learning tasks to the total amount of time they need. Carroll (1963) argued that time actually spent on learning is defined as equal to the smallest of three variables: (a) opportunity (time allowed for learning), (b) perseverance (the amount of time students are willing to engage actively in learning), and (c) aptitude (the amount of time needed to learn under optimal instructional conditions). Numerous studies and meta-analyses have confirmed the validity of the Carroll model. It was the basis for Bloom's concept of mastery learning (Bloom 1968) and is also related to 'direct instruction' as described by Rosenshine (1983).

The Walberg model

Walberg (1984) formulated an encompassing model of educational productivity which is based on the main factors of the Carroll model and included an additional category of environmental variables. Aptitude, instruction and the psychological environment are seen as major direct causes of learning. They also influence one another and are in turn influenced by feedback on the amount of learning that takes place. The Walberg model was tested as a structural equation model on science achievement, indicating more complex, indirect relationships (Reynolds and Walberg 1992). However, as Carroll (1989) pointed out 25 years after the construction of his model, the one factor in his original model that needed further elaboration was 'quality of instruction'. In this context, making use of the principles of mastery learning and direct instruction, Creemers (1994) developed Carroll's model of learning by identifying three components within quality of instruction: curricular materials, grouping procedures and teacher behaviour. Creemers' model is described in the next section since it is based on the assumption that the influences on pupil achievement are multi-level.

Integrated multi-level educational effectiveness models

Since the mid-1980s a blending of approaches to educational effectiveness has taken place. This development is reflected in the work of researchers who have attempted to develop comprehensive models of educational effectiveness by integrating the findings of school effectiveness research, research on teacher effectiveness and the early input–output studies (Stringfield and Slavin 1992, Scheerens 1992, Creemers 1994). The main characteristics of the resulting models, which are briefly presented below, are that:

1   antecedent conditions are classified in terms of inputs, processes and context of schooling
2   the models have a multi-level structure, where schools are nested in contexts, classrooms are nested in schools and pupils are nested in classrooms or teachers.

The QUAIT/MACRO model

The QUAIT/MACRO model (quality, appropriateness, incentive and time) (meaningful goals, attention to academic focus, coordination, recruitment and training, and organisation) was developed by Stringfield and Slavin (1992) and has four levels:

1   the level of the individual pupil and learner
2   the level of (para-)professionals who are in direct interaction with pupils
3   the level of schools, comprising head teachers and other school-level personnel as well as school programmes which affect student learning and the ways pupils, teachers and parents act and interact
4   the above-school level, comprising the community, the school district, and sources of programming, funding and assessment arising from the centre (e.g. the state).

The teaching and classroom level part of the model arises from Slavin's 'theory of effective classroom organisation' which focuses on those parts of the Carroll model that are potentially in the control of the teacher. These are: *quality* (e.g. opportunity to learn, time on task and instructional principles such as teacher asks clear and appropriate questions, provides feedback and incorporates pupils' comments and interests into lessons); *appropriateness*, which concerns the difficulty level of the subject matter; *incentive*, which refers to providing stimulating motivation to learn; and *time on task*. These characteristics of effective instruction are borne not only by the teacher, but also by parents and special programmes. At school level, the principles described under the acronym MACRO are presented and thereby the model includes the human resource dimension of schooling as well as school organisational features. Features at the above-school level mentioned in the model are relationships with parents and the local community, and school funding arrangements.

What is most distinctive about this model is its dynamic dimension. This dimension is illustrated by providing scenarios of how schools could develop ineffectiveness over time, as the cumulative result of higher grade teachers having to compensate for weak teachers in lower grades, an increased proportion of disadvantaged pupils and decreased teacher morale. However, a weakness of this model is that although the QUAIT modelling on the teacher and pupil level is elaborated, this is not the case with the MACRO parts of the model.

The Creemers model

Creemers (1994) developed Carroll's model of learning by adding to the general concept of opportunity the more specific 'opportunity to learn'. In Creemers' model, time and opportunity are discerned both at the classroom level and at the school level. In this way, Creemers made a distinction between available, and actually used, time and opportunity.

Creemers' model was based on the following four assumptions. First, time on task and opportunity used at the pupil level are directly related to pupil achievement. Quality of teaching, the curriculum, and the grouping procedures influence the time on task and opportunity to learn. It is argued that some teachers may spend more time actually teaching than others who spend more time on classroom management and keeping order. Teachers are therefore seen as the central component in instruction at the classroom level. Teachers make use of curriculum materials and they select grouping procedures which may determine what is learnt. However, teaching quality, time, and opportunity at the classroom level are also influenced by factors at the school level, which may or may not promote these classroom factors. Thus, quality, time and opportunity are not the key concepts at the classroom level only, but also at the school level.

Second, the context, school and classroom levels permeate time on task and opportunities used at the pupil level. Teachers are able to influence time for learning and opportunity to learn in their classrooms through the quality of their instruction. But ultimately pupils decide how much time they will spend on their school tasks and how many tasks they will complete. Thus, pupil achievement is also determined by pupil factors such as aptitudes, social background and motivation.

Third, Creemers (1994) argues that the higher levels are conditional for the lower levels. Thus, factors at the context level should be seen as conditional for factors at the school level, factors at the school level as conditional for factors at the classroom level, and factors at the classroom level as conditional for pupil achievement. It is therefore claimed that pupil achievement should not be considered as an accomplishment either of classroom factors only (as in many studies on teacher behaviour) or of school factors only (as in many studies of school effectiveness), but as an outcome of both levels.

Fourth, Creemers (1994) claims that there are four principles operating in generating educational effectiveness. He states that the variables at the different levels should support each other in order to improve pupils' achievement. This is called the *consistency principle*. Creemers (1994: 98) argues that there should be consistency of effective characteristics within and between levels. A second formal criterion is *cohesion*, which implies that all members of the school staff must show characteristics of effective teaching. Moreover, Creemers (1994) argues that there should be *constancy*, meaning that effective instruction is provided throughout the school career of the student. Finally, the model states that there should be *control*, meaning that goal attainment and the school climate should be evaluated. Consistency, cohesion, constancy and control are formal principles, which are difficult to observe directly, but we can argue that they exist when the same factors operate across instructional components, subjects, classes and grades.

Four studies (De Jong and Westerhof 1998, Reezigt *et al.* 1999, Driessen and Sleegers 2000, Kyriakides *et al.* 2000) have been conducted in order to test the main aspects of Creemers' model. The studies by Reezigt *et al.* (1999) and Driessen and Sleegers (2000) did not produce strong evidence about the validity of the model. This was attributed to weaknesses in the methods used to collect data and to the fact that variables such as student motivation, time on task and opportunity to learn were not available. The main conclusion was that the concepts of the model should be more adequately operationalised in future research. The other two studies (De Jong and Westerhof 1998, Kyriakides *et al.* 2000) used multiple methodologies and provided empirical support for the main assumptions of Creemers' model. A study on differentiated effectiveness testing the model in relation to different criteria for measuring effectiveness, and for different groups of students, is described in the last part of this book to show how the robustness of the model might be strengthened by research into differentiated effectiveness.

Operational questions in the modelling of teacher effects: a critique of the conceptual models of educational effectiveness

When researchers try to find teacher effects and test the models of educational effectiveness, they have to face two major questions.

1 *How is effectiveness defined in terms of time?* This question draws attention to two factors which raise doubts about whether teacher effects are stable. The first factor refers to the frequency with which teacher effectiveness is determined; the second is related to the specific measurement moments in management and/or production processes by which effectiveness is gauged. However, none of the existing conceptual models of educational effectiveness, except the Creemers model, is helpful in providing answers to the operational question dealing with time stability of teacher effects. In Creemers' model there has been an assumption that stability is desirable but it has to be treated problematically given the complexity of teachers' work and life. In practice, with regard to the first factor, the prototype research on teacher effectiveness is characterised by an attempt to determine effectiveness once only. Examples of research whereby the output of teachers is determined at several points in time by conducting longitudinal studies are scarce. As far as the second factor is concerned, the point at which effectiveness is gauged is generally at the end of a school year. However, some critics of TER (e.g. Ralph and Fennessey 1983) argue that it is unreasonable to call a teacher effective simply because the average level of achievement appears to be relatively high at the end of the school year. It can therefore be claimed that since traditional TER has not provided any answers to the above question concerning the period or periods in which the measurement of teacher effects should take place, the issue of time stability of teacher effects should be included in a differentiated model.

2 *What criteria should be used as indicators of effectiveness?* Those attempting to investigate teacher effects have to provide answers to questions concerning the criteria used in order to measure

teacher effectiveness. For example, one might argue that teacher effects should be identified by looking at the capacity of teachers to promote pupils' learning in a specific subject (e.g. mathematics) or that teacher effects can be identified by looking at teachers' ability to behave as staff development facilitators of colleagues in teaching mathematics. The existing conceptual models of educational effectiveness do not treat the choice of appropriate indicators of effectiveness, so that a range of indicators needs to be considered to make an appropriate selection. We have suggested five dimensions in Chapter 6, each of which would generate criteria, and for us a model of differentiated teacher effectiveness has to incorporate the extent to which there is criterion consistency across these dimensions. The question about the appropriate criteria of measuring teacher effectiveness draws attention to a methodological issue. The type of statistical models used to estimate teacher effects can be justified only if prior decisions have been made about the groups of pupils whose progress is measured. As has been mentioned in Chapters 5 and 6, TER was based on the assumption that the effectiveness of a teacher is effectiveness for the average pupil, i.e. average with respect to aptitude, socio-economic status, etc. However, there are indications that for below-average pupils the situation is different than for average or above-average pupils (see Chapter 7). Moreover, the study reported in the last part of the book demonstrates that even in the classrooms of the most effective teachers (defined by taking into account the traditional way of measuring teacher effectiveness) the rate of progress which boys made in mathematics was greater than the rate of progress made by girls, and the rate of progress by middle-class pupils was greater than that made by other pupils. Teachers considered effective on the basis of the average progress of pupils in the class have some groups of pupils systematically being disadvantaged in their rate of learning by comparison with other groups. Conventional models of educational effectiveness ignore this issue, because effectiveness is constructed generically rather than in a differentiated way.

Benefits from testing the conceptual models through research into differentiated effectiveness

As has been argued above, the adoption of the model of differentiated teacher effectiveness proposed in Chapter 6 might provide answers to the main operational questions concerning the modelling of teacher effects. Such studies could also help us conduct in-depth testing of the existing conceptual models of educational effectiveness. We turn now to the potential benefits of testing the models of educational effectiveness through research focused on each of the five dimensions defined in Chapter 6.

The capacity of teachers to be effective across the range of work activities

The models of educational effectiveness do not take into account the capacity of teachers to be effective across the range of work activities involved in modern teaching, but only the type of activities associated with the formal instructional role. A differentiated model would examine factors associated with effectiveness in achieving for example, pastoral goals, or in the management of other adults to improve student learning, and so on. The identification of factors associated with teachers' capacity across their roles would help us identify those factors associated with all, or several, aspects and those associated only with one or some of them. Moreover, analysis of data in relation to the effectiveness of teachers in specific dimensions of their role could help us identify homogeneous groups of teachers who are less effective in some types of activities and more effective in others. Such a typology of teachers might be useful not only for building theories in the field of effectiveness but also for establishing mechanisms of formative personnel evaluation.

Teacher effectiveness and organisational context

The dimension of the model of differentiated teacher effectiveness which is focused on the various cultural and organisational contexts in which teachers work suggests that our proposed model of differential effectiveness is in line with the main assumptions of the integrated multi-level educational effectiveness models. Thus, research into this dimension of differentiated effectiveness might provide empirical support to the integrated multi-level educational effectiveness models and at the same time might explore limitations of the models based on the educational psychological approach to effective instruction. These limitations, we hypothesise, would be about the neglect of the impact that organisational and cultural context has on teachers' effectiveness in classrooms.

Consistency of teacher effects on students' achievement

Research into the consistency of teacher effects on student achieve-ment might help us develop models of effective teaching presenting factors associated with effective teaching in any subject, as well as more subject specific data. The identification of factors associated with teaching effectiveness in each subject might help test whether a generic model is sustainable. It may also clarify some of the inconsis-tencies in the literature on teacher effectiveness. For example, subject knowledge is widely perceived as a factor affecting teacher effective-ness (Scriven 1994), but the evidence is problematic (Borich 1992, Darling-Hammond 2000, Kyriakides *et al.* 2002). Monk (1994) reported that the relationship between subject knowledge and teacher effectiveness is curvilinear: a minimal level of knowledge is necessary for teachers to be effective, but beyond a certain point a negative relation occurs. It can however be assumed that research into differen-tial teacher effectiveness might reveal that the relationship between subject knowledge and student achievement might not be the same for different subjects. For some of them the relationship might be linear, for others curvilinear, or there might be no relationship. Similar benefits could arise from research investigating the consistency of teacher effect on the achievement of student in each subject com-ponent, or in aims associated with different domains (e.g. cognitive aims versus affective aims), or with teacher beliefs. For instance, the relationship of teacher self-efficacy beliefs in some subject components with student achievement gains might be different from the relation-ship in other subject components (Nielsen and Moore 2003, Finney and Schraw 2003).

Our final point on research into the consistency of teacher effects on student achievement has to do with the importance of identifying differences in the capacity of the same group of teachers to achieve dif-ferent aims of the various areas of the curriculum. Such research could help us classify teachers into homogeneous groups according to how effective they are in teaching different subjects or subject components; some teachers may be equally effective in teaching all the components of a subject whereas others are not.

Teacher effectiveness with different groups of pupils: differences in students' background factors

Research into the capacity of teachers to promote the progress of different groups of students might also help us identify factors in teaching that are most effective with students from different socio-economic groups. As was shown in Chapter 7, there is research revealing that different teacher behaviour and curricula are more effective in promoting the progress of pupils of different socio-economic status (Muijs and Reynolds 2001a, Connell 1996). However, we need to develop models which will present all those factors associated with teacher capacity to promote the progress of different groups of students. The development of such models could help us identify possible dimensions on which a policy for equal opportunities can be based. Moreover, questions such as those raised in Chapter 7 about whether teaching of students from low socio-economic groups should be focused more strongly on basic skills can be explored. In addition, the impact of other variables upon the progress of different SES groups of pupils beyond those concerning curricular materials, grouping procedures and teacher behaviour should be examined. Finally, we might be able to identify, through qualitative enquiry, the reasons teachers judged more effective with particular groups of pupils give for their effectiveness. This would contribute to understanding effectiveness in relation to social justice and inclusion.

Teacher effectiveness with different groups of pupils: differences in students' personal characteristics

Two suggestions regarding the contribution of a model illustrating the capacity of teachers to promote the progress of different groups of pupils according to their personal characteristics are provided. First, research might help us identify how existing models of educational effectiveness can be adapted to investigate the influence on progress of particular groups of students according to their personal characteristics. Second, since all these personality variables, except personality type, can be changed, it is important to identify what type of teacher behaviour might help students to improve their motivation and their self-esteem, and to help them adopt thinking styles associated with higher achievement. For example, thinking styles treated as processes can be built on and used to compensate for weaknesses (Grigorenko and Sternberg 1995). In this interpretation, styles are seen as dynamic, not as frozen forever (Grigorenko and Sternberg 1997), and thereby cannot be considered as 'bad or good' styles (Sternberg 1988, Sternberg and Grigorenko 1995). Moreover, pupils are expected to develop optimal styles for particular situations. It can therefore be argued that research on differentiated teacher effectiveness may help us identify the type of teacher behaviour which helps students to develop optimal thinking styles.

Finally, research into differentiated effectiveness which not only is focused on each dimension of effectiveness separately, but attempts to investigate the interactions between these dimensions, could help develop more differentiated models. For example, we may identify factors associated with effective teaching of specific curriculum areas taught to different SES group of students. Such specific models might appear to conflict with the intention of the effectiveness research community to establish a general theoretical framework of educational effectiveness research (Teddlie and Reynolds 2000, Kyriakides 2003a). However, such studies might help test the generalisability of a model of educational effectiveness since it would examine the extent to which the same factors are associated with student achievement across the five dimensions of difference. Thus, research investigating the effect of each dimension and their interaction effects would contribute to the development of both generic and differentiated models of teacher effectiveness by the systematic testing of their validity.

Part III
Values and policy implications

9   Effective teaching and values

The purpose of this chapter is to outline the moral basis of teaching in general, and to illustrate an argument that effective teaching is underpinned by moral values, especially in relation to the nature of learning and the classroom climate. It follows that any model of differentiated teacher effectiveness must include an analysis of the values of the schools and teachers involved in teacher effectiveness research or appraisal.

The chapter is not designed to provide a comprehensive analysis of values and education, which is far beyond its scope. Our aim is merely to illustrate the argument from a range of literature, though we are conscious that different sources could have been chosen. The values we identify with effective teaching are deliberately selective. This is because it would be arrogant for us to pretend to identify a comprehensive set of values across cultures and time and because the values underlying a particular approach to effectiveness have preferably to be identified by the teachers and the schools. That is to say, the values dimension in teacher effectiveness is the area most appropriately involving self-evaluation.

The moral framework of teaching

There is a consensus in the classic sociology literature that the processes of education are suffused with values and moral purpose. There are two broad, and related, analytical positions within this consensus, referring to the *social functions of schooling* and the *personal and professional values expected of teachers*.

The social functions of schooling

Following the French sociologist and philosopher, Emile Durkheim (1925), the education system functions for society as an apparatus for the formation, the reproduction, or the reinforcement, of moral identity and moral order. For Durkheim, society was 'a certain intellectual and moral framework, distinctive of the entire group . . . society is above all a shared consciousness and it is therefore this collective consciousness that must be imparted to the child' (cited in Durkheim 1961: vii). The role of social institutions, such as the family and the school, was therefore one of moral socialisation. It followed that Durkheim saw the apparently technical matter of the rules and routines of school and classroom life – the 'discipline of the school' – as embodying in palpable form for the child the deep structure of society's moral order. Discipline was not merely the means of enabling teachers to instruct more effectively, for it was through experiencing school discipline that the child learned a sense of duty to society.

> Too often, people conceive of school discipline so as to preclude endowing it with . . . an important moral function. Some see it in a simple way of guaranteeing superficial peace and order in the class room . . . In reality, however, the nature and function of school discipline is something altogether different . . . It is the morality of the classroom . . . The class is a small society. It is therefore both natural and necessary that it have its own morality corresponding to its size, the character of its elements, and its function. Discipline is this morality . . . It is essentially an instrument – difficult to duplicate – of moral education.
>
> (Durkheim 1961: 148–149)

Durkheim has been criticised for being unduly functionalist in his overarching emphasis on the social structure. In particular, his analysis seems to the modern sensibility too categorical, in a world where identity is thought to be more flexibly, more actively and more individually *constructed* than socially imposed (Giddens 1991). Pupils act upon the moral order of the school to shape it, as well as being shaped by it.

Nevertheless, Durkheim's general analysis of the moral order of society having to be reproduced in the moral order of the school has remained highly salient. The Organisation for Economic Cooperation and Development (OECD), for example, has argued that the school is becoming the only universally experienced site for the formation of moral identity and that this has consequences for the nature of the work of teachers (OECD 1990). Contemporary teachers are engaged in moral development as much as cognitive development.

Personal and professional values of teachers

The second position is that teachers, by virtue of their professional responsibilities, are expected to embody in their personal life a society's, or a community's, moral ideals. We draw here upon the analysis by the American educational sociologist, Willard Waller (1932): 'the teacher is supposed to represent certain ideals in the community. These ideals differ somewhat from one community to another, but there is an underlying similarity.' He illustrated his argument by citing a teacher's contract which included, *inter alia*:

> I promise to abstain from all dancing, immodest dressing, and any other conduct unbecoming to a teacher and a lady.

> I promise not to go out with any young men except in so far as it may be necessary to stimulate Sunday-school work.
>
> (Waller 1932: 43)

Waller argued (1932: 44–45) that, for teachers, meeting moral requirements laid upon them by the community might take priority over teaching effectiveness: 'the most complete ineffectiveness as a teacher does not always constitute a valid ground for dismissing a teacher . . . whereas detection in any moral dereliction causes a teacher's contract to be broken at once'.

Both these analytical positions, which reflect sociologists' interest in social control, may, at first reading, seem extreme or anachronistic and, in Waller's case, too locally situated. However, there are modern versions of these positions.

For example, the value assumptions for European teachers were made explicit by the Council of Europe (1985):

> The initial training of teachers should prepare them for their future contribution to teaching about human rights in their schools. For example, future teachers should:
> (i) be encouraged to take an interest in national and world affairs;

(ii) be taught to identify and combat all forms of discrimination in schools and society and be encouraged to confront and overcome their own prejudices.

(cited in Pollard 1997: x)

Likewise, the code of ethics of the Australian College of Education states:

A teacher's responsibility for the initiation of members of society into its cultures will involve not only teaching of knowledge . . . But also the development of commitment to its highest values . . . Colleagues should be treated with respect without discrimination on grounds of status, sex, race, colour, national origin or religious or political belief and such respect should be encouraged in others.

(cited in Haynes 1998: 178)

Contemporary analyses tend to focus particularly on the moral implications of the teacher's professional relationship with pupils and parents. Soder (1990: 74) argues that the imbalance in power between pupil and teacher carries its own moral imperative: 'It is precisely because children are compelled and children are defenceless and have low status that teaching has moral obligations and thus moral praiseworthiness'. Sockett (1990: 234) likewise claims that 'Teachers must be known by parents and children as people they can trust'. And Tomlinson (1995: 63) characterises the self-sacrificing attitude expected of teachers: 'There is a self-forgetting concentration on the needs of the pupil and a continuing agony better to understand those needs'.

These kinds of claim, (despite their apparent affection for overblown expression, and a tendency to conflate empirical and normative language), reflect the general moral framework of teaching. However, our concern is not with the general values in an education system so much as the values underlying conceptions of effectiveness in teaching. Thompson (1995: 23–45) makes the connection between these general values and the activities of teaching. She argues that the teaching profession has three related ethical frames, namely an ethic of *care*, an ethic of *competence* and an ethic of professional *commitment*. It is in the second frame that teaching effectiveness and values are demonstrable, since it includes learning relationships, and knowledge of pedagogy: 'knowledge of pedagogy can be regarded as **the** moral imperative of the profession as, to put it bluntly, teachers and schools must be able to demonstrate that learning and development take place because of their expertise' (Thompson 1995: 32).

For Thompson (1995: 9), teachers cannot operate without a conception of an ethical basis for their teaching. Drawing on Starratt (1994), she argues that:

> Every teacher has an educational platform which expresses the normative assumptions, principles, beliefs and values that guide their teaching activity and usually encompass the aim of education, the teacher's preferred pedagogy; the image of the learner; the social significance of the student's learning . . . the most important things students should learn. Seldom are these stated explicitly, but they are nonetheless highly influential in their teaching.

Of course the particular values differ in different societies, and within the same society will change over time to reflect changes in culture. Likewise the conceptions of teaching and learning, and the values underlying them, will necessarily change. However, for us, any model of teacher effectiveness will need to elaborate the values upon which it is premised.

Values and effective teaching

The question therefore is not whether rather general values exercise an influence on teachers so much as whether they frame more specific values associated with effective teaching. Although there are exceptions (Dunne and Wragg 1994, Kyriacou 1997b), for the most part the educational effectiveness literature has tended to adopt a model that appears at first sight value-free; the model adopts a measure of student outcome or progress, and attempts to establish the most efficient school or classroom processes for achieving it. It is not value-free so much as based in a value system of instrumental pragmatism, in which ends are taken for granted and means pursued without reference to them. There is rarely a treatment of the processes or outcomes as problematic in respect of the value assumptions that underlie them. The consequence has been that the literature has insulated effectiveness from the larger moral frame of teaching. Teacher effectiveness researchers appear not to have read Durkheim.

Yet it is clear that effectiveness in education carries value assumptions. It is a central focus for the performativity ethic (Ball 1999) and has connotations with the drive for increased productivity in systemic reform (Apple 1986). Its curricular provenance is Tyler's rational curriculum model, with its stress on clearly defined objectives, processes and outcomes (Tyler 1971). In the contemporary context, it is possible to see educational effectiveness as deeply implicated in the trend to globalisation and the pressure for education systems to feed into increased economic productivity. On this assumption the values inhering in educational effectiveness are rendered problematic.

Values and differentiated teacher effectiveness

The values we identify serve to illustrate the argument. We have selected two areas of focus for values analysis in classroom effectiveness: the concept of learning, i.e. what counts as worthwhile achievement or learning; and classroom climate, including the nature of teacher–pupil relationships. We treat these separately for the purposes of analysis, but it is obvious that they are interrelated. We have chosen *independent learning* and *inclusiveness* as illustrative exemplars of values in relation to learning and classroom climate respectively, because they reflect differentiation, but they are obviously not the only values that might be used.

Effectiveness and learning: the value of independent learning

Pring (1992: 19–20) argues that it is inappropriate to consider monitoring standards without first enquiring into the value base for judgements about standards. He criticises the 'lack of explicit and detailed criteria by which judgements (about standards) are made', on the grounds that the concept of achievement has built into it 'the mastery of something worthwhile'. Standards are, on this argument, the benchmarks by which judgements about achievement are made, but they reflect often inexplicit values. They are not the values themselves. This provides Pring with a critique for international comparison of educational effectiveness: 'as society comes to value different forms of life . . . so do our moral purposes change, and so too do the standards by which we assess moral worth . . . it makes it logically impossible to make sensible comparisons of standards . . . across cultures unless those cultures share a common set of values'.

Drawing on Pring's analysis, Richards (2001: 12–13, 19) argues that the measurement of standards achieved in classrooms by the Office for Standards in Education (Ofsted) is invalid precisely because there is no examination of values:

Currently the Ofsted inspection process involves collecting, evaluating and reporting evidence but without any explicit reference to aims and values . . . Judgements of the 'effectiveness' of schools or departments are empty unless it is clear what aims are being effectively achieved or what values successfully embodied . . . The nature of the standards is presupposed; they are not discussed or seen as contentious . . . yet . . . they are dependent on values and therefore potentially contentious.

From our point of view these analyses force an examination of what counts as valuable learning – what kinds of learning should be thought worthwhile, and therefore should arise from, or be the objective for, effective teaching.

We are immediately faced with an empirical difficulty since most studies of teacher effectiveness take performance in standardised tests as the outcome measure, sometimes with the implication that it stands as proxy for other kinds of learning. There are exceptions, as Mortimore (1998) points out. Some studies have measured the impact on self-esteem or self-concept, and some have investigated performance on practical tasks. None has examined teacher effectiveness on independent learning, that is to say, the kind of teaching which encourages and enables students to learn for themselves, to develop metacognitive awareness, to take some control over the learning process by being less dependent on the teacher and more ready to challenge the received wisdom of the teacher. Such learning has not been included in the empirical studies, on the whole (see Chapter 7 for some exceptions). One obvious reason for this is that it is difficult to measure validly. Yet this kind of learning is highly valued in a world where electronic sources of information are widely accessible, where the ability to learn for oneself is in high demand in many occupations, and where the concept of lifelong learning has become increasingly important. Furthermore, we would argue that this kind of learning is intrinsically more valuable than much of the learning measured by conventional testing, irrespective of its value in the world outside school. This is because even with very young children it confers a kind of dignity upon the learners; it embodies respect for them as learners and reflects a questioning of authority relationships in teaching and learning; its underlying value position is the acknowledgement that knowledge is tentative and learning requires scepticism.

This view finds expression in Kyriacou's (1997b) text on effective teaching, where he argues that effective teachers have to respect students as learners. For teaching to be effective there has to be mutual respect and rapport between teacher and student, based on a commitment to fair treatment. He argues that teachers must show genuine care for each student's progress, must respect students as learners, and must respect them as individuals. This requires a particular value position on the nature of learning in which an appropriate degree of responsibility for learning has to be devolved to students. Teachers should set up 'learning experiences in which the views and opinions of pupils can be heard, developed and elaborated, in which pupils are given a large measure of control in shaping and carrying out learning activities' (Kyriacou 1997b: 109).

Thus, any model analysing teacher effectiveness might need to be able to accommodate this and other values held by teachers as an underlying commitment to a particular view of learning.

Effectiveness and classroom climate: the value of inclusiveness

We have argued already that, following Durkheim, we cannot conceptualise classroom effectiveness as merely instrumental, designed only to establish order and generate cognitive gains. Any classroom reflects values, for instance fairness of treatment and respect for persons, and this has been recognised, though in a token sense, in the research literature where classroom climate has been examined as a factor in teacher effectiveness (e.g. Brookover *et al.* 1979, Mortimore *et al.* 1988). However, the emphases have been on instructional related factors, such as teacher expectations, degree of openness, extent of differentiation, work-related questioning and class management. These do embody values, but the studies tend not to develop detailed analyses of the values *per se*; the classroom climate in these studies is defined primarily by a focus on work and on time on task (see Chapter 4).

The question therefore is whether a distinctive set of values associated with classroom climate can be identified. We believe that the value of 'inclusiveness' may be an interesting example here. By this we mean a respect for all pupils and a commitment to enabling all pupils to achieve their potential. Dunne and Wragg (1994) refer to an ethos in which relationships are warm, teachers hold all students in positive regard, bias and stereotyping are minimised, and students' views and perspectives are canvassed inclusively. Self-evaluation by pupils is encouraged, and (anticipating Kyriacou's argument) there is 'transfer of power and initiative based on teaching children to act responsibly ... and the curriculum is negotiated secure in the knowledge that pupils share purposes and values' (Dunne and Wragg 1994: 41).

A more elaborated analysis of inclusiveness (using a slightly different terminology) is offered by Pollard (1997). He argues that classrooms should be 'incorporative', by which is meant a classroom 'consciously designed to enable each child to act as a full participant in class activities and also to feel him or herself to be a valued member of the class' (Pollard 1997: 111). Pollard cites extensive research to classify the problems of developing such a classroom climate in four areas: ability, gender, race and social class.

Pollard claims that a competitive ethos, at odds with inclusiveness, is damaging for some individuals, because of the way differences in attainment are constructed:

> a contrast can be drawn between classes in which the strengths and weaknesses of each child are recognised and in which the particular level of achievement of each child is accepted as a starting point, and classes in which specific qualities or abilities are regarded as being of more value than others in absolute terms . . . the success of some pupils is made possible only at the cost of the relative failure of others. The overall effect is to marginalize some children, whilst the work of others is praised and regarded as setting a standard to which other children should aspire . . . an incorporative classroom will produce better classroom relationships and more understanding and respect for others than one in which emphasises the particular success of the few.
>
> (Pollard 1997: 112–113)

The value position underlying such a classroom climate is important in relationship to teaching effectiveness, but the issue is not how teachers relate to pupils of different gender or race etc., but how teachers deal with *differentiated attainment* by students. We need a model of differentiated effectiveness precisely to allow for the possibility that different teaching approaches or behaviours might be needed to respond appropriately to students with different levels of attainment. This provides a more defensible justification than one focused on particular social groups, important though they are; it reinforces the need to articulate, and to accommodate within an effectiveness model, the values that sustain it (such as, in this illustration, commitment on the teacher's part to inclusiveness).

Values outside the classroom

It has been argued in Chapter 2 that much of teachers' work occurs outside the classroom and that the extra-classroom activities need to be incorporated in any model of teacher effectiveness. There is a fuller available treatment of this dimension in respect of values than is the case within classrooms. This is partly because many education systems have a specification of professional values or of a professional code of ethics, which are binding on teachers as members of the profession, or to which teachers are expected to have regard. We have already referred to the Australian code above, cited in Haynes (1998), who provides a powerful analysis of professional values and ethics.

In England, the revised national curriculum in 2000 (DfES 2000) was accompanied by a statement of values from a 'Values Forum' in which values were identified under four headings. These were *self, relationships, society* and *the environment*, and within each section there were highly specified value positions. The statement of values did not have statutory force, but it was claimed (though not demonstrated) that there was consensus in society about these values, even though some of them – for example, 'respect for the institution of marriage' – were obviously contestable. In England also, the General Teaching Council (GTC 2001) produced a general code of ethics expressing a set of professional values required of its members. These included holding high expectations of all pupils and 'demonstrating' (presumably, like Waller's example above, in their person) values such as tolerance, honesty, fairness, an appreciation of different backgrounds and taking responsibility for their own professional development. The difficulty posed by these kinds of approaches to values for us is that they tend to lack direct connection with effectiveness. (Commitment to one's own professional development, universally invoked in professional codes, may be an exception.)

The most sustained development of an argument linking teaching effectiveness with values was made in relation to the English government's requirement that promotion in teaching should be explicitly connected to teachers' performance, mainly performance in the classroom. This argument was made by Hay McBer (DfEE 2000), a management consultancy firm contracted to develop a basis for teacher appraisal in England as part of the 'modernisation' of the teaching profession, envisaged in a Green Paper (1998). Since it would form the basis for career progression, it would need to be demonstrably equitable, or at least litigation-proof. We have shown elsewhere in this book (Chapter 5) that there were methodological uncertainties in the way it was developed (see BERA 2001), but the model created by Hay McBer had the considerable advantage that it made explicit a set of values associated with 'professionalism' which, it was claimed, had a direct connection with teacher effectiveness.

These values included *respect for others, challenge and support, confidence,* and *creating trust.* Respect for others reflected an 'underlying belief that individuals matter and deserve respect'; challenge and support reflected a 'commitment to do everything possible for each pupil and enable each pupil to be successful'; confidence involved the 'belief in one's ability to be effective and to take on challenges'; and creating trust involved 'being consistent and fair and keeping one's word'. Hay McBer claimed that such values permeated teaching, by feeding into a classroom climate that was conducive to effective teaching and learning.

Incorporating values into a model of differentiated teacher effectiveness

It is a difficult task to envisage how a model for research and appraisal might incorporate values. This is not primarily because of the technical problems associated with measurement, validity and reliability, though there are difficulties in that respect. Despite Peters' (1970, 1973) argument that there are some fundamental values in education, the real challenge arises from the fact that in different societies, in different schools, and for different individual teachers there may be differences in values. Although not extreme moral relativists, we would argue that, for this reason, any model should be developed to allow for such differences, and that the most appropriate methodology for this to happen would be through some kind of self-evaluation. Self-evaluation is, of course, a method of identifying values rather than the substantive values themselves.

There is some limited evidence that a self-evaluation approach is feasible, though we can provide only an outline here. Kyriakides *et al.* (2002) have shown that Cypriot primary school teachers could identify eight clusters of values and that these values could be the basis for both school development and teacher evaluation. In terms of validity it was possible for Kyriakides *et al.* to show that the value clusters developed in this way showed close connection with the profile of teacher effectiveness in the research literature. However, dominant among these values was 'love of children', a value not easily discernible in the Hay McBer model, though resonating with the value of respect for pupils, in the analyses by Dunne and Wragg (1994) and Kyriacou (1997b), outlined earlier.

Further research is needed to see the extent to which self-evaluation can work in other settings. But the case for self-evaluation in respect of values is convincing for three reasons. First, as has been argued earlier, differentiation in value orientation operates empirically, so that an exclusively generic model of values would be inappropriate. The model would have to incorporate a very wide set of values, and it is unlikely that a general model, appropriate across cultures and across differences in systemic developmental stages, would work. Second, self-evaluation as a method has been advocated as part of an approach to school effectiveness and improvement (MacBeath 1999) in which ownership of, and identification with, the improvement process can be embodied. Such advantages should flow from self-evaluation in teacher effectiveness also. Third, there must be some concern in democratic and pluralistic societies about the power relations associated with a general set of values to which all teachers must subscribe, and by which they should be evaluated for career progression. A common set of externally framed values would lead either to teachers pretending to espouse values to which they were not committed, in order to secure promotion, or to the appraisal process privileging inappropriately some values at the expense of others. Potentially a methodology involving self-evaluation would resolve these difficulties, since it would allow for value differences to be generated and reflected at the level of the school and the individual teacher, rather than at the level of the state.

10 Differentiated teacher effectiveness and teacher appraisal

In this chapter we will look at how the differentiated model of teacher effectiveness we have developed could be used to generate performance management and self-appraisal instruments that are linked to professional development and school improvement rather than just accountability as is currently too often the case. As well as mechanisms that more adequately encompass the full complexity of the teachers' work, this kind of instrument should provide useful feedback that can lead to enhanced teacher and school effectiveness. We will attempt to imagine an effective and flexible form of appraisal and performance management. This exercise, by its very nature, has to be a tentative one. One reason for this is that accountability and appraisal policies differ from country to country. More importantly, a complex differentiated effectiveness model might easily lead to complex, hard-to-implement instruments, which would easily become a bureaucratic rather than a developmental exercise. For this reason (and because of the evidence on effective appraisal we will discuss below), the model we are tentatively proposing focuses on self-evaluation of separate aspects of the differential model, i.e. teachers (or teams) would focus on one aspect and develop self-evaluation methods for developmental self-appraisal. Lest this seems overly vague and loose, we must stress the use of specific criteria to look at each domain.

Models of appraisal

Appraisal can fulfil two main goals – accountability and professional development – which are often seen as contradictory (Bartlett 1996). In the light of the difficulty of reconciling these goals, accountability predominates in many cases.

As well as fulfilling different goals, appraisal can be carried out by either peers or superiors of the person appraised. Peer review obviously

	Accountability	Development
Peer	Peer accountability	Peer review and development
Hierarchy	Performance target setting and review	Competence assessment and development

Figure 10.1 A model of appraisal based on Fisher (1994)

has differing connotations from review by those in a hierarchical position to the appraised. This leads to the model in Figure 10.1, proposed by Fisher (1994).

Peer review and development, according to Fisher (1994), aims to provide the appraisee with feedback to plan future professional development, and is aimed primarily at fulfilling individual goals. Competence assessment and development is likewise focused on the appraisee's development needs, but is also aimed at making judgements on performance. This is usually linked to accountability mechanisms. In competence assessment and development models there is usually an emphasis on aligning individuals to organisational goals. In peer accountability systems, individuals are brought to account for their actions by peers. This is often done where a clear external framework of standards exists, such as in the medical profession. Performance target setting and review focuses on targets for achievement. Targets are usually set for the whole organisation and then cascaded down to individual members of staff. It is this type of appraisal that is common in many educational systems. These different types of appraisal lead to different outputs, but evidence is increasing that the most common type of appraisal in education (performance target setting and review) is not the one most likely to lead to school improvement and the creation of schools as professional learning communities. This dissatisfaction with judgemental appraisal systems is also apparent in industry, where they are seen as unreliable, and detrimental to teamwork (Powney 1991).

Problems with current appraisal practices

In many countries there has, over the past few decades, been a move towards both increased accountability of the education system and the teaching profession and forms of school-based management.

These have led to an increased use of appraisal, within, and developed by, schools in those countries where central accountability is still relatively limited, as in the Netherlands (Reezigt *et al.*, forthcoming), and to the imposition of state-mandated appraisal and evaluation policies in countries where accountability and/or centralisation are strong, such as Cyprus (Kyriakides and Campbell 2003) and the UK (Reynolds and Muijs 2004).

Where accountability dominates, appraisal systems are likely to attract some hostility and often lead to teachers 'going through the motions'. Too often appraisal then becomes purely a paper exercise (Bartlett 1996). Negative attitudes towards appraisal can also result from a tendency to focus on the negatives in some schools. Appraisal imposed from without can be seen as threatening to personal autonomy, and in one study many teachers felt that the English government's appraisal system, which can be described as an attempt to combine performance target setting and review and competence assessment and development, impeded the development of schools as collaborative cultures. The stance taken towards appraisal differed depending on whether respondents were themselves part of senior management, appraisers or appraised, however. What was clear was that appraisal as it was occurring was a managerial and account-ability-focused process rather than a collegial one (Bartlett 1998). Appraisal for staff development does not suffer from these problems, but on the other hand can become disconnected from school goals if the focus is purely on the individual. The use of a more fine-grained and differentiated model, such as the one proposed here, could help alleviate some of these issues by allowing teachers to focus on positives as well as areas for development, and is likely to be better aligned with the real needs of the teaching profession in the complex educational reality that exists at present.

It is important to note, however, that whenever both goals (appraisal for accountability and appraisal for staff development) are present it is not possible to resolve these dilemmas fully. Failure to acknowledge that the dilemma exists, by, for example, denying the accountability aspect, is unlikely to be effective as managerial issues are likely to be resolved in an opaque manner rather than openly. An open acknowledgement of both goals, and a collaborative and collegial approach to appraisal, are likely to be more fruitful (Cardno 1995).

Another problem with appraisal aimed at performance assessment and accountability is that it proves very hard to use effectively in practice. In one study of companies in the English West Midlands, it was found that while respondents saw many benefits in theory, the practice was very different, with companies reporting major problems with areas such as measuring performance, time management, and identifying training needs. Imposing systems from on high on all staff was seen to lead to mistrust and in some cases (passive) resistance (Bowles and Coates 1993).

The linking of teaching to performance is always a difficult matter, as identified in a report from the English inspectorate (Ofsted 2002) on the implementation of the new performance appraisal system, where it was found that many schools involved had difficulties in setting performance targets.

Appraisal for school improvement

Where used to focus on professional development needs, appraisal can be an effective part of school improvement, with a potential to enhance the capacity to improve the school by enabling it to develop as a learning organisation. Gunter (1996) posits a number of ways in which this can occur. Self-appraisal can develop self-knowledge and mastery through personal reflection, target setting can enable learning goals to be set that can inform the school development plan, data collection can become a forum for reflection and feedback. Once appraisal becomes a continuous process that all staff go through, rather than a ritual taking place a few specific times, it can become a forum for continuous and collective learning. In order to result in lasting school improvement, teachers need to be empowered to take control of their own appraisal, albeit in collaborative groups. As in many countries teachers at present work in a system where this is not the case, achieving this will require helping teachers to gain confidence in knowing how to start self-assessment (Humphreys 1992). The model of differentiated teacher effectiveness could form a starting point for this. Other issues include providing teachers with emotional support mechanisms, acknowledging the personal biographical factors that impact on performance, and developing critical distance (Humphreys 1992). Being part of a collaborative group is crucial in providing both support and the necessary critical distance.

All this points clearly to the fact that appraisal is only likely to be an effective learning tool where teachers can take ownership and control over the process and orient it towards staff development needs. The extent to which that is the case is to a high degree dependent on the role of the appraiser in the process, and the relationship between appraiser and appraisee. Whether the appraiser or appraisee is supposed to raise points for discussion, the extent to which they are asked to give an overall judgement of performance, and whether or not any final report has to be agreed between appraiser and appraisee or is simply written by the appraiser, are examples of the former; the extent to which appraiser and appraisee differ in hierarchical position is an example of the latter. The extent to which targets are established centrally or collaboratively is another important element (Townley 1993).

In the 1998 Green Paper, the Department for Education and Skills in England set out a new appraisal system, designed to overcome problems with existing practices outlined above. However, rather than moving towards a more developmental model, accountability was strengthened, not least through attempting to link teachers' effectiveness to teachers' pay and performance management. Also, there was clearly no attempt to look at broader models of teacher effectiveness.

In order to fulfil requirements that lead to teachers crossing a threshold for increased pay, they are required to show that they meet national standards in:

- knowledge and understanding
- teaching and assessment
- teaching and classroom management
- teaching and monitoring progress
- pupil progress
- wider professional effectiveness – professional development
- wider professional effectiveness – school development
- professional characteristics.

What immediately strikes one when looking at this list is that although some attempt has clearly been made to look at a range of characteristics, the vast majority of these concentrate on classroom teaching, while the broader professional competencies of teachers as described in our text receive little attention. This becomes even clearer when one scrutinises the Ofsted report on the implementation of the appraisal strategy, which focuses almost exclusively on factors relating to classroom teaching (Ofsted 2002). Some measures exist that focus on wider competencies (for example, the instrument developed by Gaziel and Wasserstein-Warnet (2000) that focuses on teachers' relationships and collaboration with colleagues and parents, professional characteristics such as engagement in supplementary tasks and being a member of professional bodies, as well as classroom practice), but these are without exception more limited and less flexible than would seem desirable within a differentiated teacher effectiveness model.

The link of the English appraisal system with pay has been highly controversial, but in practice has had little meaning, as most applicants in the initial cohort passed the threshold after the scheme was significantly watered down following a very unfavourable reaction to the principle of performance-related pay among the teaching profession (Storey 2000, Wragg *et al.* 2001).

Towards a differentiated appraisal model

A proposed differentiated model would incorporate wider aspects of the teacher's professional role. In previous chapters we have identified a number of areas in which teachers might be differentially effective (subjects, differential pupil background, differential pupil characteristics, different roles and different contexts). This clearly leads us to a model whereby appraisal would take place in different areas, such as teaching different subjects or curriculum areas, teaching pupils with different dominant intelligences, teachers' pastoral or leadership roles, etc. Individual schools and teachers would be able to adapt and choose which areas are important within their vision and goals. This diverse perspective is likely to be fruitful both in highlighting the strengths of individual teachers and in identifying areas for development for staff. Below are some examples of what this could look like.

A school or department could collaboratively decide based on its priorities that it would want to appraise teachers or use self-appraisal in the following areas:

- teaching pupils with different intelligences
- teaching pupils with special educational needs
- developing leadership for school improvement
- becoming effective pastoral carers
- developing the teaching of problem-solving.

Within these, one would develop more fine-grained appraisal systems to look at each aspect. For example, when looking at developing pupils pastorally, one could use Freydenberg's (1997) model to assess the extent to which the following elements have been addressed:

- be competent in social skills, including the ability to manage conflict peacefully
- cultivate enquiring problem-solving habits for lifetime learning
- acquire technical and analytical capabilities to participate in a global economy

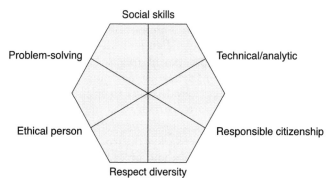

Figure 10.2 Graphical representation of appraisal: selected elements

- become ethical persons
- learn the requirements of responsible citizenship
- respect diversity in a pluralistic society.

Appraisal could then focus on the extent to which each of these needs was met in the classroom, for example by rating each on a four-point scale, the results of which could for example be graphically depicted in Figure 10.2, with longer lines indicating that this area has been more effectively or fully met. Obviously, the elements proposed here are just examples, and teams could develop their own criteria for studying specific dimensions, although reference to research evidence in the areas studied is important.

Similarly, when information on all the elements has been collated, total ratings for each area could be collected, resulting in the depiction in Figure 10.3. This would give a clear picture of where strengths and

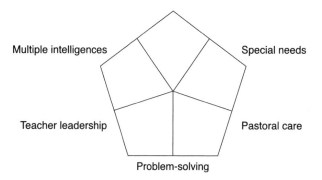

Figure 10.3 Graphical representation of appraisal: total ratings

areas for development lie, both as a whole and within sub-areas. We feel that when used in a collaborative setting, within small teams or groups, such an approach would help align individual and organisational goals and professional development needs. Metcalfe (1994) suggests using trios, in which participants take turns to take on appraiser, appraisee and observer roles. In order to ensure that working in small teams would not lead to parochialism and blindness to the bigger picture, we would suggest including staff members from other departments (or even schools) as critical friends in the process. They could look at evidence and goals, and provide a fresh perspective. We would also suggest rotating teams regularly, to ensure that staleness is avoided. As Metcalfe suggests, these groups should ideally be non-contrived and relate to existing professional relationships, possibly linked to existing school improvement teams. The latter have been found to be an effective way to promote school improvement (Hopkins and West 2000) and more generally, small, flexible teams have long been found to be the cornerstone for innovation in effective organisations (e.g. Peters and Waterman 1983). A further element of flexibility suggested by Metcalfe (1994) is the use of a professional audit approach, whereby all teachers are regarded as professional peers. Appraisal in this model takes place in professional teams, which may differ depending on the area appraised.

This model is best suited for self-appraisal in our opinion, but can also easily be adapted for use in collegial contexts. Obviously, training in the use of such an appraisal model would be helpful. As Kyriacou (1997a) has pointed out, a lack of training has led to anxiety among many placed in the appraiser role. This would serve teachers' professional development needs, highlighting areas for development.

Collecting data on performance

How can appraisal become a continuous process that can help schools become learning organisations and improve, rather than an *ad hoc* once-a-year/term jumping through hoops? This can be done by linking appraisal to teacher leadership and school improvement teams as mentioned above. These teams could continually appraise and self-appraise by collecting information on the areas identified as ones to appraise (see above), and regularly meet to discuss progress in these areas. Appraisal could in this way become almost an action research approach, where continuous interrogation of data can help develop self-reflection at the individual and organisational levels. Obviously, in order for such a system to function time will need to be freed for staff to participate.

What kind of methods could be used to collect data for (self-) appraisal and school improvement? Again, a flexible approach would seem preferable, as it is clear that within a differentiated effectiveness framework different evidence is needed of effectiveness in different areas. Methods would include interviewing, questionnaires to pupils, observation, and logs and journals.

Classroom observation methods currently form a key part of many appraisal systems, linked as they are to classroom teaching. However, while observation is undoubtedly a useful method for looking at classroom teaching, it is often used with little regard for, or knowledge of, its characteristics.

Compared to many other measures, classroom observations have the advantage of being more objective due to the outsider's perspective. The detailed recording of actual behaviours possible during classroom observation allows for fine-grained exploration of behaviours. Classroom observation has a number of disadvantages as well. Firstly, all classroom observations are by definition snapshots, and even successive observations of a teacher will only ever supply a collection of snapshots rather than a full picture of teacher behaviour over the year. Secondly, the presence of an observer in the classroom will inevitably influence the teacher's behaviour, either consciously in the form of the teacher putting on a 'performance' for the sake of the observer, or unconsciously, through increased caution or nervousness (Ward *et al.* 1981).

An important distinction in classroom observation research is that between high and low inference measures. Low inference measures require a minimal amount of observer judgement, relying largely on counting the behaviours one wants to study. High inference measures rely on more observer judgement, as when observers are asked to rate a teacher's behaviours on a rating scale (e.g. 'the teacher corrected behaviour constructively'). In general, low inference measures have the advantage of being more reliable (McConnell and Bowers 1979, Dickson 1983, Wiersma 1983, 1988). On the other hand, low inference measures are also more limited in what they are able to measure. Low inference measures by definition focus on the occurrence or not of certain easily measurable behaviours, but cannot measure the quality of use of these behaviours, and are unable to take context factors into account (Muijs 2004). One solution to the question of which measure to use could be to use both high and low inference

measures in a study. However, there is some evidence of contamina-
tion, in that a halo effect seems to occur whereby the ratings on the
different instruments influence one another (Marston and Zimmerer
1979).

Other methods of gaining information on classroom processes
(which can be used to look at differentiated teacher effectiveness in the
areas of subject, pupil background and pupil's personal characteristics) are interviewing teachers about their teaching and using pupil
questionnaires.

Interviews have the advantage of allowing the appraisee to give
her/his full understanding of her/his teaching of an interaction with
different pupil groups (for example). In-depth interviews with teachers
have the advantage of allowing the appraiser to probe the teacher in
depth on his/her teaching and thus allow more detailed findings to
emerge than questionnaires. Open questions, such as 'how is the innovation going?' will tend to elicit more open responses from the interviewee than more guided questions, such as 'are you doing x?',
which can easily lead to the interviewee giving the answer he or she
thinks the interviewer wants to hear (Guskey 2000). Following open
questions, the interviewer can move to more focused questions on
specific aspects. Interviews suffer from lower reliability, however, relying on teachers' 'there and then' memory and, if not standardised,
from lack of comparability. In-depth interviews also make a large
demand on teacher time, can be threatening to teachers and are as
expensive as classroom observation (Muijs, forthcoming).

An under-utilised method is to ask students themselves about
whether or not they have observed changes to, for example, teaching
behaviours or other school factors. Students can certainly provide
highly interesting and useful information on their teachers, but are
not always able to supply detailed information on specific behaviours.
The results on reliability of student data are unclear. In an older study,
student ratings were found to differ from classroom observation data,
therefore being likely to be a useful addition rather than a replacement
for such methods (Evertson *et al.* 1978). However, a more recent
study found high correlations between student classroom climate self-
reports and teachers' use of effective instructional behaviours as
measured through classroom observation (Padron and Waxman 1999).
The Hook and Rosenshine (1976) study likewise gives support to
the validity of the use of student ratings of teacher behaviours. One
study found student ratings of their teachers to be related to the grades
awarded to them and to suffer from halo effects (Owen 1976). Some
recent studies suggest that it is possible to develop reliable measures of

teachers' pedagogical and content knowledge to be judged by pupils, at least at the higher secondary age. Tuan *et al.* (2000) developed an instrument for Taiwanese pupils that demonstrated adequate psychometric properties, while Kyriakides (2003c) used generalisability theory to demonstrate the validity of an instrument to measure students' perceptions of teacher effectiveness in Cyprus.

Appraising those aspects of teacher effectiveness not related to classroom teaching requires some different methods. Interviewing again is a useful method, and questionnaires may be appropriate in some circumstances. However, when looking at aspects such as different role performance (e.g. leadership), different methods may be useful. Logs and journals are reflective tools in which participants are asked to record their thoughts and feelings about the professional development programme at regular intervals. They also allow participants to reflect on their own growth as learners. Participants in one study of the use of learning logs reported improved self-awareness and enhanced professional development opportunities (Barclay 1996). Guiding questions can be provided to aid this process (Guskey 2000). They can provide rich and contextualised information, especially where participants are specifically asked to record information on local characteristics and needs, as in Bonamy *et al.*'s (2001) evaluation of the Learn-Nett project.

Conclusion

In this chapter we have made some tentative steps towards proposing a model of teacher (self-)appraisal that we believe ties in both with a more differentiated model of teacher effectiveness and with an appraisal model that can foster real change and school improvement rather than bureaucratic control. We realise that this model is a first step, and clearly needs further articulation in practice. However, a differentiated and flexible model by its very nature rules out a single instrument that can be presented to participants as right for all occasions.

Used within a collegial and developmental framework, however, we feel that a differentiated appraisal model has the potential to make a positive contribution to school improvement by providing an individualised focus for development, which takes into account the full role of the teacher as a professional, and which can help counter reductionist views of the teacher as a classroom technician who merely needs to engage in the right set of all-purpose instructional behaviours.

11 Educational policy implications

The problematic relationship between educational research evidence and education policy

The purpose of this chapter is to explore the implications of the model of teacher effectiveness developed in this book for its possible contribution to education policy. We accept that the relationships between policy and research, even in a period when commitment to developing evidence-informed policy is strong (Hargreaves 1997), are highly problematic. Education policy operates in political and cultural contexts that vary across different education systems, so that evidence that is closely related to policy in one system may be tangential in another. For these reasons, and others, policy borrowing across cultures and systems has been rightly criticised for its simplistic assumptions (Alexander 2001). However, we are advocating the borrowing of evidence, methodology and theorising that may be able to be applied to policy, not the borrowing of policy itself. For this reason, our intention is to consider those implications of our model that contain the promise of applicability to some extent across education systems, rather than elements that would be limited to specific policy in one system.

In support of this position, we would point to the emergence of six features of modernising education systems, as in public sector services generally, that appear to be common, or at the very least widespread, and in which evidence about educational effectiveness will necessarily play a significant role. These are:

- the rise of the performance culture, or 'performativity', and the perceived need to measure the effectiveness of professionals for comparative purposes (Carley 1988, Ball 1999)

- the trend toward increased accountability mechanisms, 'marketisation' of education, and the perceived need for provision of information about individual and organisational effectiveness to stakeholders (Norris 1998, Power 1999, Whitty *et al.* 1998)
- the promotion of schools as learning organisations which are characterised by the use of performance data to improve school effectiveness (MacBeath *et al.* 2000)
- the widening range of responsibilities and changed demarcation of professional responsibilities under the modernisation of public services (Barber 1995, Merson 2000)
- a belief in continuous professional development and lifelong learning to improve teacher effectiveness (Fullan 1999)
- the concern for educational effectiveness in relation to inclusivity and social justice (Slee *et al.* 1998, Weiner 2002).

Our assumption in this chapter is that the evidence, methodology and theorising underlying our differentiated model of teacher effectiveness can contribute to the understanding and development of these features, while we acknowledge that different systems will be at different stages in relation to them.

Education policy

Education policy can be thought of, following Furlong and White's classification model (2001; cited in Edwards 2003), as having three interrelated aspects, namely policy *formation*, policy *implementation* and policy *evaluation*. Irrespective of its relationship to research, education policy is a problematic conception in all three respects. Policy formation is often developed behind the closed doors of the civil service, with compromise and personal ambition sometimes combining with luck, so that policy intentions are often opaque. There are harsher judgements, dismissing the rational decision-making character of policy-making; Shipman (1984) argued that horse-trading was the appropriate metaphor for the formation of policy, and Briault (cited in Kogan 1975) talked of a 'triangle of tension' between the national, local and individual school levels. Similarly, Ponting (1986), in an insider's account of policy-making in the civil service, claimed that policy-making had to be constructed as emerging *ad hoc* through a series of compromises between departments headed by powerful ministers with their own ambitions. However, he added a further complexity – the fortuitous element in the exercise – when he reported that a Secretary of State for Education in England got a highly contentious policy accepted by the cabinet because it came at the end of a long agenda and was nodded through so that the meeting could finish on schedule. Graham and Tytler (1993) noted that the drive to push ahead with a particular version of school history in what was recognised as a flawed national curriculum in England was partly energised by the desire of the then Secretary of State, Kenneth Baker, to be remembered as a great educational reformer and partly by his own deep commitment to the study of history. For outsiders to these processes, understanding the nature and purpose of any particular policy becomes much more difficult than is sometimes recognised. (See Campbell (1989) for a further discussion of this.) For this reason, the relationship of research to any policy claiming to be evidence-based is rendered uncertain.

Second, policy implementation is often driven, at least initially, by a political timetable, usually much shorter than the time-scale needed for robust trial and evaluation. So what passes for policy implementation is *de facto* a pilot for a future policy formation refined by experience. For example, in England, the policy established in the 1988 Education Reform Act, that there should be a common and compulsory curriculum in ten subjects for all pupils up to the age of 16, was amended some 12 years later to allow students to opt out of some subjects such as Modern Foreign Languages at age 14, and to add statutory provision in Citizenship for all secondary school students. What the drivers were for these changes is unclear, but they might be thought to include the shortage of modern language teachers, and the perceived difficulty in forcing students with little ability or interest in languages to study them beyond age 14. The introduction of Citizenship might be interpreted as driven largely by the concerns in the Home Office about a lack of civic awareness, including alienation from politics, and excess of antisocial behaviour in public spaces among young people. However, there might equally be a quite rational basis for its introduction, given that most other countries teach Citizenship, sometimes within a subject called Social Studies, and that its omission from the original 1988 curriculum arose, as with other cross-curricular themes, from a policy framing the statutory curriculum exclusively in terms of the conventional subjects of the traditional secondary school in England. It follows that it is difficult to know when what is thought to be a policy being implemented has ended its trial period and has become established.

Third, evaluation of policy is affected by the above two factors, because uncertainty about formation and implementation renders evaluation of policy difficult. If it is not known what the intentions of policy-makers were, or whether what is being implemented is the established policy or not, the focus for evaluation becomes fuzzy or can be only formative in purpose, not summative. For example, by the mid-1990s, it was widely held among educational researchers (e.g. Black 1996, Campbell 1996, Lawton 1996) that the education reforms in England following the introduction, through the 1988 Education Reform Act, of the national curriculum were failing to achieve their three stated main objectives: there was little evidence of improving literacy and numeracy standards; the reformed curriculum and assessment arrangements had had to be routinely and substantially amended because of their impracticability; and parental choice of school was being provided for in a limited way only. However, four years later, the judgement of the chief civil servant in the Department of Education, Sir Michael Bichard, was quite the opposite. The 1988 reform policy had been a considerable success because its objectives had been concerned with creating a consumer-led market in education in order to reduce the power of the producers – the teacher associations and the Local Education Authorities. According to Bichard, producer power had been effectively broken by devolution of management, especially the management of education funding and staff appointments, to the governing bodies of the individual schools. The way to evaluate the policy was not in terms of the stated objectives for the curriculum, standards and choice, but in terms of the redistribution of power in the system. (See Bichard, cited in Campbell 2001.)

It follows for us that the relationship between research evidence and education policy is uncertain, has to be constructed tentatively, and is permanently open to revision in the light of changed circumstances. Moreover we accept Edwards' (2003: 4) point that 'policy is shaped by many, often conflicting, interests and pressures so that even the hardest evidence can only be part of that shaping'.

Nevertheless, in the field of educational effectiveness there is reason to expect that the relationship can be somewhat more direct than in some other fields. Evidence about effective teaching, gathered from the USA and the Pacific Rim countries, fed into the English government's national strategies on teaching literacy and numeracy in primary schools (Muijs and Reynolds 2001a), even though the policies embodying the strategies were adapted to the English system. Likewise, some systems adopting policies for teacher appraisal are drawing upon cross-system evidence about teacher effectiveness for that purpose, according to Teddlie (2003). More strikingly, Teddlie shows that defects in the evidence (for example, the separation of teacher effectiveness from school effectiveness) are reflected in defects in the policies. None of this removes the uncertainty from the research–policy connection, but it does suggest that in teacher effectiveness, research evidence has played a part in policy formation and implementation and offers the promise that it can continue to do so.

There are five areas of education policy to which our model may be thought to contribute:

- the conception of teacher effectiveness underlying policy
- policies on teacher appraisal
- policies on teacher training
- policies on school improvement
- policies on inclusivity and social justice.

The conception of teacher effectiveness underlying policy

The most fundamental area is the conception of teacher effectiveness. We have shown that the principal emphasis in recent ideas of teacher effectiveness is narrow in conception, being restricted to classroom instruction and mainly to instruction in the national language and in mathematics. We have argued that what is needed is a broader conception to incorporate teachers' work outside the classroom and to include a wider range of subjects in which different classroom behaviour may need to be exhibited by teachers to realise learning. Effectiveness would also need to be concerned with the management of adults other than teachers in classrooms. The conventional conception is, moreover, defective in three other ways: in the kind of historical perspective that would have provided the idea of 'power to teach'; in articulating value assumptions about learning and teacher–learner relationships; and in the extent to which differentiated effectiveness with different groups of pupils, in different contexts, etc., is emphasised.

The leading edge of contemporary research, however (e.g. Hopkins and Reynolds' (2001) notion of context specificity, Teddlie and Stringfield's (1993) evidence about variation in teaching approaches depending upon social context, Teddlie's (2003) meta-analysis of teacher evaluation), is ahead of policy formation generally and would support the need for policy change. Without a substantive conceptual change in the direction indicated above to what counts as teacher effectiveness, it is difficult to see how the other changes we outline could be realised.

Policies on teacher appraisal

We have discussed research on teacher appraisal, and the role that teacher effectiveness research has played in this respect, in Chapter 10. Many systems are moving toward the establishment of criteria or competences by which teachers' effectiveness can be assessed for purposes of salary level or promotion, and also for the identification of development needs (see Teddlie (2003) for an international set of case studies on this aspect). There will need to be four research-derived elements in any such evaluation mechanism. First, that effectiveness should be differentiated by the five elements we have explored in this book, perhaps especially in relation to the teaching of pupils of different ages, different attainment, and from different social and ethnic backgrounds. Depending upon the purposes for which teacher appraisal is established in policy, this element would allow for teachers' strengths and development needs to be identified. Second, as we argue in Chapter 9, teacher appraisal should include a values analysis in order that judgements about effectiveness can take account of the values underlying teaching and learning held by the individual teacher, the school and the system. In this sense also, therefore, differentiation would need to be incorporated since there will be differences in values at the individual, school and system levels. Third, as we argue in Chapter 6, the gathering of evidence about teacher effectiveness should include self-evaluation, which could provide a basis, though not the only basis, for sampling the wide range of teacher effectiveness behaviour involved in our model. Finally, teacher appraisal cannot logically or ethically be separated out from the organisational context within which teachers work, so that the evidence collected should take account of the interactions between the school, the department and the individual teacher. We have argued elsewhere (Campbell *et al.* 2003) that this would have the further advantage of a reciprocal accountability: from the individual to the department or school, and from the school or department to the individual.

Policies on teacher training

The dichotomy between initial teacher training and the continuing professional development of teachers is gradually being eroded, as systems start to incorporate training that is coherent and developmental across each phase of a professional career.

Initial teacher training, whatever its formal regulations, is fundamentally about the development of teacher effectiveness. The debates about initial teacher training have been twofold: about locus and control of training, and the concept of effectiveness. Issues around locus and control include the balance of practice and theory and the role played by practitioners in the training process, and the nature of partnerships between universities, schools and the state. This has been a longstanding debate, as Robinson (2004) shows, and has been in full swing for over a century in the USA and the UK. Our model has little to offer on this issue.

On the second issue, the debate has been about the extent to which the concept of effectiveness should be defined in an instrumental manner, primarily focused on generic, criterion-referenced competences of planning, teaching, classroom management and assessment of learning; or whether initial teacher training should enable students to become reflective practitioners, and to be inducted into value orientations, and into theories about learning and the relationship between schooling and society. There is some scepticism about the extent to which a short practice-oriented postgraduate training period can achieve such ambitious goals as reflectivity, value clarification and psychological and social theorising (Berliner 1992, Macintyre 1992). These it is argued should be developed in the post-initial phase, after classroom effectiveness has been demonstrated. Policy based on this approach is established in Northern Ireland, where a three-phase model (initial, induction, and continuing professional development) operates, and a similar though somewhat looser model is emerging in England. However, in these systems the linkages between phases are fragile in practice and it has yet to be shown that the more ambitious goals are achievable.

From the point of view of our model, the stage when, in a professional career, different elements of effectiveness are focused on, is a matter for policy in the particular system. Our concern is with the evidence about effectiveness that might be fed into policies on teacher training. Our model suggests that four elements should be incorporated at some stage. First, the instructional skills demonstrated to have an effect on student performance in tests should be part of teacher training (almost certainly initial teacher training), but with the recognition of the limitations of the measures. These skills include planning, structuring, questioning and whole-class interactive teaching and the systematic use of formative feedback. These skills are well established in the empirical research literature, as Reynolds and Muijs (2000) show, and, moreover, they have a striking resonance with the models in the late nineteenth and early twentieth century in England, the rest of Europe and the USA, analysed by Robinson in Chapter 3 and elsewhere (Robinson 2004). However, secondly, we would argue that training should involve differentiation in skills according to subject, age phase, pupil personal characteristics and pupil background factors. This would help reduce the gap between theory based on generic competences and the reality of teaching in different contexts with different subjects and different groups of pupils. Third, training should involve analysis of values inherent in the intended learning, since there would be something bizarre about professional training, however instrumentally conceived, if the trainees cannot identify what is worthwhile about the nature of the learning they are effecting.

The final element is the personal character of the teacher. We are not thinking here of the studies of teacher personality traits, measured on psychometric instruments, carried out in America and elsewhere, which have been shown not to be related in general to pupil learning outcomes (see Chapter 4). We are referring to the ability of the teacher to integrate theory and practice in the particular setting of the particular classroom – 'power to teach', as outlined in Chapter 3. This personal ability to match and adjust theory to particular practice in a powerful and lively way is more than classroom charisma; it is the capacity to differentiate general pedagogical principles to the unique context of teaching. It may help explain some of the hitherto un-explained variance at the classroom level found in many effectiveness studies. Effective teaching is not the pedagogical equivalent of painting by numbers, but is 'the science of the art of teaching' (Galton 1999: 125), and we believe that recently both training and research have been the poorer for their neglect of this idea.

Policies on school and teacher improvement

Modern approaches to school improvement (e.g. Fullan 1999, MacBeath 1999, MacBeath *et al.* 2000) are based on ideas of ownership of change by school staff and on school self-evaluation. Under these approaches accountability mechanisms external to the school are supplemented, or in some cases replaced, by development mechanisms internal to it. However, the school improvement movement grew out of the school effectiveness movement (Creemers 1994, Mortimore 1998) and the modern approaches noted above depend upon the creation and use of effectiveness data, whether at the level of the school or of the individual teacher. Thus our model relates to policies for school improvement by enabling data on teacher effectiveness to be drawn upon as part of the data available for school self-evaluation. There are three areas of particular importance here.

Our model will provide data on the interactions between the levels of the individual teacher and the department and whole-school levels. This should enable a school development plan to identify the strengths and development needs of individual teachers and, most importantly, to recognise the strengths and development issues at the school level which can help support teacher improvement. That is to say, our model assumes that teacher effectiveness is not simply an individual responsibility – a matter of praise or blame for the individual teacher – but is a whole-school responsibility. Teacher effectiveness and school effectiveness are interrelated. Moreover, the data that can help realise this reciprocal accountability can be made available through the methodology of the model.

Second, in principle at least, despite practical and logistical difficulties of timetabling, the model also offers schools the promise of improved deployment of staff expertise; teachers demonstrably more effective with particular groups of pupil, such as those with special educational needs, or older students, might be used to teach these groups more, or might provide school-based training for other staff. Qualitative evidence on effectiveness would be especially important here if teachers have to articulate the reasons and methods that they believe make them more effective with particular groups of pupils.

Thirdly, there is almost no direct evidence showing that teacher development strategies pay off in terms of improved pupil outcomes. This is partly because direct causal links are difficult to demonstrate and partly because evidence linking teacher development with improved pupil outcomes, whether in behaviour or learning or both, is rarely sought, according to Campbell *et al.* (2002). Our model would enable much more valid measurement of teacher effect associated with teacher development to be made, and possibly with school development also.

Policies on inclusivity and social justice

School effectiveness research, and to a lesser extent teacher effectiveness research, has been criticised for doing little to address the problems of social injustice and exclusion (Thrupp 1999, Slee *et al.* 1998, Weiner 2002). In radical form, this criticism sees the school effectiveness movement as reactionary because it appears to ignore the inequalities of social and intellectual capital in a class-based system, and provides a basis for attributing responsibility for poor educational performance to schools rather than to a social-class based political economy. We think that some of this criticism is misplaced for two reasons. First, it criticises school effectiveness researchers for not achieving objectives that they did not attempt to achieve (Hopkins and Reynolds 2001). Second, some studies (Mortimore 1998) have developed a social perspective, showing that the effectiveness of some schools is significantly higher than that of other schools with pupil intakes with similar social characteristics. As Mortimore argues, this kind of evidence challenges social and educational determinism, and, furthermore, has attempted to identify the features of the most effective schools. Nevertheless there is some force in the view that an approach to educational effectiveness that largely ignores the social, economic and political context within which the education system functions is at least open to question.

There is also the conclusion (Goldstein and Woodhouse, cited in Weiner 2002) that the models available are only as good as the data they incorporate, the robustness and validity of which are sometimes exaggerated. Because of this danger of over-ambitiousness in respect of data collection we have tried in this section of the book to be even more tentative than elsewhere.

Nevertheless, our model of teacher effectiveness can contribute to this issue because of the differentiation incorporated into it. Our assumption, based on some research in the USA (Brookover *et al.* 1979, Teddlie and Stringfield 1993), is that teachers will be effective to different degrees with different categories of pupil, and that effectiveness with pupils in circumstances of poverty and deprivation may require substantively different instructional and motivational skills, and possibly different pedagogical frames (Bernstein 1975), from those required for teaching pupils from more affluent homes and therefore with greater social and intellectual capital. There is currently inadequate research, so this dimension of our work in particular will need further investigation.

Conclusion

The model we propose is tentative and exploratory and cannot deliver all that researchers and policy-makers might wish in the short term. It needs further testing and research before the kinds of contributions outlined above are realisable. The model might also seem too complex for schools to engage with, although it need not involve high levels of bureaucracy as some performance measurement models do. As part of the contribution to testing the model through research, the following chapter reports a hitherto unpublished study using the model in which aspects of differentiated teacher effectiveness are investigated.

Part IV

Differentiated teacher effectiveness research: the model in practice

12 A study of aspects of differentiated effectiveness

The purpose of this chapter is to illustrate the application of the model on differentiated teacher effectiveness in a specific research project. The project was conducted to develop a theoretical framework of educational effectiveness research based on Creemers' (1994) comprehensive model of educational effectiveness. Creemers' model and the main findings of the four studies conducted to test its validity (De Jong and Westerhof 1998, Reezigt *et al.* 1999, Driessen and Sleegers 2000, Kyriakides *et al.* 2000) have been presented in Chapter 8 and referred to elsewhere in the book. Six issues arising from these studies influenced the design of the study.

- The unexplained variance (more than 25%) at the pupil level, which might require further variables to be included in the model (Kyriakides *et al.* 2000).
- The decision of Creemers to include SES in his model enables testing of the idea that pupil attainment was not entirely determined by academic and social background characteristics (Rutter *et al.* 1979, Reynolds 1976, Reynolds and Sullivan 1979).
- The capacity of teachers to perform effectively with different groups of pupils according to their personal characteristics, such as thinking style, personality, motivation (Reezigt *et al.* 1999, Driessen and Sleegers 2000, Kyriakides *et al.* 2000, Opdenakker and Van Damme 2000). Evidence supporting a strong relation between achievement, personality and thinking style (Kline 1983, Sternberg 1985, Fontana 1986, Jonassen and Grabowski 1993, Braden 1995, Furnham 1995) suggests that if the variables type of personality and thinking style are taken into account more variance at the pupil level might be explained.
- The consistency of educational effects, i.e. the extent to which the factors found to be associated with educational effectiveness are

the same irrespective of the criterion used to measure effectiveness. There is some evidence that the results of school effectiveness research (SER) are heavily dependent on the choice of outcome measures used (Opdenakker and Van Damme 2000, Teddlie and Reynolds 2000). Our model suggests that effectiveness in different subjects and in components (also called domains) within subjects, and in different broad domains (cognitive and affective), should be investigated.

- The relationship between generic and differentiated effectiveness, and whether there is an empirical basis for a theory of differentiated teacher effectiveness (see Campbell *et al.* 2003). If Creemers' model could be tested in relation to different criteria of measuring effectiveness and for different groups of students, the robustness of the theory would be strengthened.

Research aims

The summary above suggests the need to operationalise variables in three dimensions: student personal characteristics; subjects, subject components and different domains; and student background factors.

The study therefore attempted to examine the extent to which:

1 the variables 'personality' and 'thinking style' explain variances of achievement at student level and should be included in Creemers' model
2 the variables mentioned in Creemers' model are associated with the effectiveness in teaching the two main subjects of the Cyprus curriculum (i.e. Mathematics and Greek Language) and components within them, and the effectiveness in achieving affective outcomes
3 the variables mentioned in Creemers' model are associated with teacher effectiveness for different groups of pupils
4 homogeneous groups of teachers can be established according to effectiveness with different groups of pupils in Mathematics, Greek Language and in the development of positive attitudes towards the school.

Methods

A study measuring the effectiveness of 32 primary schools and 81 teachers in teaching Mathematics and Greek Language and in helping pupils to develop positive attitudes towards the school was conducted in Cyprus in order to test the main aspects of Creemers' model. Stratified sampling was used to select the 32 Cypriot primary schools. Stratified sampling involves dividing the population into homogeneous groups, each group containing subjects with similar characteristics, and then a random selection from each group is taken (Cohen *et al.* 2000). Thus, the primary schools were divided into four groups. The variables taken into account for dividing the schools into these groups were the location of the school (rural or urban), and the size of the school (small (fewer than six teachers) or big). The choice of the school sample in each group was random. All the Year 6 pupils ($N = 1721$) from each class ($N = 81$) of the school sample were chosen. The chi-square test did not reveal any statistically significant difference between the research sample and the population in terms of pupils' sex. Moreover, the *t*-test did not reveal any statistically significant difference between the research sample and the population in terms of the size of class and of the length of teaching experience of the teacher sample.

Over 30 variables which might enhance time spent learning and opportunity used to learn on the part of students are presented in Creemers' model. These variables can be measured in different ways, which makes testing the model a very complex task. In order to test the main assumptions of the model a selection was made of all possible variables, which were categorised as context, time, opportunity and quality factors.

Dependent variables: cognitive and affective outcomes of schools

Data on pupils' cognitive achievement in Mathematics and Greek Language were collected by using two forms of assessment (external assessment and teacher assessment). A questionnaire was also developed in order to measure pupils' attitudes toward peers, teachers, school and learning, considered as appropriate measures of affective outcomes of schools (Cheng 1993). The questionnaire and the two forms of assessment in Mathematics and Greek Language were administered to all pupils of the school sample who were at the beginning of Year 6 in September 2001. They were also administered to them when they were at the end of Year 6 (i.e. June 2002). The constructions of the tests and the questionnaire were subject to controls for reliability and validity.

Structural equation modelling procedures were used to examine the construct validity of the Language and the Mathematics tests

(Kyriakides and Gagatsis 2003). In addition, the concurrent validity of each test was examined by taking into account data from teachers' reports. Teachers were asked to complete a report for each pupil indicating whether the child had acquired each skill of Mathematics and Language curriculum for Year 6 (Ministry of Education 1994). More specifically, teachers were asked to rate pupils as 'developing competence', 'competent' or 'above average' for each section. These responses were scored 0, 1 and 2 respectively. Using the Spearman correlation coefficient it was possible to identify significant correlations ($p < .001$) between findings gathered from the written tests and findings from teachers' assessment for each aspect of pupils' knowledge in Mathematics and Greek Language. All the values of Spearman correlation coefficients were higher than 0.35 and lower than 0.63. The concurrent validity of the test is satisfactory since the use of both internal and external ways of assessment provides a basis for triangulation of data (Cohen *et al.* 2000).

As far as the predictive validity of each test is concerned, the multiple correlations between attainment at the beginning of Year 6 and attainment at the end of Year 6 in each subject were higher than 0.65 and provided a satisfactory starting point for value-added analysis. The combination of teacher-completed checklist and the written test provided the best indicator of pupils' subsequent attainment in each subject, better than either type of assessment in isolation. For this reason, it was decided that the dependent variables on pupils' achievement in each subject could arise from a calculation of the average of each pupil's score in the written test and the relevant teacher's report form.

A first-order Confirmatory Factor Analysis model designed to test the multidimensionality of a theoretical construct (Byrne 1998) was used in order to examine the construct validity of the questionnaire used to collect measures of affective outcomes of schools. The findings of the first-order factor standard error of the mean (SEM) analysis generally affirmed the theory upon which the questionnaire was developed, since criteria fit for a four first-order factor model (scaled $\chi^2 = 69.2$, d.f. $= 48$, $p < .011$; RMSEA $= 0.029$ and CFI $= 0.976$) provided values that are in line with the generally accepted guidelines for model fit. Thus, a decision was made to consider the four-factor structure as reasonable and the analysis proceeded and the parameter estimates were calculated. However, the relatively high values of the factor intercorrelations (i.e. higher than 0.48) revealed that a higher order model which could explain the correlations among the four first-order factors could be developed. This model hypothesised that: (a) responses to the questionnaire could be explained by four first-order factors and one second-order factor; (b) each questionnaire item would have a nonzero loading on the factor it was designed to measure, and zero loadings on all other factors; (c) error terms associated with each item would be uncorrelated, and (d) covariation among the four first-order factors would be explained by their regression on the second-order factor. The fit statistics (scaled $\chi^2 = 63.6$, d.f. $= 46$, $p < .008$; RMSEA $= 0.027$ and CFI $= 0.979$) were acceptable. By comparing the second-order factor model with the theoretical first-order factor model, we could identify a minor decrease of the RMSEA (from 0.029 to 0.027) and a very minor increase of the CFI (from 0.976 to 0.979). Thus, the single second-order model was considered appropriate (Maruyama 1998) and thereby the analysis proceeded and the parameter estimates were calculated. In terms of theory, the second-order factor, which has been identified through SEM analysis, represents a general measure of affective outcomes of schools. For this reason, it was decided that the dependent variable on students' attitudes towards schools could arise from a calculation of the average of each pupil's scores in each of the four parts of the questionnaire measuring pupils' attitudes towards peers, teachers, school and learning respectively.

The reliability of the data from the two forms of assessment and from the administration of the questionnaire was measured by calculating the relevant values of Cronbach Alpha for the scales used to measure pupils' knowledge in Mathematics and Language and the four subscales of the questionnaire concerning pupils' attitudes. The values of Cronbach Alpha for the scales used to measure pupils' responses to the two forms of assessment and the four subscales of the questionnaire are shown in Table 12.1. We can observe that all values of Cronbach Alpha were higher than 0.82 and this implies that we can be confident about the reliability of the measures used to collect data on student cognitive and affective outcomes (Cronbach 1990).

The following paragraphs present the variables defined at the level of the pupil, the classroom and the school. Questionnaires to pupils of Year 6, teachers and head teachers were administered in order to collect data about the variables used to test Creemers' model. In addition, observations were conducted in order to measure teacher behaviour in the classroom. The procedures used for measuring each variable were similar to those followed by Kyriakides *et al.* (2000).

Table 12.1 Internal consistency reliability for each domain of the two forms of assessment in Mathematics and Language and for each subscale of the inventory measuring affective outcomes of schools administered at the beginning and at the end of school year 2001–2002

Instrument/Domains and subscales	Cronbach Alpha	
	Beginning	End
A) Mathematics: written test		
Total test score	.91	.92
Domain 1: Numbers and calculations	.88	.90
Domain 2: Handling data (data representation, analysis, and probability)	.90	.89
Domain 3: Measurement	.88	.87
Domain 4: Geometry	.91	.89
Domain 5: Solving problems	.89	.88
B) Mathematics: teacher assessment		
Total test score	.88	.89
Domain 1: Numbers and calculations	.87	.86
Domain 2: Handling data (data representation, analysis, and probability)	.90	.88
Domain 3: Measurement	.86	.89
Domain 4: Geometry	.87	.86
Domain 5: Solving problems	.86	.87
C) Greek Language: written test		
Total test score	.88	.89
Domain 1: Reading and comprehension	.86	.87
Domain 2: Writing	.85	.87
Domain 3: Listening	.85	.86
D) Greek Language: teacher assessment		
Total test score	.88	.87
Domain 1: Reading and comprehension	.85	.85
Domain 2: Writing	.86	.88
Domain 3: Listening	.87	.89
E) Questionnaire on affective outcomes		
Total scale:	.88	.87
Subscale 1: Attitudes towards peers	.87	.87
Subscale 2: Attitudes towards teachers	.84	.85
Subscale 1: Attitudes towards schools	.83	.87
Subscale 1: Attitudes towards learning	.86	.86

Variables at the pupil level

Aptitude

The model states aptitude as one of the variables that influence time spent and opportunity used. Aptitude refers to the degree in which a pupil is able to perform the next learning task. For the purpose of this study, it consists of prior knowledge of each subject (i.e. Mathematics and Greek Language) emerging from the two forms of baseline assessment, and their attitudes towards education emerging from students' responses to the questionnaire administered at the beginning of the school year.

Pupil background factors

Information was collected on three pupil background factors: pupil's age, pupil's sex, and pupil's socio-economic status (SES). Five SES variables were available: the educational level of the father, the educational level of the mother, the social status of father's job, the social status of mother's job and the economic situation of the family. Relevant information for each child was taken from the school records. The SES scores were measured on a seven-point scale ranging from lower to higher social class.

Motivation in Mathematics and Greek Language

Motivation in each subject was measured in two different ways: as *perseverance* and as *subject motivation*. The perseverance scale for each subject consisted of ten items of the questionnaire administered to all pupils which asked them to indicate the extent to which they put effort into learning Mathematics (five items) and Greek Language (five items). The scales used had a range from 1 to 4 (never = 1, and 4 = always) and the scores were averaged so the lowest score was 1 and the highest was 4. Analysis of the data revealed a relatively homogeneous scale for both Mathematics ($a_m = 0.82$) and Greek Language ($a_1 = 0.81$). Two six-item scales were also developed to measure pupils' motivation for Mathematics and for Greek Language. Pupils could score from 0 to 1 on each of the items. After recoding, a score of 0 meant that students were not motivated and a score of 1 meant that they were highly motivated. For each pupil an average score was calculated for each subject and both scales were homogeneous ($a_m = 0.82$ and $a_1 = 0.86$).

Expectations

Expectations were measured through eight items of the questionnaire asking each pupil to indicate the extent to which his/her parents and his/her friends believe that it is important to do well in Mathematics ($n = 4$) and Language ($n = 4$). For each pupil an average score was calculated ranging from 0 to 1. Similarly, expectations concerning the achievement of affective aims were measured through eight questionnaire items asking pupils to indicate the extent to which his/her parents and his/her friends believe that it is important to develop positive attitudes towards peers, teachers, schools and learning. Analysis of the data revealed that the three scales concerning expectations in mathematics, language and affective school outcomes were homogeneous ($a_m = 0.83$, $a_l = 0.79$, and $a_{af} = 0.86$).

Students' personality

Students' personality was measured by 'the personality inventory' which included a total of 50 items, ten for each of the 'Big Five' factors of personality. The items included in this inventory were selected according to the results of a previous study so as to represent the main facets involved in each of the Big Five factors (Demetriou *et al.* 2003) and they were drawn from an extended Greek version of an inventory addressed to the Big Five factors (Besevegis *et al.* 1996). The items addressing agreeableness referred to altruism (e.g. I am compassionate, I care about other people's problems) and compliance (e.g. I am understanding, I am kind). The items addressing neuroticism referred to emotional reactivity (e.g. I get angry easily, I like to get things my own way) and emotional instability (e.g. I am nervous, I tend to react negatively to everything). The items addressing conscientiousness referred to order and will to achieve (e.g. I am orderly, I am organised) and to school performance (e.g. I am diligent, I am lazy). The items addressed to openness to experience referred to intellect (e.g. I am clever, I learn easily) and to openness (e.g. I am inventive, I take initiatives). The items that addressed extroversion referred to sociability (e.g. I am outgoing, I am sociable) and introversion (e.g. I am lonely, I shut myself off). Based on the results of an exploratory factor analysis of students' responses to the 50 items of the personality inventory (explaining 66% of the total variance), three mean scores were created for each student to represent his/her performance on each of the five factors of personality. Thus, the first-order factor structure of the personality inventory was investigated to determine whether the five factors of personality defined in the literature explain the variability in the 15 mean scores, or whether there is a single latent factor that can explain better the variability in these scores. The findings of the first-order factor SEM analysis generally affirmed the theory upon which the inventory was developed. Although the scaled chi-square for the five-factor structure ($\chi^2 = 125.8$, d.f. $= 80$, $p < .001$) as expected was statistically significant, the RMSEA (0.030) and the CFI (0.969) both met the criteria for acceptable level of fit. Thus, a decision was made to consider the five-factor structure as reasonable and the analysis proceeded and the parameter estimates were calculated. It was found out that all parameter estimates were statistically significant ($p < .001$) and that the correlations among the five factors were positive but smaller than 0.13. The low values of the factor intercorrelations provided support for the separation of the five factors in the personality inventory. This finding is also in line with the fact that there is no single general factor in personality (Kohnstamm and Mervielde 1998). Thus, for each pupil an average score was calculated for each of the five factors and all scales were homogeneous (i.e. the values of Cronbach Alpha were higher than 0.77).

Students' thinking style

Students' thinking style was measured by a short version of the 'Thinking Styles Inventory' which included a total of 60 items. The items included in this inventory were selected according to the results of a previous study (Demetriou *et al.* 1999) so as to represent the thinking styles of each of the five dimensions of mental self-government (Sternberg 1988). As far as the dimension of *functions* is concerned, the questionnaire included three items addressing the *legislative* style (e.g. When I have to undertake a task, I like to deal with it by using my own ideas), six items addressing the *executive* style (e.g. I like to follow definite rules or directions when I have to solve a problem or do a task), and four items addressing the *judicial* style (e.g. I like to check and rate opposite points of view or conflicting ideas). In regard to *forms*, four items addressed the *monarchic style* (e.g. When I try to reach a decision, I tend to focus on one major factor), four items addressed the *hierarchical style* (e.g. I like to make a list of the tasks I have to do and order them by their importance), four items addressed the *oligarchic style* (e.g. When I have to undertake a lot of important tasks, I begin with doing the things that my teachers and myself consider as most important), and four items addressed the *anarchic style* (e.g. I like to tackle all kinds of problems, even seemingly trivial ones). In regard to *levels*, three items addressed the *local style* (e.g. I like dealing with problems that require paying attention to details), and three items addressed the *global style* (e.g. I am more interested in the final product of a project than in its details). As far as the dimension of *scope* is concerned, four items in the battery addressed the *internal style* (e.g. I like to work alone on a task or a problem), and five items addressed the *external style* (e.g. I enjoy working in a team). Finally, the dimension of *leaning* included three items addressing the *liberal style* (e.g. I like questioning old ideas and ways of dealing with things and seek better and new ways), and three items addressing the *conservative style* (e.g. When faced with a problem, I like to use a traditional way to solve it). Based on the results of exploratory factor analyses of students' responses to the items of each of the five dimensions of mental self-government, it was possible to identify factors representing each thinking style but the oligarchic style. Thus, for each pupil an average score was calculated for each of the 12 thinking styles and the value of Cronbach Alpha for the scale of each thinking style was higher than 0.72.

Time factors

Time on task during classes was measured in two different ways. First, each pupil was asked to estimate the proportion of time she/he paid attention during a typical lesson in each subject separately. Second, teachers were asked to rank the pupil to the degree she/he paid attention to the Greek and Mathematics lessons. For purposes of comparability the teacher rankings were transformed to standard scores.

Opportunity factors

Time spent doing homework and time spent on private tuition were seen as measures of the opportunity factor. Culturally, private tuition in Cyprus is very important and a high percentage of pupils attend private lessons. Thus, pupils were asked to report the average amount of time spent on homework and on private tuition in Mathematics and in Greek Language.

Explanatory variables at classroom level

At the classroom level there are three main variables which accounted for learning on the part of pupil: time, opportunity and the quality of instruction. Time and opportunity are supposed to influence directly pupil's learning whereas the quality of instruction is supposed to have an impact on time and opportunity. Moreover, variables concerned with the context of each classroom, such as the average baseline score, the average SES score, and the percentage of girls were measured. The contextual factors were aggregated from the pupil level data.

We were also able to use some variables concerning the characteristics of teachers, and especially background characteristics such as sex, length of teaching experience, and length of experience in teaching each subject to Year 6 pupils. As far as teachers' subject and pedagogy knowledge is concerned, which is a variable not included in the Creemers' model but examined in TER, we collected data on whether teachers were holders of postgraduate qualifications and on whether they attended postgraduate courses on teaching Mathematics and/or on teaching Greek Language.

Quality of teaching

In the literature there is a debate as to whether quality of teaching is best evaluated by independent observers or by pupils (Aleamoni 1981, Fraser 1995a). Both methods have advantages and disadvantages. Advantages claimed for questionnaires to pupils are that they are based on pupils' experiences over many lessons and that they have been found to account for more variance in student learning outcomes than have directly observed variables (Ellet 1997, Fraser 1995b). On the other hand, the judgements of independent observers are seen as more reliable and valid than the judgements of pupils (Rosenshine and Furst 1973). In this study, quality of teaching was measured by both independent observers and pupils.

First, it was decided to measure the quality of instruction by asking pupils to respond to 50 items of the questionnaire administered to them. The 50 items emerged from a review of the literature on teacher effectiveness (Scheerens 1990, Muijs and Reynolds 2001a, Kyriakides *et al*. 2002) and covered: (a) classroom management, (b) the form and quality of teachers' organised lessons, and (c) classroom climate. More specifically, key indicators of effective classroom management included: good preparation of the classroom and installation of rules and procedures at the beginning of year; smoothness and momentum in lesson pacing; consistent accountability procedures and clarity about when and how students can get help and about what options are available when they finish (Doyle 1986). Items concerning the form and quality of teachers' organised lessons were divided into those that involve teachers' skills in giving information (structuring), asking questions (soliciting) and providing feedback (reacting). Finally, as far as classroom climate is concerned, students were asked to provide information regarding the extent to which their classroom environment was businesslike and supportive for the students (Walberg 1986). Although it was not practical to include in the questionnaire items reflecting all the elements of quality of teaching as described in the extended analysis of Scheerens and Bosker (1997: 123–133), it can be claimed that the three dimensions of teacher behaviour which were examined covered the most consistently replicated findings of TER (see Chapter 4). Thus, pupils were asked to indicate the extent to which their teacher used certain ways of teaching in Mathematics and in Greek Language on a four-point scale (never = 1, 4 = always). The scores were transformed so that 1 indicated poor practice and 4 good practice. Thus, the score for each teacher was the mean score of the Year 6 pupils of the class she/he taught in each questionnaire item. A generalisability study on the use of students' ratings on this questionnaire provided further support for the use of pupil surveys for teacher evaluation (Kyriakides 2003c).

An eight-factor model was derived from exploratory factor analysis of students' responses to items dealing with teaching practice in Mathematics, since it was found that eight eigenvalues were greater than 1. Moreover, 68% of the total variance was attributable to the first eight factors and this means that a model with eight factors could be considered adequate to represent the data. The rotated factor matrix which was derived by using the varimax rotation procedure revealed that the 50 questionnaire items could be classified into eight factors, which consisted of items which refer to teachers ability in: (1) maintaining appropriate classroom behaviour, (2) maintaining attention on lesson, (3) giving information, (4) asking questions, (5) providing feedback, (6) providing practice and application opportunities, (7) establishing a businesslike and supportive environment, and (8) establishing positive relationships with students. High inter-item reliability was identified, with all item–total correlations within each factor being highly significant ($p < .001$). Acceptable levels of internal consistency were indicated by Cronbach's Alpha coefficients ranging from .72 to .81 for all the factors. Similar results emerge from analysing student responses to items concerning teaching in Greek Language. Thus, these eight subscales (factors) were taken as the operationalisation of quality of teaching in each subject as perceived by pupils, and for each teacher 16 different scores for quality of teaching were generated, by calculating the classroom average of each factor score in each subject.

Second, high-inference observation measures were used in order to collect data about the quality of teaching. Observations were carried out by three members of the research team and inter-rater reliability was satisfactory ($r = 0.65$, $p < .01$). Further details about the observation instrument may be found in Kyriakides (2002). The Extended Logistic Model of Rasch (Andrich 1988) was used to analyse the data collected through observations of teacher behaviours and a scale was created and analysed for reliability, fit to the model, meaning and validity. Analysis of the data revealed that the instrument had satisfactory psychometric properties but its reliability should be improved. The conceptual design of the instrument for three subscales concerning classroom management (i.e. similar to items of factors 1 and 2 emerging from student ratings), the form and quality of teachers' organised lessons (i.e. similar to factors 3 up to 6) and classroom climate (similar to factors 7 and 8) was also confirmed. Thus, these three subscales were taken as the operationalisation of quality of teaching in each subject as emerged from external observations and thereby for each teacher six different scores for his/her quality of teaching were generated, by calculating the relevant Rasch person (i.e. teacher) estimate in each subscale.

Time factors

Anderson's (1995) definition of instruction time was taken into account in order to estimate the total time spent teaching on the part of teacher. Thus, the total of lessons cancelled and the total of lessons officially intended to be spent on mathematics, but used for other purposes, was subtracted from the total of lessons allocated to mathematics in the whole year. This gave the actual time spent teaching mathematics. The same approach was used in order to estimate the actual time spent teaching Greek Language.

Opportunity to learn

Opportunity to learn was measured through six items of the questionnaire to teachers concerned with the amount of homework their pupils were usually asked to undertake in Greek Language. For each teacher an average score was calculated ranging from 0 to 1. The same approach was used in order to measure opportunity to learn in

Mathematics. Analysis of the data revealed that both scales were homogeneous ($a_m = 0.83$ and $a_1 = 0.79$).

Explanatory variables at school level

Context

In order to investigate the school effect, school contextual factors such as the average prior knowledge score in each subject, the average SES score and the proportions of girls were measured. These factors are all aggregated from the pupil-level data. Moreover, the type of school was taken into account and schools were divided into small (fewer than six teachers) and big (more than five teachers).

In Creemers' model, the school level is considered conditional for the classroom level. Its influence on outcomes is mediated by the classroom factors. Therefore, only those factors conditional for the quality of instruction, time and opportunity to learn are seen as important at the school level and were measured in this study. School effectiveness factors as well as climate factors have often been operationalised as perceptions of people (Anderson 1982, Creemers and Reezigt 1999). Although perceptions lack objectivity, objective indicators of school climate are hard to use (Teddlie and Meza 1999). In addition, Hoy *et al.* (1990) argue that perceptions of climate factors may differ from one person to another in the same organisation. For example, school rules about classroom instruction perceived by the head teachers may differ from the quality of school rules perceived by the teachers. For this reason, it was decided to use two different methods to collect data about the school effectiveness factors. First, all teachers of the 32 sample schools were asked to answer a questionnaire concerning the school effectiveness factors, described below. The score for each school was the mean score of its teachers for each scale used to measure the school effectiveness factors. The same questionnaire was also administered to the head teachers of these 32 schools. For each school effectiveness factor, an average score of its head teacher's responses to the relevant questionnaire items was calculated.

Quality factors

At the school level we can distinguish conditions for the quality of instruction with respect to the educational aspects concerning *rules and agreements about aspects of classroom instruction*, especially grouping procedures and teacher behaviour. Six items were used to create a scale measuring the existence of school rules and agreements about classroom instruction in teaching Mathematics. Similar items were used to measure the existence of school rules and agreements about instruction in teaching Greek Language. More specifically, teachers and head teachers were asked to give their opinions on a five-point scale ranging from 1 (there are no rules and the teacher is autonomous) to 5 (there are clear rules which have to be followed by the teachers). A similar approach was used to measure the existence of school rules in terms of how teachers can help their pupils develop positive attitudes towards peers, teachers, school and learning. Analysis of teachers' responses revealed three homogeneous scales which were used to measure the degree of autonomy of teachers about classroom instruction in teaching Mathematics ($a_t = .78$), in teaching Language ($a_t = .81$) and in achieving the main affective aims of education ($a_t = .80$). One-way analysis of variance revealed that the variation of teachers' responses between the schools in each of the three scales was substantially greater ($p < .001$) than that within schools. It was therefore decided to use the mean score of all teachers in a school as the score of the school in each of the three main criteria for measuring educational effectiveness. Data from head teachers' responses revealed three homogeneous scales which were used to measure head teachers' attitudes towards the degree of auton-omy of teachers about: (a) classroom instruction in Mathematics ($a_h = .77$), (b) classroom instruction in Greek Language ($a_h = .78$) and (c) ways of improving schools' affective outcomes ($a_h = .74$).

Conditions for the quality of instruction was also measured by investigating the *school policy on students' assessment*. Twelve items of the questionnaire administered to both teachers and head teachers were concerned with rules and agreements related to the assessment system of the school, such as the assumptions on which the construc-tion of tests was based, the use of common tests for parallel classes, the use of different methods for monitoring pupils' progress and the use of assessment data for diagnostic and remedial teaching. Data emerging from teachers' and head teachers' responses revealed that the two scales were homogeneous ($a_t = .83$ and $a_h = .80$). Both schools with an assessment system attempting to achieve mainly sum-mative purposes and schools with an assessment policy focused on the formative purposes of assessment were identified.

Time factors

The measurement of time factors at school level emerged from six items asking teachers and head teachers to evaluate the quality of school *rules about time use*, including the school policy on homework, pupil absenteeism and cancellation of lessons. Teachers and head teachers were asked to give their opinions on the usefulness of the school rules about time use. The scale used had a range from 1 to 4 (not useful at all = 1, very useful = 4). Analysis of teachers' responses revealed a relatively homogeneous scale ($a_t = .78$) which could be used to measure teachers' attitudes about the appropriateness of school rules. However, the reliability of data from head teachers' responses to the items of this scale was not satisfactory ($a_h = .36$) and it was decided that the measure of time factors at school level could only arise from the scale mean score of all teachers of each of the 32 schools.

Opportunity to learn

The curriculum is considered a variable which determines conditions for the opportunity to learn at school level because it determines the content taught, the activities to be performed in the classroom or at home and the testing of pupils. In our sample both the Mathematics and the Greek Language curriculum are uniform since they are nationally prescribed, so that it was impossible to investigate the effect of the curriculum. Creemers *et al.* (1992) argue that consensus about the 'mission' of the school can be seen as another indication of the conditions for the opportunity to learn at the school level. Teachers and head teachers were asked to give their opinions on a five-point scale ranging from 1 (there is no consensus about the mission of our school) to 5 (there is absolute consensus about the mission of our school). One-way analysis of variance revealed that the variation of teachers' responses to each item between the schools was substantially greater ($p < .001$) than that within schools. It was therefore decided to use the mean scale score of all teachers in a school as the score of the school. Data from head teachers' responses revealed that the reliability of the scale was not satisfactory ($a_h = .41$). Thus, head teachers' views about the mission of their school were not taken into account.

Results

Creemers' model was tested using 'MLwiN' (Rasbach and Woodhouse 1995) because the observations are interdependent and because of multi-stage sampling since pupils are nested within classes and classes within schools. The dependency has an important consequence. If pupils' achievement within a class or a school has a small range, institutional factors at class or school level may have contributed to it (Snijders and Bosker 1999). Generally dependency can be attributed to the fact that pupils within the same school share the same school environment and communicate with each other and to the fact that pupils within the same class share the same teacher. Multi-level analysis is a method of analysis which cannot cope with missing data. However, the pupils and teachers were asked to complete the questionnaires when they were at the school (with permission given by the Ministry of Education) so that we had full data from 32 schools, 81 classes and 1,721 pupils. In order to achieve the first two research aims, different analyses of data were conducted in order to examine the extent to which the variables in Creemers' model show the expected effects on each of the three dependent variables.

Thus, the first part of this section refers to the results of multi-level analysis in respect to the teaching of mathematics and in respect to each domain of the Mathematics curriculum, whereas results concerning factors associated with effectiveness in teaching Greek Language and its domains are presented in the second part. The third part refers to factors associated with effectiveness in the achievement of affective outcomes of schools. The above multi-level analyses help us identify factors associated with the progress of the whole group of students of our sample. In order to provide answers concerning the third aim of this study, we examine the associations between sex, social-class and teacher effect with primary pupils' progress in achieving: (a) cognitive aims in Mathematics, (b) cognitive aims in Greek Language, and (c) affective aims of schools. The results of these analyses are briefly presented in the fourth part of this section. Finally, we present results of cluster analysis used to identify homogeneous groups of teachers according to their effectiveness in Mathematics, in Language and in affective school outcomes.

Effectiveness in teaching Mathematics

The first step in the analysis is to determine the variance at individual, class and school level without explanatory variables (null model or model 0). The variance in the empty model is 134.41. Of the total variance 98.52 (standard error (SE) = 18.08), 20.43 (SE = 7.22) and 15.45 (SE = 3.98) is accounted for the individual, class and school level. The variance at each level reaches statistical significance ($p < .05$)

and this implies that MLwiN can be used. Table 12.2 shows that 73.3% of the variance is at the pupil level, 15.2% is at the class level and 11.5% is at the school level.

In model 1 the context variables at pupils' level are added to the empty model. The figures of the third column of Table 12.2 show that model 1 explains 51.2% of the total variance and that 8.1% is unexplained at the school level, 9.2% at the classroom level and 31.5% at the pupil level. The likelihood statistics (χ^2) show a significant change between the null model and model 1 ($p < .001$). More specifically, it reveals that adding gender background improves model 1 and that boys achieve higher scores than girls in Mathematics. Prior knowledge in mathematics is the strongest effect in predicting the mathematics achievement score. The analysis revealed an increase of 2.18 for each unit in prior knowledge. Moreover, the socio-economic background (SES) has a strong effect on mathematics achievement score since one unit difference in SES score seems to represent 2.04 difference in math score. Effect strength is a function of the ratio of the coefficient to the standard error and, since the standard error is smaller in the case of prior knowledge (.09) than SES (.12), the effect of prior knowledge in Mathematics is the strongest effect in predicting the math achievement score. Finally, the values of standard errors show that the effects of contextual factors are significant. The smallest effect, gender background, is more than 4 times its standard error and the strongest effect, the prior knowledge, is more than 24 times its standard error. We need to bear in mind here that effect size is not necessarily a reliable guide to effect stability (Heck and Thomas 2000).

In model 2 all the variables at the pupil level except those concerning personality type and thinking style were entered (i.e. 'perseverance', 'math pleasure', 'expectations', 'pupil's self-rated attentiveness', 'teacher-rated attentiveness', 'homework' and 'private tuition'). It was found that 'math pleasure', 'expectations', 'teacher-rated attentiveness' and 'homework' had significant effects. However, these effects are not stronger than prior knowledge and social background. The effect of attentiveness is represented negatively because the lower the score on the scale, the higher is the rating of the attentiveness of pupil. 'Pupil's self-rated attentiveness' had a small but significant effect. However, when 'teacher-rated attentiveness' was entered the effect of 'pupil's self-rated attentiveness' disappeared. The figures of the fourth column of Table 12.2 reveal that model 2 explains 59.1% of the variance and that 24.3% is unexplained at the pupil level, 8.8% at the class level and 7.8% at the school level. The likelihood statistics reveal a statistically significant reduction from model 1 to model 2, which justifies the selection of model 2.

In model 3 the variables at the pupil level which are not included in Creemers' model (i.e. the five types of personality type and the 12 thinking styles) were entered. It was found that two types of personality (i.e. 'conscientiousness' and 'openness to experience') and two thinking styles (i.e. 'executive' and 'liberal') had significant effects. The figures of the fifth column of Table 12.2 reveal that model 3 explains 66.3% of the variance and that 17.6% is unexplained at the pupil level, 8.5% at the class level and 7.6% at the school level. Moreover, the likelihood statistics reveal a statistically significant reduction from model 2 to model 3, which justifies the selection of model 3. Having controlled for both pupil contextual factors and pupil factors mentioned in Creemers' model, the results of model 2 show that 24.3% of the pupil-level variation remained unexplained. By adding the variables at pupil level concerning students' personality and thinking style, the percentage of pupil-level variation remaining unexplained is reduced to 17.6%. Thus, model 3 reveals that although not all personality and thinking style measures were related to achievement gains, the inclusion of these two variables significantly improves the explained percentage of achievement variation at pupil level.

In model 4 the explanatory variables at classroom level were entered. Since the content of learning is considered important, the prior knowledge level of the class was added to the model as a contextual factor. The average SES was also considered as a measure of the context of each class. The following observations arise from the sixth column of Table 12.2. First, the two contextual factors at classroom level showing statistically significant effect were the average prior knowledge in Mathematics and the average SES. Second, none of the variables concerning background characteristics of the classroom teacher was found to be statistically significant. The variables measuring teachers' subject knowledge and teachers' pedagogy knowledge showed very small but significant effects when they were taken in isolation but when entered together none of them had a statistically significant effect. Third, almost all the explanatory variables at classroom level which are included in Creemers' model had a significant effect. The only two variables which did not have a significant effect were the classroom climate measured through external observation and the time on task. It is also important to note that despite the fact that all the variables measuring quality of teaching through pupils' opinions were found to be related with student achievement in mathematics, teachers' abilities to provide practice and application opportunities and to

Table 12.2 Parameter estimates and (standard errors) for the analysis of Mathematics achievement (pupils within classes, within schools)

Factors	Model 0	Model 1	Model 2	Model 3	Model 4	Model 5
Fixed part (intercept)	37.4 (1.31)	37.2 (1.15)	38.2 (0.86)	39.5 (0.78)	41.8 (0.46)	41.9 (0.44)
Pupil level						
Context						
Prior knowledge in maths		2.18 (0.09)	2.13 (0.09)	2.12 (0.09)	2.09 (0.08)	2.03 (0.07)
Sex		−0.82 (0.17)	−0.81 (0.17)	−0.81 (0.16)	−0.78 (0.07)	−0.76 (0.07)
Socio-Economic Status (SES)		2.04 (0.12)	2.03 (0.13)	2.01 (0.11)	2.02 (0.12)	1.96 (0.10)
Motivation						
Perseverance			NSS*			
Math pleasure			1.44 (0.35)	1.42 (0.32)	1.42 (0.31)	1.43 (0.34)
Expectations			1.24 (0.31)	1.21 (0.29)	1.22 (0.28)	1.22 (0.29)
Opportunity used						
Pupil's self-rated attentiveness			NSS			
Teacher-rated attentiveness			−0.99 (0.36)	−0.98 (0.35)	−0.97 (0.36)	−0.98 (0.34)
Time on task						
Homework			0.75 (0.12)	0.73 (0.10)	0.74 (0.11)	0.72 (0.09)
Private tuition			NSS			
Personality						
Emotional stability				NSS		
Conscientiousness				0.73 (0.11)	0.72 (0.10)	0.70 (0.09)
Openness to experience				0.84 (0.11)	0.83 (0.12)	0.82 (0.10)
Agreeableness				NSS		

Thinking style

Legislative	NSS		
Executive	0.78 (0.08)	0.79 (0.09)	0.77 (0.08)
Judicial	NSS		
Global	NSS		
Local	NSS		
Liberal	0.70 (0.11)	0.70 (0.10)	0.69 (0.09)
Conservative	NSS		
Hierarchic	NSS		
Monarchic	NSS		
Anarchic	NSS		
Internal	NSS		
External	NSS		

Classroom level

Context

Average prior knowledge in Maths	2.34 (0.40)		2.20 (0.33)
Average SES	1.44 (0.44)		1.40 (0.42)
Percentage of girls	NSS		

Teacher characteristics

Sex	NSS		
Experience in maths teaching	NSS		
Postgraduate studies in education	NSS		
Specialisation in Mathematics	NSS		

Quality of teaching
A) *Student questionnaire*

Maintaining appropriate classroom behaviour	0.82 (0.09)		0.81 (0.09)
Maintaining attention on lesson	0.91 (0.09)		0.92 (0.09)

continued on next page

Table 12.2 (continued)

Factors	Model 0	Model 1	Model 2	Model 3	Model 4	Model 5
Giving information					0.96 (0.08)	0.97 (0.08)
Asking questions					0.95 (0.09)	0.95 (0.09)
Providing feedback					1.10 (0.09)	0.92 (0.10)
Providing practice and application opportunities					1.11 (0.09)	0.99 (0.09)
Creating a supportive environment					0.85 (0.09)	0.84 (0.09)
Positive relationships with pupils					0.70 (0.09)	0.73 (0.09)
B) External observations						
Classroom management					0.89 (0.09)	0.86 (0.09)
Quality of organised lessons					0.92 (0.08)	0.91 (0.08)
Classroom climate					NSS	
Time on task						
Time spent teaching					NSS	
Opportunity to learn						
Amount of homework assigned					0.01 (0.002)	0.01 (0.002)
School level						
Context						
Average SES						1.12 (0.35)
Average prior knowledge in Maths						1.08 (0.32)
Percentage of girls						NSS
School type						NSS
Quality of instruction						
A) Questionnaire to teachers						
Rules and agreements about aspects of classroom instruction in Maths						0.72 (0.25)

Rules and agreements about ways of improving affective outcomes						0.62 (0.22)
Assessment system focused on formative purposes						0.78 (0.15)
B) Questionnaire to head teachers						
Rules and agreements about classroom instruction in Maths						NSS
Rules and agreements about ways of improving affective outcomes						NSS
Assessment system focused on formative purposes						0.76 (0.13)
Time factors						
Rules about time use						NSS
Opportunity to learn						
Consensus about the 'mission' of the school						NSS
Variance components						
School	11.5%	8.1%	7.8%	7.6%	7.4%	4.3%
Class	15.2%	9.2%	8.8%	8.5%	4.8%	4.8%
Pupil	73.3%	31.5%	24.3%	17.6%	17.2%	17.2%
Absolute	134.41	65.59	54.97	45.29	39.51	35.34
Explained		51.2%	59.1%	66.3%	70.6%	73.7%
Significance test						
χ^2	1225.60	896.67	778.68	638.67	510.45	443.01
Reduction		328.93	117.99	140.01	168.22	67.44
Degrees of freedom		3	4	4	13	6
p-value		.001	.001	.001	.001	.001

* NSS = no statistically significant effect.

provide feedback have the strongest effect in predicting the Mathematics achievement score whereas their ability to develop positive
relations with pupils has the weakest effect. Finally, model 4 explains
71.6% of the variance and 7.4% is unexplained at the school level,
3.8% at the classroom level and 17.2% at the pupil level. A statistically significant reduction between model 3 and model 4 has been
observed, and justifies the choice of model 4.

In model 5 the variables at school level were entered. The following observations arise from the figures in the seventh column of
Table 12.2. First, the two contextual factors at school level which
had a statistically significant effect were the average prior knowledge
in Mathematics and the average SES. The same contextual factors at
classroom level had a statistically significant effect. Second, the
gender background and the school type had no statistically significant
effect. Third, all the variables concerning the quality of instruction at
school level which were measured by taking into account teachers'
opinions had a statistically significant effect, whereas the two variables
concerning the establishment of rules and agreements at school level
measured through head teachers' opinions did not have a significant
effect. Fourth, variables concerning time factors and opportunity to
learn did not have a significant effect. Finally, model 6 explains
75.8% of the variance and 3.8% remains unexplained at the school
level, 3.2% at the classroom level and 17.2% at the pupil level. The
reduction of the likelihood statistic between model 4 and model 5 is
67.44 points and this is a statistically significant change ($p < .001$).

Multi-level analyses of students' achievement in each domain of Mathematics

A brief summary of the results from multi-level analyses of students'
achievement in each domain of Mathematics separately is provided in
this section. The most important findings concerning factors associated
with students' achievement in the five Mathematics domains are as
follows.

First, students' prior knowledge in each domain was found to be the
strongest effect in predicting the relevant Mathematics achievement
score. Similarly, the average prior knowledge level of the class and
the average prior knowledge level of the school showed statistically
significant effect when they were included in model 4 and model 5
respectively. SES was the other contextual variable which was found
to be related with student achievement. However, the effect size of

SES was much smaller in the case of geometry and much stronger in the case of problem-solving.

Second, in each analysis, adding gender background improves model 1. However, the effect of gender background was not consistent since boys achieved higher scores than girls in geometry, measurement, handling data and problem-solving but girls achieved higher scores in numbers and calculations.

Third, all the variables which were added in model 2 and found to be related with mathematics achievement (i.e. motivation, expectations, teacher-rated attentiveness and homework) were also related with achievement in each domain of Mathematics. The only exception is the variable measuring expectations, which was not associated with achievement in geometry. Moreover, achievement in problem-solving was predicted by perseverance and pupil's self-rated attentiveness, which do not have any effect in achievement in any other Mathematics domain.

Fourth, as far as the effect of the five types of personality is concerned, openness to experience is associated with each Mathematics domain except numbers and calculation. Moreover, openness to experience has a stronger effect on achievement in problem-solving than achievement in any other Mathematics domain. On the other hand, conscientiousness was found to be related with all the Mathematics domains except geometry and measurement. The other variable which was included in model 3 was the various types of thinking style. However, there was almost no consistency in relation to the effect of types of thinking style on achievement in each Mathematics domain.

Fifth, none of the variables concerning background characteristics of the classroom teacher was found to be statistically significant except pedagogic knowledge, which was related with measurement. On the other hand, amount of homework assigned was related with achievement in each of the five Mathematics domains.

Sixth, all the variables used to measure quality of teaching except the measure of classroom climate through external observations are associated with student achievement in each Mathematics domain. However, differences in the size of their effects on students' achievement in each domain were found. More specifically, 'providing feedback' was found to be among the two variables with the strongest effects on all the domains but geometry. Moreover, 'providing practice and application opportunities' was found to be one of the two variables with the strongest effects on geometry, measurement, and number and calculations. Similarly, 'asking questions' was found to be one of the two variables with the strongest effects upon 'problem-solving' and 'handling data'. On the other hand, 'positive relationships with pupils' had the weakest effect on achievement in each component except 'problem-solving'.

Finally, consistency was identified in the effect of variables concerning the quality of teaching at school level on students' achievement in each component of Mathematics. More specifically, the establishment of a formative assessment system at the school level is strongly related with achievement in each component. Moreover, the variables at school level on 'time factors' and 'opportunity to learn' are not related to achievement in any component except that 'time factors' is related to achievement in numbers and calculations. Furthermore, the variable concerning teachers' opinions about 'rules and agreements about ways of improving schools' affective outcomes' is not related to achievement in any component but problem-solving.

Effectiveness in teaching Greek Language

We can observe in Table 12.3 that the variance in the empty model (model 0) is 154.23. Of the total variance, 113.36 (SE = 19.03), 25.91 (SE = 7.52) and 14.96 (SE = 3.88) is accounted for the individual, class and school level. The variance at each level reaches statistical significance ($p < .05$) and this implies that MLwiN can be used.

In model 1 the context variables at pupil level are added to the empty model. This model explains 47.7% of the total variance and 8.9% is unexplained at the school level, 12.6% at the classroom level and 30.8% at the pupil level. The likelihood statistics show a significant change between the null model and model 1 ($p < .001$). Prior knowledge in Language is the strongest effect in predicting the Language achievement score. Moreover, adding gender background improves model 1 and girls achieve higher scores than boys in Language. Finally, SES has a strong effect on Language achievement score.

In model 2 all the variables at the pupil level except those concerning personality type and thinking style were entered. It was found that 'language pleasure', 'expectations', 'pupil's self-rated attentiveness', 'teacher-rated attentiveness' and 'homework' had significant effects but none of them is stronger than prior knowledge and SES. The figures of the fourth column of Table 12.3 reveal that model 2 explains 56.9% of the variance and that 22.2% is unexplained at the pupil level, 12.2% at the class level and 8.7% at the school level. Moreover, the likelihood statistics reveal a statistically significant reduction from model 1 to model 2, which justifies the selection of model 2.

In model 3 the five types of personality and the 12 thinking styles were entered. It was found that the two types of personality (i.e. 'conscientiousness' and 'openness to experience') and the two thinking styles (i.e. 'executive' and 'liberal') which had significant effect on achievement in Mathematics (see Table 12.2) had significant effect on Language achievement. However, in the case of Language achievement, global thinking style also had significant effect on student achievement. The figures of the fifth column of Table 12.3 reveal that model 3 explains 64.7% of the variance and that 15.5% is unexplained at the pupil level, 11.7% at the class level and 8.1% at the school level. Moreover, the likelihood statistics reveal a statistically significant reduction from model 2 to model 3, which justifies the selection of model 3. Thus, model 3 of the analysis of language achievement reveals that although not all personality and thinking style measures were related to achievement gains, the inclusion of these two types of measures significantly improves the explained percentage of achievement variation at pupil level in language. The same conclusion has been drawn from the multi-level analysis of students' gains in Mathematics achievement.

In model 4 the explanatory variables at classroom level were entered. The following observations arise from the sixth column of Table 12.3. First, the two contextual factors at classroom level showing statistically significant effect were the average prior knowledge in language and the average SES. Second, the only variable concerning background characteristics of the classroom teacher which was found to be statistically significant was pedagogic knowledge. However, this variable has the weakest effect on students' achievement since the ratio of its coefficient estimate to its standard error is the smallest of all the variables at the classroom level which were found to be related to student achievement. Third, almost all the explanatory variables at classroom level which are included in Creemers' model had a significant effect. The only two variables which did not have a significant effect were the classroom climate measured through external observation and the time on task. Fourth, a comparison of the effect size of the variables measuring quality of teaching through pupils' opinions on student achievement in Language reveals similar findings to those from the analysis of students' achievement in Mathematics (see Table 12.2). More specifically, teachers' ability to provide feedback has the strongest effect in predicting both the Mathematics and Language achievement score whereas their ability to develop positive

Table 12.3 Parameter estimates and (standard errors) for the analysis of Greek Language achievement (pupils within classes, within schools)

Factors	Model 0	Model 1	Model 2	Model 3	Model 4	Model 5
Fixed part (intercept)	34.4 (1.27)	35.2 (1.05)	36.1 (0.86)	37.3 (0.58)	37.8 (0.49)	38.2 (0.42)
Pupil level						
Context						
Prior knowledge in language		2.08 (0.09)	2.08 (0.09)	2.10 (0.09)	2.09 (0.08)	2.07 (0.08)
Sex		0.92 (0.15)	0.89 (0.15)	0.88 (0.16)	0.89 (0.15)	0.89 (0.15)
Socio-Economic Status (SES)		2.06 (0.12)	2.07 (0.13)	2.08 (0.11)	2.06 (0.11)	2.07 (0.11)
Motivation						
Perseverance			NSS*			
Language pleasure			1.41 (0.35)	1.41 (0.34)	1.40 (0.35)	1.42 (0.34)
Expectations			1.21 (0.31)	1.20 (0.29)	1.22 (0.30)	1.22 (0.30)
Opportunity used						
Pupil's self-rated attentiveness			−0.89	−0.86	−0.87	−0.88
			(0.32)	(0.31)	(0.30)	(0.30)
Teacher-rated attentiveness			−0.95	−0.92	−0.91	−0.92
			(0.32)	(0.31)	(0.30)	(0.30)
Time on task						
Homework			0.85 (0.21)	0.83 (0.20)	0.84 (0.21)	0.85 (0.19)
Private tuition			NSS			
Personality						
Emotional stability				NSS		
Conscientiousness				0.73 (0.15)	0.72 (0.14)	0.72 (0.13)
Openness to experience				0.84 (0.11)	0.83 (0.12)	0.82 (0.11)
Agreeableness				NSS		

Thinking style			
Legislative	NSS		
Executive	0.78 (0.12)	0.79 (0.14)	0.77 (0.11)
Judicial	NSS		
Global	0.71 (0.16)	0.70 (0.15)	0.71 (0.15)
Local	NSS		
Liberal	0.70 (0.14)	0.70 (0.14)	0.69 (0.15)
Conservative	NSS		
Hierarchic	NSS		
Monarchic	NSS		
Anarchic	NSS		
Internal	NSS		
External	NSS		
Classroom level			
Context			
Average prior knowledge in language		2.14 (0.35)	2.10 (0.33)
Average SES		1.44 (0.44)	1.63 (0.42)
Percentage of girls		NSS	
Teacher characteristics			
Sex		NSS	
Experience in language teaching		NSS	
Postgraduate studies in education		0.71 (0.24)	
Specialisation in Greek Language		NSS	
Quality of teaching			
A) Student questionnaire			
Maintaining appropriate classroom behaviour		0.82 (0.09)	0.81 (0.09)
Maintaining attention on lesson		0.91 (0.09)	0.92 (0.09)

continued on next page

Table 12.3 (continued)

Factors	Model 0	Model 1	Model 2	Model 3	Model 4	Model 5
Giving information					0.96 (0.08)	0.97 (0.08)
Asking questions					1.05 (0.09)	1.07 (0.09)
Providing feedback					1.09 (0.09)	1.08 (0.09)
Providing practice and application opportunities					0.91 (0.09)	0.93 (0.09)
Creating a supportive environment					0.83 (0.09)	0.84 (0.09)
Positive relationships with pupils					0.68 (0.08)	0.69 (0.08)
B) External observations						
Classroom management					0.83 (0.09)	0.82 (0.08)
Quality of organised lessons					0.79 (0.08)	0.80 (0.08)
Classroom climate					NSS	
Time on task						
Time spent teaching					NSS	
Opportunity to learn						
Amount of homework assigned					0.01 (0.003)	0.01 (0.002)
School level						
Context						
Average SES						1.01 (0.34)
Average prior knowledge in language						1.02 (0.31)
Percentage of girls						NSS
School type						NSS
Quality of instruction						
A) Questionnaire to teachers						
Rules and agreements about aspects of classroom instruction in language						0.71 (0.21)

Rules and agreements about ways of improving affective outcomes						0.64 (0.21)
Assessment system focused on formative purposes						0.75 (0.13)
B) Questionnaire to head teachers						
Rules and agreements about classroom instruction in language						NSS
Rules and agreements about ways of improving aspects of affective outcomes						NSS
Assessment system focused on formative purposes						0.73 (0.11)
Time factors						
Rules about time use						NSS
Opportunity to learn						
Consensus about the 'mission' of the school						NSS
Variance components						
School	9.7%	8.9%	8.7%	8.1%	7.9%	4.0%
Class	16.8%	12.6%	12.2%	11.7%	4.6%	4.6%
Pupil	73.5%	30.8%	22.2%	15.5%	15.5%	15.4%
Absolute	154.23	80.66	66.47	54.44	43.18	37.01
Explained		47.7%	56.9%	64.7%	72.0%	76.0%
Significance test						
χ^2	1045.27	733.14	598.75	478.74	369.62	290.29
Reduction		312.13	134.39	120.01	109.12	79.33
Degrees of freedom		3	5	5	14	6
p-value		.001	.001	.001	.001	.001

* NSS = no statistically significant effect.

relations with pupils has the weakest effect in both cases. Finally, model 4 explains 73.0% of the variance and 7.9% is unexplained at the school level, 3.6% at the classroom level and 15.5% at the pupil level. A statistically significant reduction between model 3 and model 4 has been observed and justifies the choice of model 4.

In model 5 the variables at school level were entered. The following observations arise from the figures in the seventh column of Table 12.3. First, the two contextual factors at school level which had a statistically significant effect were the average prior knowledge in Language and the average SES. Second, almost all the variables concerning the quality of instruction at school level had a statistically significant effect, whereas variables concerning time factors and opportunity to learn did not have a significant effect. Finally, model 6 explains 77.7% of the variance and 3.3% remains unexplained at the school level, 3.6% at the classroom level and 15.4% at the pupil level. The reduction of the likelihood statistic between model 5 and model 6 is 69.33 points, and this is a statistically significant change ($p < .001$).

Multi-level analyses of students' achievement in each domain of language

The most important results from multi-level analyses of students' achievement in each domain of teaching Greek Language are as follows.

First, *pupils' prior knowledge in each domain of language* was found to be the strongest effect in predicting the relevant achievement score in language. Similarly, the average prior knowledge level of the class and the average prior knowledge level of the school show statistically significant effect when they were included in model 4 and model 5 respectively. SES was the other contextual variable, which was found to be related with student achievement in each component of Language.

Second, the effect of gender background was consistent in the case of Language teaching but not in the case of Mathematics. Girls achieved higher scores than boys in each component of Greek Language.

Third, all the variables which were added in model 2 related to Language achievement (i.e. motivation, expectations, teacher-rated attentiveness and homework) were also related to achievement in each component of Language. However, motivation in the case of writing has much stronger effect than in any other component.

Fourth, as far as the effect of the five types of personality is concerned, openness to experience is found to be associated with each component except listening. Moreover, openness to experience has a stronger effect on achievement in writing than achievement in any other component. On the other hand, conscientiousness was found to be related with all components except listening. The other variable which was included in model 3 was the various types of thinking style. However, there was almost no criterion consistency in relation to the effect of types of thinking style on achievement in Language.

Fifth, none of the variables concerning background characteristics of the classroom teacher was found to be statistically significant, except pedagogic knowledge, which was related with all components except reading and comprehension. On the other hand, amount of homework assigned was found to have a strong effect on achievement in each component.

Sixth, all the variables used to measure quality of teaching, except the measure of classroom climate through external observations, are associated with student achievement in each Language component. However, differences in the size of their effects on students' achievement in each component were found.

Finally, consistency was identified in the effect of variables concerning the quality of teaching at school level on students' achievement in each Language component. As with Mathematics, the establishment of a formative assessment system at the school level is strongly related to achievement in each component. Moreover, the variables 'time factors' and 'opportunity to learn' are not related to achievement in any Language component but writing. Furthermore, the variable concerning teachers' opinions about 'rules and agreements about ways of improving schools' affective outcomes' is not related to achievement in any component. However, the variable concerning 'rules and agreements about classroom instruction' is related to achievement in writing only, a finding out of line with the effect of independent variables on Language attainment.

Effectiveness in achieving affective outcomes of schools

Table 12.4 reveals that the variance in the empty model (model 0) is 140.29. Of the total variance, 100.86 (SE = 17.03), 24.97 (SE = 7.24) and 14.45 (SE = 3.81) is accounted for the individual, class and school level. The variance at each level reaches statistical significance ($p < .05$) and this implies that MLwiN can be used. In model 1 the

Table 12.4 Parameter estimates and (standard errors) for the analysis of affective outcomes (pupils within classes, within schools)

Factors	Model 0	Model 1	Model 2	Model 3	Model 4	Model 5
Fixed part (intercept)	34.4 (1.27)	35.2 (1.05)	36.1 (0.86)	37.3 (0.58)	37.8 (0.49)	38.2 (0.42)
Pupil level						
Context						
Prior attitudes		2.38 (0.09)	2.39 (0.09)	2.38 (0.09)	2.39 (0.09)	2.39 (0.08)
Sex		0.90 (0.18)	0.89 (0.17)	0.88 (0.18)	0.89 (0.18)	0.89 (0.18)
Socio-Economic Status (SES)		1.26 (0.14)	1.27 (0.13)	1.28 (0.14)	1.26 (0.13)	1.27 (0.13)
Expectations			1.10 (0.31)	1.10 (0.29)	1.11 (0.30)	1.11 (0.30)
Time on task						
Homework			NSS			
Personality						
Emotional stability				0.71 (0.12)	0.70 (0.12)	0.72 (0.12)
Conscientiousness				0.72 (0.14)	0.71 (0.14)	0.73 (0.13)
Openness to experience				NSS		
Agreeableness				NSS		
Extroversion				NSS		
Thinking style						
Legislative				NSS		
Executive				0.78 (0.12)	0.79 (0.12)	0.78 (0.11)
Judicial				NSS		
Global				NSS		
Local				NSS		
Liberal				0.70 (0.14)	0.70 (0.14)	0.69 (0.14)
Conservative				NSS		

Hierarchic	NSS		
Monarchic	NSS		
Anarchic	NSS		
Internal	NSS		
External	0.71 (0.16)	0.70 (0.15)	0.71 (0.15)
Classroom level			
Context			
Average prior level of attitudes		2.04 (0.33)	2.10 (0.33)
Average SES		1.04 (0.41)	1.43 (0.42)
Percentage of girls		NSS	
Teacher characteristics			
Sex		NSS	
Experience in teaching		NSS	
Postgraduate studies in education		0.79 (0.22)	0.79 (0.22)
Specialisation in any subject		NSS	
Quality of teaching			
A) *Student questionnaire*			
Maintaining appropriate classroom behaviour		0.72 (0.12)	0.71 (0.12)
Maintaining attention on lesson		0.71 (0.10)	0.72 (0.10)
Giving information		NSS	
Asking questions		NSS	
Providing feedback		NSS	
Providing practice and application opportunities		NSS	
Creating a supportive environment		0.93 (0.09)	0.94 (0.09)

continued on next page

Table 12.4 (continued)

Factors	Model 0	Model 1	Model 2	Model 3	Model 4	Model 5
Positive relationships with pupils					0.98 (0.08)	0.99 (0.08)
B) External observations						
Classroom management					0.83 (0.09)	0.82 (0.09)
Quality of organised lessons					NSS	
Classroom climate					1.02 (0.10)	1.03 (0.10)
Opportunity to learn						
Amount of homework assigned					0.01 (0.003)	0.01 (0.002)
School level						
Context						
Average SES						1.02 (0.31)
Average prior attitudes						1.01 (0.34)
Percentage of girls						NSS
School type						NSS
Quality of instruction						
A) Questionnaire to teachers						
Rules about ways of improving affective outcomes						0.94 (0.11)
Assessment system focused on formative purposes						0.65 (0.23)
B) Questionnaire to head teachers						
Rules about ways of improving affective outcomes						0.99 (0.12)

	Model 1	Model 2	Model 3	Model 4	Model 5	Model 6
Assessment system focused on formative purposes						NSS
Time factors						
Rules about time use						NSS
Opportunity to learn						
Consensus about the 'mission' of the school						0.84 (0.12)
Variance components						
School	14.3%	13.4%	131%	13.0%	12.9%	6.9%
Class	17.8%	16.5%	16.2%	16.2%	5.6%	5.6%
Pupil	67.9%	24.8%	20.2%	13.8%	13.5%	13.4%
Absolute	140.29	76.73	69.44	60.32	44.89	36.33
Explained		45.3%	50.5%	57.0%	68.0%	74.1%
Significance test						
χ^2	1124.25	912.12	847.73	718.42	577.3	487.97
Reduction		212.13	64.39	129.31	141.12	89.33
Degrees of freedom		3	1	5	10	6
p-value		.001	.001	.001	.001	.001

* NSS = no statistically significant effect.

context variables at pupils' level are added to the empty model. The figures of the third column of Table 12.4 show that model 1 explains 45.3% of the total variance and that 9.4% is unexplained at the school level, 16.5% at the classroom level and 28.8% at the pupil level. The likelihood statistics (χ^2) shows a significant change between the null model and model 1 ($p < .001$). More specifically, it reveals that adding gender background improves model 1 and that girls achieved affective aims at higher level than boys. Moreover, prior level of their attitudes towards education is the strongest effect in predicting their final score on a scale measuring their attitudes towards education. Furthermore, SES has a strong effect on the development of positive attitudes towards education. However, the effect of prior level of attitudes towards education is the strongest effect in predicting the development of their attitudes. Finally, the size of the effect of SES is correlated to a much higher degree with cognitive than affective gains (see Tables 12.2, 12.3 and 12.4).

In model 2 the variables 'expectations' and 'homework' were entered but only 'expectations' was found to have significant effect on the achievement of affective aims of schools. The figures in the fourth column of Table 12.4 reveal that model 2 explains 51.5% of the variance and that 23.2% is unexplained at the pupil level, 16.2% at the class level and 9.1% at the school level. Moreover, the likelihood statistics reveal a statistically significant reduction from model 1 to model 2, which justifies the selection of model 2.

In model 3 the variables at the pupil level which are not included in Creemers' model (i.e. the five types of personality and the 12 thinking styles) were entered. It was found that two types of personality traits ('conscientiousness' and 'emotional stability') and three thinking styles ('executive', 'liberal', 'external') had significant effect on final achievement of affective outcomes. The figures of the fifth column of Table 12.4 reveal that model 3 explains 58.0% of the variance and that 16.8% is unexplained at the pupil level, 16.2% at the class level and 9% at the school level. Moreover, the likelihood statistics reveal a statistically significant reduction from model 2 to model 3, which justifies the selection of model 3. Thus, model 3 reveals that the inclusion of measures of personality and thinking styles significantly improves the explained percentage of achievement variation at pupil level in the affective aims of education. This finding also emerged from the multi-level analysis of factors associated with students' cognitive gains in mathematics and language.

In model 4 the explanatory variables at classroom level were entered. The following observations arise from the sixth column of

Table 12.4. First, the two contextual factors at classroom level showing statistically significant effect were the average prior level of attitudes towards schooling and the average SES. Second, the only variable concerning background characteristics of the classroom teacher found to be statistically significant was pedagogy knowledge. Third, all the variables at classroom level concerning quality of teaching had a significant effect except those which refer to the quality of teacher's organised lessons as measured through observations or pupils' ratings. Fourth, a comparison of the effect size of the variables measuring quality of teaching reveals that those which refer to classroom climate have stronger effects than those concerning classroom management. Finally, model 4 explains 69.0% of the variance and 8.9% is unexplained at the school level, 5.6% at the classroom level and 16.5% at the pupil level. A statistically significant reduction between model 3 and model 4 has been observed and justifies the choice of model 4.

The following observations arise from the figures in the seventh column of Table 12.4. First, the two contextual factors at school level which had a statistically significant effect were the average prior attitude towards education and the average SES. Second, the two variables measuring 'rules and agreements about ways of improving schools' affective outcomes' and the variable 'consensus about the mission of the school' were associated with affective aims. Finally, model 6 explains 74.1% of the variance and 3.9% remains unexplained at the school level, 5.6% at the classroom level and 16.4% at the pupil level. The reduction of the likelihood statistics between model 5 and model 6 is 109.77 points and this is a statistically significant change ($p < .001$).

Multi-level analyses of students' achievement in each of the four factors concerning schools' affective outcomes

The most important results which emerge from comparison of the multi-level analyses of students' attitudes towards peers, teachers, school and learning are as follows.

First, prior attitudes in each of the four factors has the strongest effect in predicting the relevant factor score at the end of school year. Similarly, both the average prior level of attitudes towards each factor at the class and at the school level show statistically significant effect when included in models 4 and 5 respectively. SES was the other contextual variable which was found to be related with the development of positive attitudes towards each factor except the development of positive attitudes towards peers.

Second, the effect of gender background was relatively consistent since girls achieved higher scores than boys in each factor of the affective aims of education except in the development of positive attitudes towards peers. Third, the two variables which were added in model 2 (expectations and homework) were related with each factor measuring the achievement of affective aims of schools. Fourth, as far as the effect of the five types of personality is concerned, 'conscientiousness' was found to be related with the development of students' attitudes towards each of the four factors. However, consistency was not identified either in relation to the effect of 'emotional stability', which was found to be related with the development of positive attitudes towards school and learning, or in relation to the effect of 'extroversion', which was found to be related with attitudes towards peers only. Fifth, there was no consistency in the effect of most of the types of thinking style on the development of positive attitudes towards each of the four factors used to measure the affective outcomes of schools. For example, the effect of the liberal style on the development of positive attitudes towards learning is significant, but a negative relation of the liberal thinking style with the development of positive attitudes towards teachers was found.

Sixth, the only variable concerning background characteristics of the classroom teacher which was found to be statistically significant was pedagogic knowledge. However, it is only related with the development of positive attitudes towards learning and with the development of attitudes towards teachers. As far as the effect of explanatory variables at classroom level is concerned, most of the variables used to measure quality of teaching were related with the development of positive attitudes towards education. However, there was no consistency in their effects. It is also important to note that comparison of the parameters of the variables at classroom level and their standard errors reveals that variables measuring the classroom climate had the strongest effect on students' achievement of each aspect of the affective school outcomes. Finally, variables concerning the classroom management and the amount of homework assigned were found to have strong effect on the development of positive attitudes towards learning and schools.

Consistency was identified in the effect of variables concerning the quality of teaching at school level on the development of positive attitudes towards teachers, peers, learning and schools. More specifically, the establishment of rules and agreements about ways of improving schools' affective outcomes at the school level is strongly related with the development of positive attitudes towards peers, teachers, schools and learning. Furthermore, the variable concerning the establishment of a formative assessment system was related with the development of all factors except attitudes towards peers.

Differentiated teacher effectiveness in relation to sex and social class

This section presents findings concerning the third aim of this study and is an attempt to identify the association of sex, social class and teacher effect with pupils' progress in achieving cognitive aims in Mathematics and Greek Language and in achieving the most important affective aims. In order to examine whether there are differentiated teacher effects, we analyse the results from the random effects from each model used to examine the impact of contextual pupil variables on pupils' progress. The second, third and fourth columns of Table 12.5 illustrate the random effects from the model used to examine the impact of contextual factors on pupils' progress in Mathematics, Language and affective outcomes respectively. The following observations arise from Table 12.5.

First, there were significant differences between teachers in the progress in each dependent variable made by their pupils, as indicated by the significant variation in teacher intercepts shown in the 'between teachers' section of Table 12.5. To test whether teachers were also differentially effective in relation to pupils' prior attainment in mathematics, the coefficient for the score derived from pupils' assessment at the beginning of Year 6 (baseline score) in Mathematics was also allowed to vary randomly at level 2. It was then decided to plot the relationship between the baseline score and the score at the end of Year 6 for each teacher. Significant differences ($p < .001$) between teachers in the slope of the lines illustrating the relationship between baseline score in Mathematics and the score of pupils at the end of Year 6 were found. It was also found that the teacher effects were large, and pupils with the same baseline score achieved markedly higher scores at the end of Year 6 in some classes than in others. However, for the great majority of teachers the regression lines did not overlap. Thus, the differential teacher effects in relation to prior attainment were relatively modest. This implies that the teachers that were more effective for pupils with low attainment in Mathematics at the beginning of Year 6 were also usually the most effective for pupils with high attainment in Mathematics at the beginning of Year 6. The

Table 12.5 Estimates and (standard errors) showing random effects of pupil background factors on progress used to investigate differentiated teacher effectiveness in each of the three dependent variables

Random part	Mathematics		Language		Affective aims	
Between teachers (Level 2)						
Intercept	0.094*	(0.021)	0.096*	(0.020)	0.082*	(0.018)
Intercept/Sex	0.001	(0.001)	0.001	(0.001)	0.001	(0.001)
Intercept/Working social class	−0.004	(0.003)	−0.004	(0.004)	−0.003	(0.003)
Intercept/Upper-middle social class	0.005	(0.004)	0.005	(0.005)	0.004	(0.004)
Intercept/Baseline	0.008	(0.007)	0.008	(0.006)	0.009	(0.008)
Sex	0.007*	(0.001)	−0.006*	(0.001)	0.005*	(0.001)
Sex/Working social class	0.003	(0.003)	0.003	(0.002)	0.002	(0.003)
Sex/Upper-middle social class	0.002	(0.001)	−0.002	(0.002)	0.001	(0.001)
Sex/Baseline	0.004	(0.003)	0.005	(0.004)	0.005	(0.003)
Working social class	−0.006*	(0.001)	−0.007*	(0.001)	−0.005*	(0.001)
Upper-middle social class	0.008*	(0.002)	0.009*	(0.003)	0.006*	(0.002)
Baseline	0.015*	(0.005)	0.019*	(0.006)	0.017*	(0.006)
Between pupils (Level 1)						
Intercept	0.523*	(0.025)	0.503*	(0.021)	0.483*	(0.020)
Intercept/girls**	0.021	(0.011)	0.019	(0.010)	0.023	(0.012)
Intercept/working social class**	0.015	(0.009)	0.012	(0.009)	0.017	(0.010)
Intercept/upper-middle social class**	0.017	(0.009)	0.012	(0.008)	0.015	(0.008)
Intercept/baseline**	−0.211*	(0.003)	−0.181*	(0.002)	−0.201*	(0.004)
Intra-teacher correlation	0.132		0.153		0.128	

* Coefficients significant at $p < .05$.
** Although the fit of the model was improved by allowing separate variances of these factors, these results are not directly relevant to the main findings of this study.

same procedure was used in order to test whether teachers were differentially effective in relation to pupils' prior attainment in language and in the achievement of affective aims. No differentiated teacher effectiveness in relation to baseline score in any of the outcome measures was identified.

As is shown in Table 12.5, the same procedure was followed in order to examine whether there was any differentiated teacher effectiveness in relation to sex and social class. More specifically, to test whether the size of the difference between boys and girls varied across teachers, the coefficient for the attainment of boys as a group was allowed to vary randomly at level 2. While the size of the difference between girls and boys varied across teachers, this variation was not statistically significant in any of the three analyses made for each dependent variable. As can be seen in Table 12.5, tests were also made for differential teacher effects in relation to whether pupils belong to the working or middle social class and in relation to whether pupils belong to the upper-middle or middle social class. Neither of these estimates was proved significant (see Table 12.5). It can therefore be claimed that there is no evidence that teachers are differentially effective for different social and gender groups in promoting pupils' progress in any of the three outcome measures. A similar conclusion emerged from a study conducted in Cyprus in relation to differentiated school effectiveness and might be attributed to the absence in Cyprus of any policy on equal opportunities, both nationally and at school level (Kyriakides 2003b). This finding may therefore not be an indication of the lack of differentiated teacher effectiveness in relation to pupils' background characteristics; it implies that further research in countries with a policy promoting equal opportunities is needed.

Homogeneous groups of teachers according to their capacity to promote pupils' progress in three different outcome measures

The last part of this section examines whether teachers are equally effective in promoting the progress of their pupils in Mathematics, in Greek Language and in the development of positive attitudes towards education. Based on the results of multi-level analyses of pupils' progress in each dependent variable, teachers were classified into three groups according to whether they were among the most effective, among the least effective, or in the group of teachers who were neither the most nor the least effective. Table 12.6 presents the number of teachers in each of the three groups constructed for each dependent variable. We can observe that the distributions of whether teachers can be considered among the most effective, or the typical, or the least effective in each of the three dependent variables are similar. However, only 53 out of 81 teachers (65.4%) are considered equally effective across the three ways of measuring effectiveness. This implies that there may be significant differences between the extent to which teachers are effective in Mathematics, Language and in the affective aspects of education. For this reason, we decided to examine further teachers' effectiveness across the three school outcome measures by using Ward's clustering method. Eight homogeneous groups of

Table 12.6 Number of teachers of each of the eight cluster groups and of the whole sample of Cypriot teachers according to the extent to which they are considered effective in each of the three outcome school measures

Effective groups in each measure		Cluster I (N = 5)	Cluster II (N = 7)	Cluster III (N = 41)	Cluster IV (N = 5)	Cluster V (N = 6)	Cluster VI (N = 8)	Cluster VII (N = 4)	Cluster VIII (N = 5)	Sample (N = 81)
Maths	Least		7			1		4		12
	Typical			41		5	8		5	59
	Most	5			5					10
Language	Least		7					1	5	13
	Typical			41	5	6		3		55
	Most	5					8			13
Affective	Least		7					3	2	12
	Typical			41	5		8	1	3	58
	Most	5				6				11

teachers were derived from the cluster analysis since the agglomeration schedule shows a fairly large increase in the value of the distance measure from an eight-cluster (32.6) to a seven-cluster solution (28.5). The following observations about the characteristics of each of these eight cluster groups of teachers arise from Table 12.6.

First, the first three cluster groups comprise teachers who are equally effective across the three school outcome measures. Five teachers are among the most effective teachers in Mathematics, Language and in achieving affective aims of education. On the other hand, seven teachers are among the least effective teachers across the three outcomes of teacher effects. Second, the next three cluster groups comprise teachers who are among the most effective in only one out of the three outcome measures. Teachers of cluster 4 are considered as among the most effective in Mathematics but are neither among the most effective nor among the least effective in language and in the affective aspects of education. Similarly, teachers in cluster 5 are considered as among the most effective in the affective domain but not in the achievement of cognitive aims dealing with Language and Mathematics. Finally, teachers in cluster 6 are among the most effective in language but not in mathematics or in the affective aspects of education. The last two cluster groups comprise teachers who are among the least effective in achieving cognitive aims in one of the two core subjects. Cluster 7 comprises teachers who are among the least effective in mathematics but not all of them are considered as least effective teachers in the other two outcome measures. Similarly, teachers in cluster 8 are among the least effective in language but not in mathematics or in the achievement of the affective aims of education. These findings suggest that the groups of teachers represent differentiated effectiveness across subjects and across cognitive and affective domains.

Implications for research development

Our study revealed that the influences on pupil achievement are multi-level. Classrooms have unique effects on pupil learning, independently of factors operating at the school and individual levels. Moreover, by controlling for both pupil factors and classroom contextual factors, variables at school level explained variation in achievement at school level. This finding supports the main assumptions of Creemers' model and is in line with the findings of the studies conducted in order to examine the validity of the model (De Jong and Westerhof 1998, Kyriakides *et al.* 2000).

However, the most important finding is that most of the variables in Creemers' model showed the expected effects, irrespective of the criterion used to measure effectiveness. Thus, the results show the importance of the main factors in the model – time spent, opportunity to learn and the quality of instruction – since they predicted achievement in both Language and Mathematics and in their components. Moreover, the main assumptions of the model were tested in relation to the achievement of affective aims of primary education. Thus, this study provides further empirical support to Creemers' model.

As far as the aim of the study concerning the identification of additional variables at the student level is concerned, it was found that two types of personality were related to achievement gains in both subjects, and conscientiousness was found to be related with students' gains across the three outcome measures of this study. A similar finding emerged in relation to the effect of thinking styles. It was also found that after all the student variables were entered in the relevant multi-level models, most of the unexplained variance was at the student level. However, the unexplained variance at student level of each model of this study is smaller than the variances remaining unexplained in those studies which did not take into account students' personality and thinking style. It can therefore be argued that both personality and thinking style should be included in Creemers' model and should be considered as predictors of cognitive and affective gains. However, further research is needed in order to identify whether other variables at pupils' level could be related to achievement.

Finally, there is the issue of differentiated effectiveness. The picture arising from this one study, which was not able to include all possible variables, and did not examine teachers' roles outside the classroom, or take account of the organisational context, is mixed, suggesting the need for both generic and differentiated models as a basis for further research. In the present study there was some limited evidence to support the further exploration of a differentiated model. First, some variables were found to be related with student achievement across the three outcome measures, and within each aspect of the three measures. Other variables were found to be related with some outcome measures but not others. Second, there was no criterion consistency in the effect of some variables. Third, we identified different groups of teachers according to how effective they were in achieving different aims of education. Further research is also needed to identify those factors which explain why teachers belong in a particular cluster group. This might call particularly for qualitative data on the explanations that teachers themselves give for their differentiated effectiveness. On other dimensions of differentiation, such as effectiveness with different socio-economic groups, gender and ability, there was less differentiated effectiveness, at least as measured here, than might have been hypothesised. We therefore conclude that further research on differentiated teacher effectiveness may be required to improve both theory building, generic and differentiated, and methodological development.

Bibliography

Ackerman, P. L. (1996) 'A theory of adult intellectual development: process, personality, interests, and knowledge', *Intelligence*, 22: 227–257.

Ackerman, P. L. (1997) 'Personality, self-concept, interests, and intelligence: which construct doesn't fit?', *Journal of Personality*, 65: 172–239.

Ackerman, P. L. and Heggestad, E. D. (1997) 'Intelligence, personality, and interests: evidence for overlapping traits', *Psychological Bulletin*, 121: 219–245.

Adams, J. (1907) *The Practice of Instruction*, London: National Society.

Adey, P. and Shayer, M. (1994) *Really Raising Standards. Cognitive Intervention and Academic Achievement*, London: Routledge.

Aldrich, R. (1995) *School and Society in Victorian Britain*, London: The College of Preceptors.

Aleamoni, L. M. (1981) 'Student rating of instruction', in J. Millman (ed.) *Handbook of Teacher Evaluation*, London: Sage.

Alexander, R. (2001) *Culture and Pedagogy*, Oxford: Blackwell.

Anderson, B. D. and Dorsett, R. (1981) 'Production of academic achievement as a function of teachers' training, experience and salaries', paper presented at the annual meeting of the American Educational Research Association, Los Angeles, CA, April 1981.

Anderson, C. S. (1982) 'The search for school climate: a review of the research', *Review of Educational Research*, 52 (3): 368–420.

Anderson, L. W. (1995) 'Time, allocated and instructional', in L. W. Anderson (ed.) *International Encyclopaedia of Teaching and Teacher Education*, Oxford: Elsevier.

Anderson, R., Greene, M. and Loewen, P. (1988) 'Relationships among teachers' and students' thinking skills, sense of efficacy and student achievement', *Alberta Journal of Educational Research*, 17: 86–95.

Andrich, D. (1988) 'A general form of Rasch's Extended Logistic Model for partial credit scoring', *Applied Measurement in Education*, 1 (4): 363–378.

Apple, M. (1986) *Teachers and Texts: a Political Economy of Class and Gender*, New York: Routledge and Kegan Paul.

Askew, M., Rhodes, V., Brown, M., William, D. and Johnson, D. (1997) *Effective Teachers of Numeracy: Report of a Study Carried Out for the Teacher Training Agency*, London: King's College London, School of Education.

Aubrey, C. (1993) 'An investigation of the mathematical competencies which young children bring into school', *British Educational Research Journal*, **19** (1): 27–41.

Ball, S. (1999) 'Performativity and fragmentation in "postmodern" schooling', in J. Carter (ed.) *Postmodernity and the Fragmentation of Welfare*, London: Routledge.

Bamburg, J. D. (1994) *Raising Expectations to Improve Student Learning*, North Central Regional Educational Lab., Oak Brook, IL.

Bandura, A. (1986) 'Regulation of cognitive processes through perceived self-efficacy', *Developmental Psychology*, **25** (5), 729–735.

Barber, M. (1995) 'Reconstructing the teaching profession', *Journal of Education for Teaching*, **21** (1): 75–85.

Barclay, J. (1996) 'Assessing the benefits of learning logs', *Education and Training*, **38** (2): 30–38.

Barrett, L. A. (1991) 'Relationship of observable teaching effectiveness behaviors to MBTI personality types', paper presented at the International Conference of the Association for Psychological Type, Richmond, VA, July.

Barth, P., Haycock, K., Jackson, H., Mora, K., Ruiz, P., Robinson, S. and Wilkins, A. (1999) *Dispelling the Myth. High Poverty Schools Exceeding Expectations*, Washington, DC: The Education Trust.

Bartlett, S. (1996) 'Teacher appraisal: who is kidding who?', *British Journal of In-Service Education*, **22** (1): 7–17.

Bartlett, S. (1998) 'Teacher perceptions of the purposes of staff appraisal: a response to Kyriacou', *Teacher Development*, **2** (3): 479–490.

Bassey, M. and Mortimore, P. (2001) 'Report on methodological seminar on Hay McBer inquiry into teacher effectiveness', *Research Intelligence*, **76**: 5–9.

Bemis, K. A. and Cooper, J. G. (1967) *Teacher Personality, Teacher Behavior and Their Effects upon Pupil Achievement*, Albuquerque: University of New Mexico.

Bennett, N. (1976) *Teaching Styles and Pupil Progress*, London: Open Books.

BERA (British Educational Research Association) (2001) 'Report on the methodological seminar on the Hay McBer inquiry into Teacher Effectiveness', *Research Intelligence*, **76**: 5–9.

Berliner, D. (1992) 'Some characteristics in experts in the pedagogical domain', in F. Oser, A. Dick and J. Patry (eds) *Effective and Responsible Teaching: the New Synthesis*, San Francisco, CA: Jossey-Bass.

Bernstein, B. (1971) *Class, Codes and Control, Vol. 1: Theoretical Studies towards a Sociology of Language*, London: Routledge and Kegan Paul.

Bernstein, B. (1975) *Class, Codes and Control, Vol. 3: Towards a Theory of Educational Transmissions*, London: Routledge and Kegan Paul.

Besevegis, E., Pavlopoulos, V. and Mourousaki, S. (1996) 'Children's personality characteristics as assessed by parents in natural language', *Psychology: The Journal of the Hellenic Psychological Society*, 3 (2): 46–57.

Bichard, M. (2001) Address to the Department for Education and Employment, cited in R. J. Campbell (2001) 'The colonisation of the primary curriculum', in R. Phillips and J. Furlong (eds) *Education Reform and the State: Twenty Years of Politics, Policy and Practice*, London: RoutledgeFalmer.

Bidwell, C. E. and Kasarda, J. D. (1980) 'Conceptualizing and measuring the effects of school and schooling', *American Journal of Education*, 88: 401–430.

Black, P. (1996) 'The shifting scenery of the National Curriculum', in C. Chitty and B. Simon (eds) *Education Answers Back*, London: Lawrence and Wishart.

Bloom, B. S. (1968) *Learning for Mastery*, Washington, DC: ERIC.

Boles, K. C. (1992) 'School restructuring by teachers: a study of the teaching project at the Edward Devotion School', paper presented at the Annual Meeting of the American Educational Research Association, San Francisco, CA, 20–24 April.

Boles, K. and Troen, V. (1994) 'Teacher leadership in a professional development school', paper presented at the annual meeting of the American Educational Research Association, New Orleans, LA, April.

Bonamy, J., Charlier, B. and Saunders, M. (2001) '"Bridging tools" for change: evaluating a collaborative learning network', *Journal of Computer-Assisted Learning*, 17: 295–305.

Borich, G. D. (1992) *Effective Teaching Methods*, 2nd edn, New York: Macmillan.

Borich, G. D. (1996) *Effective Teaching Methods*, 3rd edn, New York: Macmillan.

Bowles, M. L. and Coates, G. (1993) 'Image and substance: the management of performance as rhetoric or reality?', *Personnel Review*, 22 (2): 3–21.

Braden, J. P. (1995) 'Intelligence and personality in school and educational psychology', in D. H. Saklofske and M. Zeidner (eds) *International Handbook of Personality and Intelligence*, New York: Plenum Press.

Brennan, R. L. (1983) *Elements of Generalizability Theory*, Iowa City, IA: American College Testing Publications.

Briault, E., cited in M. Kogan (1975) *Educational Policy Making: a Study of Interest Groups and Parliament*, London: Allen and Unwin.

Brookover, W. B., Beady, C., Flood, P., Schweitzer, J. and Wisenbaker, J. (1979) *Schools, Social Systems and Student Achievement: Schools Can Make a Difference*, New York: Praeger.

Brophy, J. E. (1986) 'Teaching and learning Mathematics: where research should be going', *Journal for Research in Mathematics Education*, 17 (5): 323–346.

Brophy, J. E. (1992) 'Probing the subtleties of subject matter teaching', *Educational Leadership*, 49 (May): 4–8.

Brophy, J. and Everston, L. (1976) *Learning from Teaching: a Developmental Perspective*, Boston, MA: Allyn and Bacon.

Brophy, J. E. and Good, T. L. (1986) 'Teacher behaviour and student achievement', in M. C. Wittrock (ed.) *Handbook of Research on Teaching*, New York: Macmillan.

Brown, B. W. and Saks, D. H. (1986) 'Measuring the effects of instructional time on student learning: evidence from the beginning teacher evaluation study', *American Journal of Education*, 94: 480–500.

Brown, S. and McIntyre, R. (1993) *Making Sense of Teaching*, London: St Edmundsbury Press.

Bryk, A. S. and Raudenbush, S. W. (1992) *Hierarchical Linear Models*, New York: Sage.

Byrne, B. (1998) *Structural Equation Modeling with LISREL, PRELIS, and SIMPLIS: Basic Concepts, Applications and Programming*, Mahwah, NJ: Lawrence Erlbaum Associates.

Byrne, C. J. (1983) 'Teacher knowledge and teacher effectiveness: a literature review', paper presented at the Annual Meeting of the Northwestern Educational Research Association, Ellenville, NY.

Cameron, K. S. (1984) 'The effectiveness of ineffectiveness', *Research in Organizational Behavior*, 6: 235–285.

Campbell, R. J. (1989) 'HMI and aspects of public policy for the primary school curriculum', in A. Hargreaves and D. Reynolds (eds) *Education Policies: Controversies and Critiques*, London: Falmer.

Campbell, R. J. (1996) 'The National Curriculum in primary schools: a dream at conception, a nightmare at delivery', in C. Chitty and B. Simon (eds) *Education Answers Back*, London: Lawrence and Wishart.

Campbell, R. J., Kyriakides, L., Muijs, D. and Robinson, W. (2003) 'Differential teacher effectiveness: towards a model for research and appraisal', *Oxford Review of Education*, 29 (4): 240–253.

Campbell, R. J., Lindsay, G. and Phillips, E. (2002) 'Professional development of primary school headteachers: the paradox of ownership', *School Leadership and Management*, 22 (4): 359–370.

Campbell, R. J. and Neill, S. R. St J. (1994a) *Primary Teachers at Work*, London: Routledge.

Campbell, R. J. and Neill, S. R. St J. (1994b) *Secondary Teachers at Work*, London: Routledge.

Cardno, J . (1995) 'Diversity, dilemmas and defensiveness: leadership challenges in staff appraisal contexts', *School Organisation*, 15 (2): 117–131.

Carley, M. (1988) *Performance Monitoring in a Professional Public Service*, London: Policy Studies Institute.

Carnoy, M. (1976) 'Is compensatory education possible ?', in M. Carnoy and H. M. Levin (eds) *The Limits of Educational Reform*, New York: David McKay.

Carroll, J. B. (1963) 'A model of school learning', *Teacher College Record*, 64: 723–733.

Carroll, J. B. (1989) 'The Carroll Model: a 25 year retrospective and prospective view', *Educational Researcher*, 18: 26–31.

Chan, C.-C., Chan, K.-Y., Cheung, W.-M., Ngan, M. and Yeung, V.-M. (1992) 'Primary school teacher self concept: its relationship with teacher behaviors and students' educational outcomes', *Primary Education*, 3 (1): 9–28.

Cheng, Y. C. (1993) 'Profiles of organisational culture and effective schools', *School Effectiveness and School Improvement*, 4 (2): 85–110.

Cheng, Y. C. and Tsui, K. T. (1996) 'Total teacher effectiveness: new conception and improvement', *International Journal of Educational Management*, 10 (6): 7–17.

Cheng, Y. C. and Tsui, K. T. (1999) 'Multimodels of teacher effectiveness: implications for research', *The Journal of Educational Research*, 92 (3): 141–150.

Chidolue, M. E. (1996) 'The relationship between teacher characteristics, learning environment and student achievement and attitude', *Studies in Educational Evaluation*, 22 (3): 263–274.

Claparede, E. (1991) *Experimental Pedagogy*, trans. by M. Louch and H. Holman from the 4th edn of *Psychologie de l'Enfant et Pedagogie Experimentale*, London: Edward Arnold.

Clemson-Ingram, R., and Fessler, R. (1997) 'Innovative programs for teacher leadership', *Action in Teacher Education*, 19 (3): 95–106.

Cohen, D., Manion, L. and Morrison, K. (2000) *Research Methods in Education*, 5th edn, London: RoutledgeFalmer.

Coleman, J. S., Campbell, E. Q., Hobson, C. F., McPartland, J., Mood, A. M., Weinfield, F. D. and York, R. L. (1966) *Equality of Educational Opportunity*, Washington, DC: US Government Printing Office.

Compayre, G. (1886) *The History of Pedagogy* (translated by W. H. Payne), Boston: D. C. Heath and Company.

Connell, N. (1996) *Getting off the List: School Improvement in New York City*, New York: New York City Educational Priorities Panel.

Connell, R. (1985) *Teachers' Work*, Sydney: Allen and Unwin.

Cooley, W. W. (1981) 'Understanding achievement test variables', in N. Sovick, H. M. Eikel and A. Lysne (eds) *On Individualized Instruction: Theories and Research*, Oslo: Universitetsforlagel.

Costin, F. and Grush, J. E. (1973) 'Personality correlates of teacher–student behavior in the college classroom', *Journal of Educational Psychology*, 65 (1): 35–44.

Cox, J. (2002) 'Effective pastoral care', paper presented at the Annual Meeting of the American Educational Research Association, New Orleans, LA, April.

Crawford, J. and Impara, J. C. (2001) 'Critical issues, current trends and possible futures in quantitative methods', in V. Richardson (ed.) *Handbook of Research on Teaching*, 4th edn, Washington, DC: AERA.

Creemers, B. P. M. (1994) *The Effective Classroom*, London: Cassell.

Creemers, B. P. M. (1996) *Effective Schools and Effective Teachers: an International Perspective*, CREPE Occasional Paper, Warwick: University of Warwick.

Creemers, B. and Reezigt, G. J. (1999) 'The role of school and classroom climate in elementary school learning environments', in H. J. Freiberg (ed.) *School Climate: Measuring, Improving and Sustaining Healthy Learning Environments*, London: Falmer.

Creemers, B. P. M., Reezigt, G. J. and Werf, M. P. C. (1992) *Development and Testing of a Model for School Learning*, Groningen: RION.

Croll, P. (1996) 'Teacher–pupil interaction in the classroom', in P. Croll and N. Hastings (eds) *Effective Primary Teaching*, London: David Fulton.

Cronbach, L. J. (1990) *Essentials of Psychological Testing*, 3rd edn, New York: Harper and Row.

Cronbach, L. J., Gleser, G. C., Nanda, H. and Rajaratnam, N. (1972) *The Dependability of Behavioral Measurements: Theory of Generalizability Scores and Profiles*, New York: Wiley.

Darling-Hammond, L. (2000) 'Teacher quality and student achievement: a review of state policy evidence', *Education Policy Analysis Archives*, 8 (1): http://epaa.asu.edu/epaa/v8n1/.

Day, C., Harris, A. and Hadfield, M. (2000) 'Grounding knowledge of schools in stakeholder realities: a multi-perspective study of effective school leaders', *School Leadership and Management*, 21 (1): 19–42.

De Corte, E. and Greer, B. (1996) 'Mathematics teaching and learning', in D. C. Berliner and R. Calfee (eds) *Handbook of Educational Psychology*, New York: Macmillan.

De Jager, B. (2002) 'Teaching reading comprehension: a comparison of direct instruction and cognitive apprenticeship on comprehension skills and meta-cognition', unpublished thesis, University of Groningen.

De Jong, R. and Westerhof, K. J. (1998) 'Empirical evidence of a comprehensive model of school effectiveness: a multi-level study in Mathematics in the first year of junior general education in the Netherlands', paper presented at the 10th ICSEI, Manchester.

De Paepe, M. (1987) 'Social and personal factors in the inception of experimental research in education (1880–1914): an exploratory study', *History of Education*, 16: 4: 275–298.

Demetriou, A., Kazi, S. and Georgiou, S. (1999) 'The emerging self: the convergence of mind, personality, and thinking styles', *Developmental Science*, 2: 387–422.

Demetriou, A., Kyriakides, L. and Avraamidou, C. (2003) 'The missing link in the relations between intelligence and personality', *Journal of Research in Personality*, in press, see http://www.sciencedirect.com/science/journal/00926566

Department for Education and Employment (DfEE) (2000) *Research into Teacher Effectiveness, a Model of Teacher Effectiveness*, Report by Hay McBer to the Department for Education and Employment, London: DfEE.

Department for Education and Skills (DfES) (2000) *The National Curriculum, Handbooks for Primary and Secondary Teachers*, London: DfES.

Dickson, G. E. (1983) 'The competency assessment of teachers using high and low inference measurement procedures: a review of research', paper presented at the World Assembly of the International Council on Education for Teaching, Washington, DC, 11–15 July.

Douglas, J. W. B. (1964) *The Home and the School*, London: MacGibbon and Kee.

Doyle, W. (1986) 'Classroom organisation and management', in M. C. Wittrock (ed.) *Handbook of Research on Teaching*, New York: Macmillan.

Driessen, G. and Sleegers, P. (2000) 'Consistency of teaching approach and student achievement', *School Effectiveness and School Improvement*, 11 (1): 57–79.

Dunham, J. (1984) *Stress in Teaching*, Sydney: Croom Helm.

Dunne, R. and Wragg, E. R. (1994) *Effective Teaching*, London: Routledge.

Durkheim, E. (1925) *L'education Morale*, Paris: Libraire Felix Alcan.

Durkheim, E. (1961) *Moral Education*, trans. by E. K. Wilson and H. Schnurer, New York: Free Press of Glencoe.

Duthie, J. (1970) *Primary School Survey*, Edinburgh: Scottish Education Department.

Edmonds, R. E. (1979) 'Effective schools for the urban poor', *Educational Leadership*, 37: 15–27.

Edwards, T. (2003) 'Report of the Colloquium', in BERA, *Educational Policy and Research across the UK*, Southwell: British Educational Research Association, 3–10.

Ellet, C. D. (1997) 'Classroom-based assessments of teaching and learning', in J. H. Stronge (ed.) *Evaluating Teaching: a Guide to Current Thinking and Best Practice*, Thousand Oaks, CA: Sage.

Ernest, P. (1999) 'Forms of knowledge in mathematics and mathematics education: philosophical and rhetorical perspectives', *Educational Studies in Mathematics*, 38 (1): 67–83.

Etzioni, A. (1969) *The Semi-professions and Their Organisation*, Glencoe: Free Press.

Everston, C. M., Anderson, C., Anderson, L. and Brophy, J. (1980) 'Relationships between classroom behaviour and student outcomes in Junior High Math and English classes', *American Educational Research Journal*, 17 (1): 43–60.

Everston, C. M., Anderson, C., Anderson, L. and Brophy, J. (1978) 'Process-outcome relationships in the Texas Junior High School Study', paper presented at the annual meeting of the American Educational Research Association, Toronto, March.

Evetts, J. (1990) *Women Teachers in Primary Education*, London: Methuen.

Fennema, E. and Loef-Franke, M. (1992) 'Teachers' knowledge and its impact', in D. A. Grouws (ed.) *Handbook of Research on Mathematics Teaching and Learning*, New York: Macmillan.

Findlay, J. (1902) *Principles of School Practice*, London: Macmillan.

Findlay, J. (1903) 'The training of teachers', an inaugural lecture delivered at the opening of the Department of Education in the Victoria University Manchester, October 1903, Manchester: Sherratt and Hughes.

Finney, S. J. and Schraw, G. (2003) 'Self-efficacy beliefs in college statistics courses', *Contemporary Educational Psychology*, **28**: 161–186.

Fisher, C. M. (1994) 'The difference between appraisal schemes: variation and acceptability', *Personnel Review*, **23** (8): 33–49.

Fontana, D. (1986) *Teaching and Personality*, New York: Basil Blackwell.

Fraser, B. J. (1995a) 'Students' perceptions of classrooms', in L. W. Anderson (ed.) *International Encyclopaedia of Teaching and Teacher Education*, Oxford: Elsevier.

Fraser, B. J. (1995b) 'Classroom environments', in L. W. Anderson (ed.) *International Encyclopaedia of Teaching and Teacher Education*, Oxford: Elsevier.

Freydenberg, E. (1997) *Adolescent Coping: Theoretical and Research Perspectives*, New York: Routledge.

Fullan, M. (1999) *Change Forces: the Sequel*, London: Falmer.

Furnham, A. (1995) 'The relationship of personality and intelligence to cognitive learning style and achievement', in D. H. Saklofske and M. Zeidner (eds) *International Handbook of Personality and Intelligence*, New York: Plenum Press.

Gahagan, D. M. and Gahagan, G. A. (1970) *Talk Reform. Explorations in Language for Infant School Children*, London: Routledge and Kegan Paul.

Galton, M. (1989) *Teaching in the Primary Classroom*, London: David Fulton.

Galton, M. (1999) *Crisis in the Primary Classroom*, London: David Fulton.

Galton, M. and Blyth, W. A. L. (eds) (1989) *Handbook of Primary Education in Europe*, London: David Fulton/Council of Europe.

Galton, M., Simon, B. and Croll, P. (1980) 'Pupil progress in the basic skills', in M. Galton and B. Simon (eds) *Progress and Performance in the Primary Classroom*, London: Routledge.

Galton, M. and MacBeath, J. (with Page, C. and Steward, S.) (2002) *A Life in Teaching? The Impact of Change on Primary Teachers' Lives*, Cambridge: Faculty of Education, University of Cambridge.

Galton, M., Simon, B. and Croll, P. (1980) *Inside the Primary Classroom*, London: Routledge and Kegan Paul.

Gardner, H. (1983) *Frames of Mind*, New York: Basic Books.

Gardner, H. (1993) *Multiple Intelligences: the Theory in Practice*, New York: Basic Books.

Gaziel, H. M. and Wasserstein-Warnet, M. M. (2000) 'Validité des instruments de decision pour l'evaluation des enseignants?', *European Journal of Teacher Education*, **23** (2): 175–188.

General Teaching Council (GTC) (2001) *Code of Professional Values and Practice for Teachers*, London: GTC.

Giddens, A. (1991) *Modernity and Self-identity: Self and Society in the Late Modern Age*, Stanford, CA: Stanford University Press.

Gipps, C. (1996) *What We Know About Effective Primary Teaching*, London: Tufnell Press.

Gipps, C., McCallum, B. and Hargreaves, E. (2001) *What Makes a Good Primary Teacher? Expert Classroom Strategies*, London: RoutledgeFalmer.

Goldstein, H. (1976) 'Whose values in education?', *Bias*, 3 (1): 1–7.

Goldstein, H. (1995) *Multilevel Statistical Models*, London: Edward Arnold.

Good, T. L. (1979) 'Teacher effectiveness in the elementary school: what we know about it now', *Journal of Teacher Education*, 30 (2): 52–64.

Good, T. L., Grouws, D. A. and Ebmeier, D. (1983) *Active Mathematics Teaching*, New York: Longman.

Graham, D. and Tytler, D. (1993) *A Lesson for Us All: the Making of the National Curriculum*, London: Routledge.

Green, J. (1913) 'Teachers, doctors and Madame Montessori', *Journal of Experimental Pedagogy*, 2 (1): 43–53.

Green, J. and Birchenough, C. (1911) *A Primer of Teaching Practice*, London: Longman.

Green Paper (1998) Cm. 4164, *Teachers: Facing the Challenge of Change*, London: Stationery Office.

Griffin, G.A. and Barnes, S. (1986) 'Using research findings to change school and classroom practice: results of an experimental study', *American Educational Research Journal*, 23 (4): 572–586.

Grigorenko, E. L. and Sternberg, R. J. (1995) 'Thinking styles', in D. H. Saklofske and M. Zeidner (eds) *International Handbook of Personality and Intelligence*, New York: Plenum Press.

Grigorenko, E. L. and Sternberg, R. J. (1997) 'Styles of thinking, abilities, and academic performance', *Exceptional Children*, 63: 295–312.

Grundy, S. and Bonsor, S. (2000) 'The new work order and Australian schools', in C. Day, A. Fernandez, T. Hauge and J. Moller (eds) *The Life and Work of Teachers*, London and New York: Falmer.

Guildford, J. (1980) 'Cognitive styles: what are they?', *Educational and Psychological Measurement*, 40: 715–735.

Gunter, H. (1996) 'Appraisal and the school as a learning organisation', *School Organisation*, 16 (1): 89–100.

Guskey, T. R. (2000) *Evaluating Professional Development*, Thousand Oaks, CA: Corwin Press.

Guthrie, L. F., Guthrie, G. P., Van Heusden, S. and Burns, R. (1989) *Principles of Successful Chapter 1 Programs*, San Francisco, CA: Far West Laboratory for Educational Research and Development.

Hammersley, M. (1991) *Reading Ethnographic Research*, London: Longman.

Hammersley, M. and Atkinson, P. (1983) *Ethnography: Principles and Practice*, London: Tavistock.

Hanushek, E. A. (1979) 'Conceptual and empirical issues in the estimation of educational production functions', *Journal of Human Resources*, **14**: 351–388.

Hargreaves, D. (1997) 'In defence of research for evidence-based teaching', *British Educational Research Journal*, **23** (4): 405–419.

Harris, A. (2000) 'Effective leadership and departmental improvement', *Westminster Studies in Education*, **23**: 81–90.

Harris, A. (2001) 'Department improvement and school improvement: a missing link?', *British Educational Research Journal*, **27** (4): 478–503.

Harris, A. (2002) *School Improvement: What's in it for Schools?*, London: Falmer Press.

Harris, A., Muijs, D. and Gunraj, J. (2004) *Teacher Leadership. Principles and Best Practice. A Report for the GTC and the NUT*, Warwick: University of Warwick.

Hay McBer (2000) *A Model of Teacher Effectiveness*, London: DfEE.

Haynes, F. (1998) *The Ethical School*, London: Routledge.

Heck, R. H. (2002) 'Multilevel modeling with SEM', in G. A. Marcoulides and R. E. Schumacker (eds) *New Developments and Techniques in Structural Equation Modeling*, Mahwah, NJ: Lawrence Erlbaum Associates.

Heck, R. H. and Thomas, S. L. (2000) *An Introduction to Multilevel Modeling Techniques*, Mahwah, NJ: Lawrence Erlbaum Associates.

Heim, J. and Perl, L. (1974) *The Educational Production Function: Implications for Educational Manpower Policy*, Institute of Public Employment Monograph No. 4, Ithaca, NY: Cornell University.

Helsby, G. (1999) *Changing Teachers' Work*, Buckingham: Open University Press.

Henchey, N. (2001) *Schools That Make a Difference: Final Report. Twelve Canadian Secondary Schools in Low-Income Settings*, Kelowna, BC: Society for the Advancement of Excellence in Education.

Henson, R. K. (2001) 'Teacher self-efficacy: substantive implications and measurement dilemmas', keynote address given at the Educational Research Exchange, Texas A&M University, January.

Hersh, S. B. (1990) 'Observing special and regular education classrooms', paper presented at the Annual Meeting of the American Educational Research Association, Boston, MA, April.

Hilsum, S. and Cane, B.S. (1971) *The Teacher's Day*, Windsor: National Foundation for Educational Research.

Hilsum, S. and Strong, C. (1978) *The Secondary Teacher's Day*, Windsor, National Foundation for Educational Research.

HMI (Her Majesty's Inspectorate) (1994) *Primary Education in Italy*, London: Department for Education and Science.

Hook, C. M. and Rosenshine, B. V. (1976) 'Accuracy of teacher reports of their classroom behaviour', *Review of Educational Research*, **49** (1): 1–11.

Hopkins, D. and Reynolds, D. (2001) 'The past, present and future of school improvement: towards the Third Age,' *British Educational Research Journal*, 27(4): 459–476.

Hopkins, D. and Reynolds, D. (2002) *The Past, Present and Future of School Improvement*, London: DfES.

Hopkins, D. and West, M. (2000) 'Appraisal in action: issues and examples from schools in Kent', *Learning Resources Journal*, 11 (1): 16–21.

Hoy, W. K., Tarter, C. J. and Bliss, J. R. (1990) 'Organisational climate, school health and effectiveness: a comparative analysis', *Educational Administration Quarterly*, 26 (3): 260–279.

Hoyle, E. (1974) 'Professionality, professionalism and control in teaching', in V. Houghton, R. McHugh and C. Morgan (eds) *Management in Education*, London: Ward Lock.

Hoyle, E. (1995) 'Changing conceptions of a profession', in H. Busher and R. Saran (eds) *Managing Teachers as Professionals in Schools*, London: Kogan Page.

Hoyle, E. and John, P. (1995) *Professional Knowledge and Professional Practice*, London: Cassell.

Hoyle, R. H. (ed.) (1995) *Structural Equation Modelling: Concepts, Issues and Applications*, Newbury Park, CA: Sage.

Humphreys, K. (1992) '"I must be crackers" – Teacher self-appraisal for professional development: reflection based on a case study of a group of teachers', *School Organisation*, 12 (2): 115–125.

ILO (International Labour Office) (1981) *Report of the Joint Meeting on Conditions of Work of Teachers* (1981), Geneva: ILO.

ILO (International Labour Office) (1991) *Teachers: Challenges of the 1990s; second Joint Meeting on the Conditions of Work of Teachers* (1991), Geneva: ILO.

Jamieson, J. L. and Brooks, D. M. (1980) 'Pupil perceptions of teacher presage and process variables and their relationship to pupil perceptions of instructional effectiveness', paper presented at the Annual Meeting of the Southwest Educational Research Association, San Antonio, TX, February.

Jarjoura, D. (1982) *Best linear prediction of composite universe scores (ACT Technical Bulletin No. 40)*, Iowa City, IA: ACT.

Jencks, C. (1972) 'A reappraisal of the most controversial document of our time', in H. Full (ed.) *Controversy in American Education*, 2nd edn, New York: Macmillan.

Jencks, C., Smith, M., Acland, H., Bane, M. J., Cohen, D., Gintis, H., Heyns, B. and Michelson, S. (1972) *Inequality: a Reassessment of the Effects of Family and Schooling in America*, New York: Basic Books.

Johnson, B. (1997) 'An organizational analysis of multiple perspectives of effective teaching: implications of teacher evaluation', *Journal of Personnel Evaluation in Education*, 11: 69–87.

Johnstone, M. (1993) *Teachers' Workload and Associated Stress*, Edinburgh: The Scottish Council for Research in Education.

Jonassen, D. H. and Grabowski, B. L. (1993) *Handbook of Individual Differences, Learning and Instruction*, Mahwah, NJ: Lawrence Erlbaum Associates.

Katz, M. (1975) *Class, Bureaucracy and Schools. The Illusion of Educational Change in America*, New York: Praeger.

Katzenmeyer, M. and Moller, G. (2001) *Awakening the Sleeping Giant. Helping Teachers Develop as Leaders*, 2nd edn, Thousand Oaks, CA: Corwin Press.

Keane, D. F. (1968) 'Relationships among teacher attitude, student attitude, and student achievement in elementary school arithmetic', unpublished doctoral thesis, University of Florida, Gainesville.

Kline, P. (1983) *Personality Measurement and Theory*, London: Hutchinson.

Kline, R. B. (1998) *Principles and Practice of Structural Equation Modeling*, New York: The Guilford Press.

Kogan, M. (1975) *Educational Policy-making: a study of interest groups and Parliament*, London: Allen & Unwin.

Kohnstamm, G. A. and Mervielde, I. (1998) 'Personality development', in A. Demetriou, W. Doise and K. F. M. van Lieshout (eds) *Life-span Developmental Psychology*, London: Wiley.

Kolb, D. (1973) *Toward a Typology of Learning Styles and Learning Environments: an Investigation of the Impact of Learning Styles and Discipline Demands on the Academic Performance, Social Adaptation and Career Choices of MIT Seniors*, Cambridge, MA: MIT Press.

Kyriacou, C. (1980) 'Stress, health and schoolteachers: a comparison with other professions', *Cambridge Journal of Education*, 10: 154–159.

Kyriacou, C. (1997a) 'Appraisers' views of teacher appraisal', *Teacher Development*, 1 (1): 35–41.

Kyriacou, C. (1997b) *Effective Teaching in Schools: Theory and Practice*, 2nd edn, Cheltenham: Stanley Thorne.

Kyriakides, L. (2001) *Contemporary Research in Educational Studies*, Nicosia: University of Cyprus.

Kyriakides, L. (2002) *A Rasch Measurement Model Analysis of a Teacher Observation System*, Nicosia: University of Cyprus.

Kyriakides, L. (2003a) 'A theoretical framework for school effectiveness research based on Creemers' model: an empirical study', paper presented at the 84th Annual Meeting of the American Educational Research Association, Chicago, IL.

Kyriakides, L. (2003b) 'Differential school effectiveness in relation to sex and social class: some implications for policy evaluation', *Educational Research and Evaluation*.

Kyriakides, L. (2003c) *The Use of Generalisability Theory in Analyzing Student Ratings of Instruction: Implications for the Evaluation of Teaching*, Nicosia: University of Cyprus.

Kyriakides, L. and Campbell, R. J. (2003) 'Teacher evaluation in Cyprus: some conceptual and methodological issues arising from teacher and school effectiveness research', *Journal of Personnel Evaluation in Education*, **17** (1): 21–40.

Kyriakides, L., Campbell, R. J. and Christofidou, E. (2002) 'Generating criteria for measuring teacher effectiveness through a self-evaluation approach: a complementary way of measuring teacher effectiveness', *School Effectiveness and School Improvement*, **13** (3): 291–325.

Kyriakides, L., Campbell, R. J. and Gagatsis, A. (2000) 'The significance of the classroom effect in primary schools: an application of Creemers' comprehensive model of educational effectiveness', *School Effectiveness and School Improvement*, **11** (4): 501–529.

Kyriakides, L. and Gagatsis, A. (2003) 'Score validity of the mathematical patterns test: developmental assessment of Cypriot primary pupils' skills in mathematical patterns, *Structural Equation Modeling: a Multidisciplinary Journal*.

Kyriakides, L. and Telemachou, K. (2002) 'Integrating formative and summative functions of national assessment in Mathematics through positioning pupils' errors on a Rasch scale', in A. Gagatsis (ed.) *Learning in Mathematics and Science and Educational Technology*, Nicosia: University of Cyprus.

Labaree, D. (2000) 'Educational researchers living with a lesser form of knowledge', in C. Day *et al.* (eds) *The Life and Work of Teachers*, London: Falmer.

Lagemann, E. (2000) *An Elusive Science: the Troubling History of Education Research*, London: The University of Chicago Press.

Larson, S. M. (1980) 'Proletarianisation and educated labour', *Theory and Society*, **9** (1): 131–175.

Lauder, H., Jamieson, I. and Wikeley, F. (1998) 'Models of effectiveness: limits and capacities', in R. Slee, G. Weiner and S. Tomlinson (eds) *School Effectiveness for Whom? Challenges to the School Effectiveness and School Improvement Movement*, London: Falmer.

Lawton, D. (1996) 'Is there coherence and purpose in the National Curriculum?', in C. Chitty and B. Simon (eds) *Education Answers Back*, London: Lawrence and Wishart.

Ledoux, G. and Overmaat, M. (2001) *Op Zoek Naar Succes. Een onderzoek naar Basisscholen die Meer en Minder Succesvol Zijn voor Autochtone en Allochtone Leerlingen uit Achterstandsgroepen*, Amsterdam: SCO-Kohnstamm Instituut.

Lein, L., Johnson, J. F. and Ragland, M. (1996) *Successful Texas Schoolwide Programs: Research Study Results*, Austin, TX: The University of Texas at Austin, The Charles A. Dana Center.

Leinster-Mackay, D. (2002) 'Frank Hayward, British Neo-Herbartian extraordinaire: an examination of his educational writings', *History of Education Society Bulletin*, **69**: 26–28.

Leithwood, K. and Steinbach, R. (2002) *Successful Leadership for Especially Challenging Schools*.

Leverne, B. (1991) 'Relationship of observable teaching effectiveness behaviors to MBTI personality types', paper presented at the International Conference of the Association for Psychological Type, Richmond, VA, July.

Levin, H. M. (1970) 'A cost-effectiveness analysis of teacher selection', *Journal of Human Resources*, 5 (1): 24–33.

Lieberman, A. (1988) 'Teachers and principals: turf, tension and new tasks', *Phi Delta Kappa*, **69**: 648–653.

Lieberman, A., Saxl, E. R. and Miles, M. B. (2000) 'Teacher leadership: ideology and practice', in *The Jossey-Bass Reader on Educational Leadership*, 339–345, Chicago, IL: Jossey-Bass.

Lindsay, G. and Muijs, D. (2003) 'Raising the attainment of underachieving white boys, black African boys and black Caribbean boys in Newham', report for London Borough of Newham Educational Scrutiny Committee, CEDAR, University of Warwick, Coventry.

Linn, R. L. (1986) 'Quantitative methods in research on teaching', in M. C. Wittrock (ed.) *Handbook of Research on Teaching*, New York: Macmillan.

Little, J. W. and McLaughlin, M. W. (eds) (1993) *Teachers' Work: Individuals, Colleagues and Contexts*, New York: Teachers College Press.

Lortie, D. (1969) 'The balance of control and autonomy in elementary school teaching', in A. Etzioni (ed.) *The Semi-professions and their Organisation*, New York: Free Press.

Louis, K. S. and Smith, B. (1990) 'Teacher working conditions', in P. Reyes (ed.) *Teachers and their Workplace*, New York: Sage.

MacBeath, J. (ed.) (1998) *Effective School Leadership: Responding to Change*, London: Paul Chapman.

MacBeath, J. (1999) *Schools Must Speak for Themselves: the Case for School Self-evaluation*, London: Routledge.

MacBeath, J., Schratz, M., Jakobsen, L. and Meuret, D. (2000) *Self-evaluation in European Schools*, London: RoutledgeFalmer.

McConnell, J. W. and Bowers, N. D. (1979) 'A comparison of high inference and low inference measures of teacher behaviours', paper presented at the Annual Meeting of the American Educational Research Association, San Francisco, CA.

McHugh, B. and Stringfield, S. (1998) *Implementing a Highly Specific Curricular, Instructional and Organisational High School Design in a High Poverty Urban Elementary School: Three Year Results*, Baltimore, MD: Johns Hopkins University, Centre for Research on the Education of Students Placed At Risk.

McIntyre, D. (1992) 'Theory, theorising and reflection in initial teacher education', in J. Calderhead and P. Gates (eds) *Conceptualising Reflection in Teacher Education*, London: Falmer.

Maden, M. (ed.) (2001) *Success Against the Odds: Five Years On*, London: Routledge.

Mandeville, G. K. and Liu, Q. (1997) 'The effect of teacher certification and task level on Mathematics achievement', *Teaching and Teacher Education*, **13** (4): 397–407.

Marcoulides, G. and Kyriakides, L. (2002) 'Applying the Rasch and Extended Generalizability Theory Models: discrepancies between approaches', *Proceedings of the 12th IOMW Conference*, New Orleans, LA.

Marsh, H. W. and Parker, J. W. (1984) 'Determinants of student self-concept: is it better to be a large fish in a small pond even if you don't learn to swim as well?', *Journal of Personality and Social Psychology*, **47** (1): 213–231.

Marston, P. T. and Zimmerer, L. K. (1979) *The Effect of Using More than One Type of Teacher Observation System in the Same Study*, see http://www.askeric.org, ERIC ED206712.

Martin, N. K. (1995) 'Beliefs regarding classroom management style: relationships to particular teacher personality characteristics', paper presented at the Annual Meeting of the American Educational Research Association, San Francisco, CA, April.

Maruyama, G. M. (1998) *Basics of Structural Equation Modeling*, Thousand Oaks, CA: Sage.

Mayer, J. D. and Cobb, C. D. (2000) 'Educational policy on emotional intelligence: does it make sense?', *Educational Psychology Review*, **12**: 163–183.

Mayer, J. D. and Salovey, P. (1993) 'The intelligence of emotional intelligence', *Intelligence*, **17** (4): 433–442.

Medley, D. M. and Crook, P. R. (1980) 'Research in teacher competency and teaching tasks', *Theory into Practice*, **19** (4): 294–301.

Medley, D. M. and Mitzel, H. E. (1963) 'Measuring classroom behaviour by systematic observation', in Gage, N. L. (ed.) *Handbook of Research on Teaching*, Chicago, IL: Rand MacNally.

Medwell, J., Poulson, L. and Wray, D. (1999) *Effective Teachers of Literacy: a Report of Research Project Commissioned by the TTA*, Exeter: School of Education, University of Exeter.

Merriam, S. M. (2001) *Qualitative Research and Case Study Applications in Education: Revised and Expanded from Case Study Research in Education*, San Francisco, CA: Jossey-Bass.

Merson, M. (2000) 'Teachers and the myth of modernisation', *British Journal of Educational Studies*, **48** (2): 155–169.

Metcalfe, C. K. (1994) 'Reappraising appraisal: a re-examination of some of the issues involved in staff appraisal in the light of a scheme of peer appraisal', *British Journal of In-Service Education*, **20** (1): 95–108.

Miller, S. (1984) *Experimental Design and Statistics*, 2nd edn, London: Routledge.

Ministry of Education (1994) *The New Curriculum*, Nicosia: Cyprus Ministry of Education.

Monk, D. H. (1992) 'Microeconomics of school productions', paper presented at the Economics of Education Section of the International Encyclopedia of Education.

Monk, D. H. (1994) 'Subject matter preparation of secondary Mathematics and Science teachers and student achievement', *Economics of Education Review*, **13** (2): 125–145.

Montgomery, A., Rossi, R., Legters, N., McDill, E., McPartland, J. and Stringfield, S. (1993) *Educational Reforms and Students Placed At Risk: A Review of the Current State of the Art*, Washington, DC: US Department of Education, OERI.

Moore, W. and Esselman, M. (1992) 'Teacher efficacy, power, school climate and achievement: a desegregating district's experience', paper presented at the Annual Meeting of the American Educational Research Association, San Francisco, CA, April.

Mortimore, P. (1991) 'Bucking the trends: promoting successful urban education', paper presented at the Times Educational Supplement/Greenwich Annual Lecture, London.

Mortimore, P. (1998) *The Road to Improvement*, Lisse: Swets and Zeitlinger.

Mortimore, P. (ed.) (1999) *Understanding Pedagogy and its Impact on Learning*, London: Sage.

Mortimore, P., Sammons, P., Stoll, L., Lewis, D. and Ecob, R. (1988) *School Matters*, Wells: Open Books.

Mosley, J. (1996) *Quality Circle Time in the Primary Classroom: Your Essential Guide to Enhancing Self-Esteem, Self-Discipline and Positive Relationships*, London: LDA.

Muijs, D. (1997) 'Predictors of academic achievement and academic self-concept: a longitudinal perspective', *The British Journal of Educational Psychology*, **67**: 263–277.

Muijs, D. (2004) 'Measuring teacher effectiveness', in D. Hopkins and D. Reynolds (eds) *The Learning Level*, London: RoutledgeFalmer.

Muijs, D. and Harris, A. (2004) 'Teacher leadership – improvement through empowerment? An overview of the literature', *Educational Management and Administration*, in press.

Muijs, D. and Reynolds, D. (2000) 'School effectiveness and teacher effectiveness: some preliminary findings from the evaluation of the Mathematics Enhancement Programme', *School Effectiveness and School Improvement*, **11** (3): 247–263.

Muijs, D. and Reynolds, D. (2001a) *Effective Teaching: Evidence and Practice*, London: Sage.

Muijs, D. and Reynolds, D. (2001b) 'Being or doing: the role of teacher behaviors and beliefs in school and teacher effectiveness in mathematics, a SEM analysis', paper presented at the Annual Meeting of the American Educational Research Association, Seattle, WA, April.

Muijs, D. and Reynolds, D. (2002) 'Teacher beliefs and behaviors: what matters', *Journal of Classroom Interaction*, **37** (2): 3–15.

Muijs, D. and Reynolds, D. (2003) 'Student background and teacher effects on achievement and attainment in Mathematics', *Educational Research and Evaluation*, **9** (1).

Musgrove, F. (1971) 'The future of the teaching profession', *Journal of Curriculum Studies* **3** (1): 19–26.

Nias, J. (1989) *Primary Teachers Talking*, London: Routledge.

Nielsen, I. L. and Moore, K. A. (2003) 'Psychometric data on the mathematics self-efficacy scale', *Educational and Psychological Measurement*, **63** (1): 128–138.

Norris, N. (1998) 'Curriculum evaluation re-visited', *Cambridge Journal of Education*, **28**: 207–220.

Nuttall, D., Goldstein, H., Prosser, R. and Rasbach, J. (1989) 'Differential school effectiveness', *International Journal of Educational Research*, **13**: 769–776.

OECD (Organisation for Economic Cooperation and Development) (1990) *The Teacher Today: Tasks, Conditions, Policies*, Paris: OECD.

Office of Manpower Economics (OME) (2000) *Teachers' Workloads Diary Survey*, London: OME.

Ofsted (2002) *Performance Management of Teachers*, London: Ofsted.

Opdenakker, M.C. and Van Damme, J. (2000) 'Effects of schools, teaching staff and classes on achievement and well-being in secondary education: similarities and differences between school outcomes', *School Effectiveness and School Improvement*, **11** (2): 165–196.

Owen, S. A. (1976) 'The validity of student ratings: a critique', paper presented at the Annual Meeting of the American Educational Research Association, San Francisco, CA, April.

Ozga, J. and Lawn, M. (1981) *Teachers' Professionalism and Class*, Lewes: Falmer.

Ozga, J. and Lawn, M. (1989) 'Schoolwork: interpreting the labour process of teaching', *British Journal of Sociology of Education*, **9** (3): 323–326.

Padron, Y. N. and Waxman, H. C. (1999) 'Classroom observations of the five standards of effective teaching in urban classrooms with English language learners', *Teaching and Change*, **7** (1): 79–100.

Paterson, L. and Goldstein, H. (1991) 'New statistical methods of analyzing social structure: an introduction to multilevel models', *British Educational Research Journal*, **17**: 387–393.

Pellicer, L. O. and Anderson, L. W. (1995) *A Handbook for Teacher Leaders*, Thousand Oaks, CA: Corwin Press.

Peters, R. (1970) *Ethics and Education*, London: Allen and Unwin.

Peters, R. (1973) *Authority, Responsibility and Education*, 3rd edn, London: Unwin.

Peters, T. and Waterman, H. W. (1983) *In Search of Excellence: Lessons from America's Best-Run Companies*, New York: HarperCollins.

Peterson, P. L. (1977) 'Interactive effects of student anxiety, achievement orientation and teacher behavior on student achievement and attitude', *Journal of Educational Psychology*, **69**: 779–792.

Philipou, G. and Christou, C. (1997) 'A study of teachers' conceptions aboput mathematics', in E. Pehkonen (ed.) *Proceedings of the 21st International*

Conference for the Psychology of Mathematics Education, vol. 4, pp. 9–16, University of Helsinki.

Philips, J. (1996) 'Culture, community and schooling in Delta County: state assistance and school change in schools that would never change', paper presented at the Annual Meeting of the American Educational Research Association, Montreal, Quebec.

Phillips, E. (1997) 'The work of teachers in small schools', unpublished PhD thesis, University of Warwick.

Pollard, A. (1997) *Reflective Teaching in the Primary School*, London: Cassell.

Ponticell, J. A. and Zepeda, S. J. (2003) 'What does teaching excellence mean? critical conflicts in principals' and award-winning teachers' perceptions', paper presented at the Annual Meeting of the American Educational Research Association, Chicago, IL, April.

Ponting, C. (1986) *Whitehall: Tragedy or Farce?*, London: Hamish Hamilton.

Power, M. (1999) *The Audit Society: Rituals of Verification*, Oxford: Oxford University Press.

Powney, J. (1991) 'Teacher appraisal: the case for a developmental approach', *Educational Research*, 33 (2): 83–92.

PriceWaterhouseCoopers (2001) *Teacher Workload Study, Final Report*, London: DfES.

Pring, R. (1992) 'Standards and quality in education', *British Journal of Educational Studies*, 40 (1): 4–22.

Public Record Office, Kew (1908) Ed 86/24, *Practising and Demonstration Schools Memoranda, 1906–1933*.

Public Record Office, Kew (1911) Ed 119/53, *Manchester University: Fielden Demonstration Schools 1908–1911*.

Rallis, S. F. and Rossman, G. B. (2003) 'Mixed methods in evaluation contexts: a pragmatic framework', in A. Tashakkori and C. Teddlie (eds) *Handbook of Mixed Methods in Social and Behavioral Research*, Thousand Oaks, CA: Sage.

Ralph, J. H. and Fennessey, J. (1983) 'Science or reform: some questions about the effective schools model', *Phi Delta Kappan*, 64: 689–694.

Rasbach, J. and Woodhouse, G. (1995) *Mln Command Reference*, London: Multilevel Models Project, University of London.

Raykov, T. and Marcoulides, G. A. (2000) *A First Course in Structural Equation Modeling*, Mahwah, NJ: Lawrence Erlbaum Associates.

Raymont, T. (1904) *The Principles of Education*, London: Longmans.

Reezigt, G. J., Creemers, B. and De Jong, R. (forthcoming) 'The perspective from the Netherlands', *Journal of Personnel Evaluation in Education*.

Reezigt, G. J., Guldemond, H. and Creemers, B. P. M. (1999) 'Empirical validity for a comprehensive model on school effectiveness and school improvement', *School Effectiveness and School Improvement*, 10 (2): 193–216.

Relich, J. (1996) 'Gender, self-concept and teachers of Mathematics: effects on attitudes to teaching and learning', *Educational Studies in Mathematics*, 30: 179–195.

Resnick, M. D., Harris, L. J. and Blum, R. W. (1993) 'The impact of caring and connectedness on adolescent health and well-being', *Journal of Paediatrics and Child Health*, **29** (3): 27–45.

Reyes, P. (1990) (ed.) *Teachers and Their Workplace*, New York: Sage.

Reynolds, A. J. and Walberg, H. J. (1992) 'A structural model of science achievement and attitude: an extension to high school', *Journal of Educational Psychology*, **84** (3): 371–382.

Reynolds, D. (1976) 'The delinquent school', in M. Hammersley and P. Woods (eds) *The Process of Schooling*, London: Routledge and Kegan Paul.

Reynolds, D., Creemers, P. B. M., Nesselrodt, P. S., Schaffer, E. C., Stringfield, S. and Teddlie, C. (1994) (eds) *Advances in School Effectiveness Research and Practice*, Oxford: Pergamon.

Reynolds, D., Creemers, B., Stringfield, S., Teddlie, C. and Schaffer, G. (eds) (2002) *World Class Schools: International Perspectives on School Effectiveness*, London: RoutledgeFalmer.

Reynolds, D. and Muijs, R. D. (1999) 'The effective teaching of Mathematics: a review of research', *School Leadership and Management*, **19** (3): 273–288.

Reynolds, D. and Muijs, D. (2004) *The Gatsby Teacher Effectiveness Study*, London: RoutledgeFalmer.

Reynolds, D., Sammons, P., Stoll, L., Barber, M. and Hillman, J. (1996) 'School effectiveness and school improvement in the United Kingdom', *School Effectiveness and School Improvement*, **7** (2): 133–158.

Reynolds, D. and Sullivan, M. (1979) 'Bringing the schools back in', in L. Barton (ed.) *Schools, Pupils and Deviance*, Driffield: Nafferton.

Richards, C. (2001) *School Inspection in England: a Re-appraisal*, Northampton: Philosophy of Education Society of Great Britain.

Robinson, W. (2000) 'History of education in the new Millennium: retrospect and prospect in teacher training', in R. Aldrich and D. Crook (eds) *History of Education into the Twenty-First Century*, London: University of London Bedford Way Occasional Paper.

Robinson, W. (2004) *Power to Teach*, London: Woburn Press.

Rosenshine, B. (1971) *Teaching Behaviours and Student Achievement*, London: NFER.

Rosenshine, B. (1979) 'Content, time and direct instruction', in P. L. Peterson and H. J. Walberg (eds) *Research on Teaching*, Berkeley, CA: McCutchan.

Rosenshine, B. (1983) 'Teaching functions in instructional programs', *Elementary School Journal*, **83**: 335–351.

Rosenshine, B. and Furst, N. (1973) 'The use of direct observation to study teaching', in R.M.W. Travers (ed.) *Second Handbook of Research on Teaching*, Chicago, IL: Rand McNally.

Rossmiller, R. A. (1982) 'Use of resources: does it influence student achievement?', *Educational Perspectives*, **21** (1): 23–32.

Roulet, G. (200) 'Exemplary mathematics teachers: subjects, conceptions and instructional practices', in P. Ernest (ed.) *Philosophy of Mathematics Education*, **13** (http://www.ex.ac.uk/~PErnest/thesis/cover_pg.htm

Ruble, T. and Cosier, R. (1990) 'Effects of cognitive styles and decision setting on performance', *Organizational Behavior and Human Decision Processes*, **46**: 283–295.

Rutter, M., Maughan, B., Mortimore, P. and Ouston, J. (1979) *Fifteen Thousand Hours: Secondary Schools and their Effects on Children*, Wells: Open Books.

Sammons, P. and Mortimore, P. (1997) 'Differential school effectiveness: departmental variations in GCSE attainment', *School Field*, 8 (1–2): 97–125.

Sammons, P., Nuttall, D. and Cuttance, P. (1993) 'Differential school effectiveness: results from a reanalysis of the Inner Education Authority's Junior School Project data', *British Educational Research Journal*, **19** (4): 381–405.

Sammons, P., Thomas, S. and Mortimore, P. (1997) *Forging Links: Effective Schools and Effective Departments*, London: Paul Chapman.

Schaffer, E. C., Muijs, R. D., Kitson, C. and Reynolds, D. (1998) *Mathematics Enhancement Classroom Observation Record*, Newcastle upon Tyne: Educational Effectiveness and Improvement Centre.

Scheerens, J. (1990) 'School effectiveness and the development of process indicators of school functioning', *School Effectiveness and School Improvement*, 2 (1): 61–80.

Scheerens, J. (1992) *Effective Schooling: Research, Theory and Practice*, London: Cassell.

Scheerens, J. (2000) *Improving School Effectiveness*, Paris: UNESCO International Institute for Educational Planning.

Scheerens, J. and Bosker, R (1997) *The Foundations of Educational Effectiveness*, Oxford: Pergamon.

Schunk, D. H. and Rice, M. (1991) 'Learning goals and progress feedback during reading comprehension instruction', *Journal of Reading Behavior*, 23(3): 351–64.

Scriven, M. (1994) 'Duties of the teacher', *Journal of Personnel Evaluation in Education*, 8 (2): 151–184.

Searle, S. R. (1974) 'Prediction, mixed models and variance components', in F. Proschan and R. J. Serfling (eds) *Reliability and Biometry*, Philadelphia, PA: Society for Industrial and Applied Mathematics.

Seidman, I. (1998) *Interviewing as Qualitative Research: a Guide for Researchers in Education and Social Sciences*, New York: Teachers College Press.

Selleck, R. (1967) 'The scientific educationist 1870–1914', *British Journal of Educational Studies*, 15: 148–165.

Selleck, R. (1968) *The New Education 1870–1914*, London: Sir Isaac Pitman and Sons.

Sharpe, S. (1984) *Double Identity*, Harmondsworth: Penguin.

Shavelson, R. J., Hubner, L. J. and Stanton, G. C. (1976) 'Self-concept: validation of construct interpretations', *Review of Educational Research*, **46**: 407–441.

Shavelson, R. J. and Webb, N. M. (1981) 'Generalizability Theory: 1973–1980', *British Journal of Mathematical and Statistical Psychology*, 34: 133–166.

Shavelson, R. J., Webb, N. M. and Burstein, L. (1986) 'Measurement of Teaching', in M. C. Wittrock (ed.) *Handbook of Research on Teaching*, New York: Macmillan.

Shavelson, R. J., Webb, N. M. and Rowley, G. L. (1989) 'Generalizability theory', *American Psychologist*, 44 (6): 922–932.

Shayer, M. and Adey, P. (2002) *Learning Intelligence. Cognitive Acceleration Across the Curriculum*, Buckingham: Open University Press.

Shipman, M. D. (1984) *Education as Public Welfare*, London: Methuen.

Simon, B. (1994) 'Some problems of pedagogy revisited', in *The State and Education Change: Essays in the History of Education and Pedagogy*, London: Lawrence and Wishart.

Slee, R. and Weiner, G. (2001) 'Education reform and reconstructions as a challenge to research genres: reconsidering school effectiveness research and inclusive schooling', *School Effectiveness and School Improvement*, 12 (1), 83–97.

Slee, R., Weiner, G. and Tomlinson, S. (eds) (1998) *School Effectiveness for Whom? Challenges to the School Effectiveness and School Improvement Movements*, London: Falmer.

Snijders, T. and Bosker, R. (1999) *Multilevel Analysis: an Introduction to Basic and Advanced Multilevel Modeling*, London: Sage.

Sockett, H. (1990) 'Accountability, trust, and ethical codes of practice', in J. I. Goodlad, R. Soder and K. A. Sirotnik (eds) *The Moral Dimensions of Teaching*, San Francisco, CA: Jossey-Bass.

Soder, R. (1990) 'The rhetoric of teacher professionalisation', in J. I. Goodlad, R. Soder and K. A. Sirotnik (eds) *The Moral Dimensions of Teaching*, San Francisco, CA: Jossey-Bass.

Soodak, L. C. and Podell, D. M. (1996) 'Teacher efficacy: toward the understanding of a multi-faceted construct', *Teaching and Teacher Education* 12: 401–411.

Souster, D. K. (1982) 'Teacher attitude toward and student and teacher perception of teaching style and achievement', unpublished thesis, Walden University.

Stahl, S. A. (1999) 'Different strokes for different folks? A critique of learning styles', *American Educator*, 23 (3): 27–31.

Starratt, R. J. (1994) *Building an Ethical School: a Practical Response to the Moral Crisis in Schools*, London: Falmer.

Sternberg, R. J. (1985) *Beyond IQ: a Triarchic Theory of Human Intelligence*, New York: Cambridge University Press.

Sternberg, R. J. (1988) 'Mental self-government: a theory of intellectual styles and their development', *Human Development*, 31: 197–224.

Sternberg, R. J. and Grigorenko, E. L. (1995) 'Styles of thinking in school', *European Journal for High Ability*, 6: 201–219.

Stipek, D. J., Givvin, K. P., Salmon, J. M. and MacGyvers, V. L. (2001) 'Teachers' beliefs and practices related to mathematics instruction', *Teaching and Teacher Education*, 17 (2): 213–226.

Storey, A. (2000) 'A leap of faith? Performance pay for teachers', *Journal of Education Policy*, 15 (5): 509–523.

Stringfield, S. C. and Slavin, R. E. (1992) 'A hierarchical longitudinal model for elementary school effects', in B. P. M. Creemers and G. J. Reezigt (eds) *Evaluation of Educational Effectiveness*, Groningen: ICQ.

Stufflebeam, D. L. and Shinkfield, A. J. (1990) *Systematic Evaluation*, Lancaster: Kluwer-Nijhoff.

Tashakkori, A. and Teddlie, C. (eds) (2003) *Handbook of Mixed Methods in Social and Behavioral Research*, Thousand Oaks, CA: Sage.

Teddlie, C. (1994) 'The integration of classroom and school process data in school effectiveness research', in D. Reynolds, B. P. M. Creemers, P. S. Nesselrodt, E. C. Schaffer, S. Stringfield and C. Teddlie (eds) *Advances in School Effectiveness Research and Practice*, Oxford: Pergamon.

Teddlie, C. (2003) 'International comparisons of the role of teacher evaluation and educational effectiveness research on teacher and school improvement', *Journal of Personnel Evaluation in Education*.

Teddlie, C. and Meza, J. (1999) 'Using informal and formal measures to create classroom profiles', in H. J. Freiberg (ed.) *School Climate: Measuring, Improving and Sustaining Healthy Learning Environments*, London: Falmer.

Teddlie, C. and Reynolds, D. (eds) (2000) *The International Handbook of School Effectiveness Research*, London: Falmer.

Teddlie, C. and Stringfield, S. (1993) *Schools Make a Difference: Lessons Learned from a Ten Year Study of School Effects*, New York: Teachers College Press.

Thompson, A. G. (1992) 'Teachers' beliefs and conceptions: a synthesis of the research', in D. A. Grouws, *Handbook of Research on Mathematics Teaching and Learning*, New York: Macmillan.

Thompson, M. (1995) *Professional Ethics and the Teacher: an Educated Talent in the Service of Society*, monograph for the Directors of the General Teaching Council, London: GTC.

Thrupp, M. (1999) *Schools Making a Difference: Let's Be Realistic!*, Buckingham: Open University Press.

Thrupp, M. (2001a) 'Sociological and political concerns about school effectiveness research: time for a new research agenda?', *School Effectiveness and School Improvement*, 12 (1): 7–40.

Thrupp, M. (2001b) 'Recent school effectiveness counter-critiques: problems and possibilities', *British Educational Research Journal*, 27 (4): 443–458.

Tomlinson, J. (1995) 'Professional development and control: the role of the General Teaching Council', *Journal of Education for Teaching*, 21 (1): 59–68.

Townley, B. (1993) 'Performance appraisal and the emergence of management', *Journal of Management Studies*, 30 (2): 221–238.

Travers, C. J. and Cooper, C. L. (1993) 'Mental health, job satisfaction and occupational stress amongst UK teachers', *Work and Stress*, 7: 203–219.

Tuan, H.-L., Chang, H.-P., Wang, K.-H. and Treagust, D. F. (2000) 'The development of an instrument for assessing students' perceptions of teachers' knowledge', *International Journal of Science Education*, 22 (4): 385–398.

Tuckman, B. W. (1968) *A Study of the Effectiveness of Directive Versus Non-Directive Vocational Teachers as a Function of Student Characteristics and Course Format*, Washington, DC: Office of Education.

Tyler, R. W. (1971) *Basic Principles of Curriculum and Instruction*, Chicago, IL: University of Chicago Press.

Vandenberghe, R. and Huberman, A. M. (eds) (1999) *Understanding and Preventing Teacher Burnout*, Cambridge: Cambridge University Press.

Varlaam, A., Nuttall, D. and Walker, A. (1992) *What Makes Teachers Tick? A Survey of Teacher Morale and Motivation*, London: London School of Economics Centre for Educational Research.

Virgilio, L., Teddlie, C. and Oescher, J. (1991) 'Variance and context difference in teaching at differentially effective schools', *School Effectiveness and School Improvement*, 2 (2): 152–168.

Von Glasersfeldt, E. (1989) 'Constructivism in education', in T. Husen and N. Postlewaite (eds) *International Encyclopedia of Education*, Oxford: Pergamon Press.

Walberg, H. J. (1984) 'Improving the productivity of American Schools', *Educational Leadership*, 41: 19–27.

Walberg, H. J. (1986a) 'Syntheses of research on teaching', in M. C. Wittrock (ed.) *Handbook of Research on Teaching*, New York: Macmillan.

Walberg, H. J. (1986b) 'What works in a nation still at risk', *Educational Leadership*, 44 (1): 7–10.

Walberg, H. J. and Welch, W. W. (1967) *Personality Characteristics of Innovative Physics Teachers*, see http://www.askeric.org, ERIC ED015888.

Walker, A. and Cheng, Y.C. (1996) 'Professional development in Hong Kong primary schools: beliefs, practices and change', *Journal of Education for Teaching*, 22 (2): 11, 197–212.

Waller, W. (1932) *The Sociology of Teaching*, New York: John Wiley and Sons.

Wang, M. C. and Walberg, H. J. (1991) 'Teaching and educational effectiveness: research synthesis and consensus from the field', in H. C. Waxman and H. J. Walberg (eds) *Effective Teaching: Current Research*, San Francisco, CA: McCutchman.

Ward, M. D., Clark, C. C. and Harrison, G. V. (1981) 'The observer effect in classroom visitation', paper presented at the Annual Meeting of the American Educational Research Association, Los Angeles, CA, April.

Watkins, C. and Mortimore, P. (1999) 'Pedagogy: what do we know?', in P. Mortimore (ed.) *Understanding Pedagogy and its Impact on Learning*, London: Paul Chapman.

Webb, R. and Vulliamy, G. (1996) 'A deluge of directives: conflict between collegiality and managerialism in the post-ERA primary school', *British Educational Research Journal*, 22 (4): 441–458.

Weiner, G. (2002) 'Auditing failure: moral competence and school effectiveness', *British Educational Research Journal*, 28 (6): 789–804.

Welton, J. (1902) *Forms for Criticism Lessons*, London: Macmillan.

Welton, J. (1906) *Principles and Methods of Teaching*, London: University Tutorial Press.

Welton, J. (1918) *What Do We Mean by Education?*, London: University Tutorial Press.

Whitaker, P. (1983) *The Primary Head*, London: Heinemann.

Whitty, G., Power, S. and Halpin, D. (1998) *Devolution and Choice in Education: the School, the State and the Market*, Buckingham: Open University Press.

Wiersma, W. (1983) 'Assessment of teacher performance: constructs of teacher competencies based on factor analysis of observation data', paper presented at the Annual Meeting of the American Educational Research Association, Montreal, Quebec, 11–15 April.

Wiersma, W. (1988) *The Alabama Career Incentive Program: a Statewide Effort in Teacher Evaluation*, see http://www.askeric.org, ERIC ED298128.

Wittrock, M. C. (ed.) (1986) *Handbook of Research on Teaching*, New York: Macmillan.

Wooldridge, A. (1994) *Measuring the Mind Education and Psychology in England, c. 1860–c.1990*, Cambridge: Cambridge University Press.

Wragg, E. C., Wragg, C. M. and Chamberlin, P. R. (2001) 'Threshold assessment: the experiences and views of teachers', paper presented at the British Educational Research Association Annual Conference, Leeds, September.

Wright, S. P., Horn, S. P. and Saunders, W. L (1997) 'Teacher and classroom context effects on student achievement: implications for teacher evaluation', *Journal of Personnel Evaluation in Education*, 11: 57–67.

Yin, R. K. (1994) *Case Study Research: Design and Methods*, Thousand Oaks, CA: Sage.

Young, E. M. (1973) *Effect of Teacher Enthusiasm on Vocational Business Education Student Achievement*, Ann Arbor, MI: University of Michigan.

Index